EXAM CRAM

PMP C

This Cram Sheet contains the distilled, key facts about ....w this information as the last thing you do before entering the test center, paying special att..... ....ose areas in which you feel you need the most review. You can transfer any of these facts from your head onto a blank sheet of paper immediately before you begin the exam.

PROJECT MANAGEMENT FRAMEWORK

- **Project**—A temporary endeavor undertaken to create a unique product, service, or result.
- **Progressive elaboration**—Developing in steps and continuing by increments; characteristic of projects.
- **Program**—A group of related projects managed in a coordinated way to obtain benefits and control not available from managing them individually.
- **Portfolio**—A collection of projects and programs grouped together to facilitate effective management of work to meet business objectives.
- **Project life cycle**—Phases that connect the beginning of a project to its end; project life cycle phases are not the same as project management process groups or processes.

  The level of uncertainty is highest and the risk of failure is greatest at the start of a project.

  The ability of stakeholders to influence a project is highest at the start and gets progressively lower as a project continues.

  The cost of changes and of correcting errors increases as a project continues.

- **Deliverable**—A measurable, verifiable work product.
- **Process**—A set of interrelated actions/activities performed to achieve a prespecified set of products, services, or results.
- **Product-oriented processes**—Specifying and creating a project's product; typically defined by a project's life cycle and can vary by application area.

PROJECT MANAGEMENT PROCESS GROUPS

Not all project management processes apply to all projects or project phases. Process groups can overlap and interact. 47 project management processes are contained within the 5 project management process groups:

- Initiating
- Planning
- Executing
- Monitoring and controlling
- Closing

Initiating Process Group

This group formally authorizes new project or project phase. Involves 2 processes:

- **Develop project charter**—Authorizing project or project phase. It involves documenting business needs and new product, service, or result intended to satisfy requirements.

  Project charter—Defines a project's purpose, identifies objectives, and authorizes the project manager to start a project.

- **Identify stakeholders**—Identifies, describes, and classifies people and entities that might affect or be affected by project activities or outcomes.

Planning Process Group

This group defines objectives and plans a course of action required to attain objectives and the scope that the project was undertaken to address. Facilitates project planning across process groups. Involves 24 processes:

- **Develop project management plan**—Defining, preparing, integrating, and coordinating all subsidiary plans into a project management plan. Primary source for how a project will be planned, executed, monitored and controlled, and closed. Iterative and ongoing process often resulting in changes/updates to project management plan. This progressive detailing is often called "rolling wave planning."
- **Plan scope management**—Documenting how project scope will be defined, validated, and controlled and how the WBS will be created and defined through the scope management plan.
- **Collect requirements**—Determining needs and requirements of all stakeholders needed to meet project objectives.
- **Define scope**—Developing a detailed scope statement as the basis for future project decisions.
- **Create WBS**—Subdividing major project deliverables and project work into smaller, more manageable components.
- **Plan schedule management**—Documenting how the project schedule will be defined, managed, and controlled.
- **Define activities**—Identifying specific activities to be performed to produce project deliverables.

EXAM✓CRAM

PMP

Fifth Edition

Michael G. Solomon

PMP Exam Cram, Fifth Edition

ISBN-13: 978-0-7897-5370-0
ISBN-10: 0-7897-5370-7

Library of Congress Control Number: 2014950142

Printed in the United States of America

First Printing: October 2014

Trademarks

All terms mentioned in this book that are known to be trademarks or service marks have been appropriately capitalized. Pearson IT Certification cannot attest to the accuracy of this information. Use of a term in this book should not be regarded as affecting the validity of any trademark or service mark.

Warning and Disclaimer

Special Sales

For information about buying this title in bulk quantities, or for special sales opportunities (which may include electronic versions; custom cover designs; and content particular to your business, training goals, marketing focus, or branding interests), please contact our corporate sales department at corpsales@pearsoned.com or (800) 382-3419.

For government sales inquiries, please contact governmentsales@pearsoned.com.

For questions about sales outside the U.S., please contact international@pearsoned.com.

Associate Publisher
Dave Dusthimer

Executive Editor
Betsy Brown

Senior Development Editor
Christopher Cleveland

Managing Editor
Sandra Schroeder

Senior Project Editor
Tonya Simpson

Copy Editor
Kitty Wilson

Indexer
Erika Millen

Proofreader
Debbie Williams

Technical Editor
Janet Jones

Publishing Coordinator
Vanessa Evans

Multimedia Developer
Lisa Matthews

Cover Designer
Alan Clements

Compositor
Trina Wurst

Contents at a Glance

Table of Contents

About the Author

Michael G. Solomon, CISSP, PMP, CISM, is a full-time security and project management speaker, consultant, and trainer with more than 25 years of industry experience. He holds an MS in mathematics and computer science from Emory University (1998) and a BS in computer science from Kennesaw State University (1987) and is currently a PhD candidate for a computer science and informatics degree at Emory University. A former college instructor, Michael has written several IT and project management books, including *Security Illuminated* (Jones & Bartlett, 2005), *Security+ Lab Guide* (Sybex, 2005), *Computer Forensics JumpStart* (Sybex, 2005 and 2011), and *PMP Exam Cram* (Que, 2005 and 2010). He has also authored and provided the on-camera delivery of LearnKey's CISSP Prep, PMP Prep, and Computer Foundations e-Learning courses. Michael also co-authored *Auditing IT Infrastructures for Compliance* (Jones & Bartlett, 2011) and *Fundamentals of Information Systems Security* (Jones & Bartlett, 2011 and 2014), and he authored *Security Strategies in Windows Platforms and Applications* (Jones & Bartlett, 2011 and 2014).

About the Technical Editor

Janet Jones, PMP, has almost 30 years of experience in the Information Technology industry, with multifaceted skills in designing and developing business, financial, health care, and manufacturing applications, database design and administration, software design and development, system conversion and integration, process reengineering, network configuration and troubleshooting, technical training, technical writing, and significant hands-on project management. She maintains numerous IT and project management certifications and currently works as a senior consultant for a global IT consulting company. As a writer and technical editor, she has been both contributing author and technical reviewer/editor for several educational publications and other certification and certification preparation materials.

Dedication

The content of this book would not have been possible without the unyielding support of my family. I'd like to dedicate this work to three people. First, my best friend and wife, Stacey, who constantly brings out more in me than I thought possible. Second, two guys who challenge me each day to be the best I can be: my sons, Noah and Isaac.

Acknowledgments

Thanks so much to all the people at Pearson who made this project possible and actually a smooth ride. Thanks, Betsy, Chris, and Jan for keeping me on track and making suggestions that improved the quality of the work.

We Want to Hear from You!

As the reader of this book, *you* are our most important critic and commentator. We value your opinion and want to know what we're doing right, what we could do better, what areas you'd like to see us publish in, and any other words of wisdom you're willing to pass our way.

We welcome your comments. You can email or write to let us know what you did or didn't like about this book—as well as what we can do to make our books better.

Please note that we cannot help you with technical problems related to the topic of this book.

When you write, please be sure to include this book's title and author as well as your name and email address. We will carefully review your comments and share them with the author and editors who worked on the book.

Email: feedback@pearsonitcertification.com

Mail: Pearson IT Certification
            ATTN: Reader Feedback
            800 East 96th Street
            Indianapolis, IN 46240 USA

Reader Services

Visit our website and register this book at www.pearsonitcertification.com/register for convenient access to any updates, downloads, or errata that might be available for this book.

Introduction

The Project Management Professional (PMP) certification is a valued asset in the ever-evolving professional project management field. PMP certification in the professional arena ensures that employers are hiring a project manager with thorough, tested knowledge in project management principles; years of hands-on, specific experience performing project management tasks; and a commitment to continuing education in the field of project management. In addition, PMP certification gives colleagues a commonality of experience and provides opportunities for networking. PMPs share the same frame of reference in project management, regardless of the field of endeavor.

PMP-certified individuals work in a wide array of industries, from aerospace to telecommunications. Many hiring supervisors specify PMP certification as a preferred skill set when soliciting project managers.

Both private- and public-sector employers recognize the value that a PMP-certified employee brings to a project. Corporations embrace the consistent application of project management methodologies for initiating, planning, executing, controlling, and closing projects. The Project Management Institute (PMI) Project Management framework is highly praised by companies and government entities, whether they are engaged in large-scale development projects or simply undertaking small reengineering initiatives. In both scenarios, the PMI approach offers a consistent project management methodology that can be tailored to the size and complexity of the project. This framework, coupled with the PMP certification program, ensures that PMP-certified practitioners are in high demand in the workforce.

PMI has brought the art and science of project management full circle through its PMP certification program and methodology, the Project Management Body of Knowledge (PMBOK). PMI seeks to evaluate project management professionals through the application of the certification process to ensure a dependable workforce with solid credentials. The PMP certification examination tests for comprehensive project management knowledge as well as a thorough understanding of the PMBOK. This approach ensures that PMP-certified practitioners have comparable qualifications and strategic competencies in all aspects of project management. PMI advocates the practice of project management as a discipline, not unlike engineering or any other precise, science-based course of study. As such, PMI developed the PMBOK as a comprehensive framework of best practices for the implementation of project management, regardless of the specific industry.

The Project Management Institute

PMI is the premier project management organization in the world. It is a nonprofit educational group intent on advancing the practice of project management through the promotion and promulgation of widely accepted standards. It has more than 420,000 members in more than 170 countries with more than 250 charter-based local chapters. This is quite a feat for an organization that started in 1969 with five volunteers!

PMI establishes professional standards, provides continuing education opportunities for members, engages in industry-specific research, and offers certifications aimed at unifying and strengthening the discipline of project management.

If you consider yourself a project management professional and want to earn your PMP certification, consider joining PMI. You will receive a reduced rate when sitting for your PMP examination, as well as all the other benefits of PMI membership, including seminars, workshops, and other continuing education opportunities. These benefits include a community of peers that provides valuable information exchange about industry trends and access to the latest knowledge through a monthly magazine and quarterly research journals. To learn more about PMI and membership, visit PMI's website, at www.pmi.org.

What's New in the *PMBOK Guide*, Fifth Edition

PMI, as a member-driven organization, is continually evolving to meet the needs of its membership and the project management profession. To this end, the PMBOK has been revised to incorporate feedback from members and to reflect current industry practice and developments since the previous edition. If you are familiar with the previous edition—the *PMBOK Guide*, Fourth Edition—you will want to acquaint yourself with the changes in the Fifth Edition. This is particularly important if you used an earlier edition of the PMBOK to prepare for the PMP certification examination.

The new edition of the PMBOK pursues greater consistency and clarity over the Fourth Edition. The Fifth Edition also focuses on ensuring alignment with PMI standards and ISO 21500, the project management standard of the International Organization for Standardization. In addition, the *PMBOK Guide*, Fifth Edition introduces business rules to define how to handle the order and detail of information within procedure inputs, tools and techniques, and outputs. The PMBOK now incorporates redefined terms such as *Work Performance Data*, *Work Performance Information*, and *Work Performance Reports*. The new consistent terms align with the Data, Information, Knowledge, Wisdom (DIKW) model developed in the field of knowledge management.

New material has been added to this edition to reflect changes, adaptations, and additions to tools and techniques used in the current practice of project management. The number of processes in the PMBOK has increased from 42 to 47. These five processes were added:

▶ **Plan Scope Management**—Section 5.1

▶ **Plan Schedule Management**—Section 6.1

▶ **Plan Cost Management**—Section 7.1

▶ **Plan Stakeholder Management**—Section 13.2

▶ **Control Stakeholder Engagement**—Section 13.4

In addition, one process was moved to the new Stakeholder Management knowledge area:

▶ **Identify Stakeholders**—Section 10.1 moved to Section 13.1

Finally, the names of 12 processes were changed to promote consistency and clarity:

▶ **Direct and Manage Project Execution**—Section 4.3 changed to Direct and Manage Project Work

▶ **Verify Scope**—Section 5.5 changed to Validate Scope

▶ **Plan Quality**—Section 8.1 changed to Plan Quality Management

▶ **Perform Quality Control**—Section 8.3 changed to Control Quality

▶ **Develop Human Resource Plan**—Section 9.1 changed to Plan Human Resource Management

▶ **Plan Communications**—Section 10.2 changed to Plan Communications Management—Section 10.1

▶ **Distribute Information**—Section 10.3 changed to Manage Communications—Section 10.2

▶ **Report Performance**—Section 10.5 changed to Control Communications—Section 10.3

▶ **Monitor and Control Risks**—Section 11.6 changed to Control Risks

▶ **Plan Procurements**—Section 12.1 changed to Plan Procurement Management

▶ **Administer Procurements**—Section 12.3 changed to Control Procurements

▶ **Manage Stakeholder Expectations**—Section 10.4 changed (and moved) to Manage Stakeholders Engagement—Section 13.3

The *PMBOK Guide*, Fifth Edition defines a new Knowledge Area, Project Stakeholder Management. This new Knowledge Area was added to highlight the importance of stakeholders to the project management process. While PMI has always placed emphasis on stakeholders, a separate Knowledge Area makes it clear that managing stakeholders is fundamental to good project management.

All these changes resulted from PMP input that was used to streamline and clarify the PMBOK. A complete listing of all changes to the *PMBOK Guide*, Fifth Edition, is available in Appendix X1 of the PMBOK, and we also discuss these changes in more detail in Chapter 1, "Project Management Framework Fundamentals." Each change is identified in its respective chapter in the PMBOK.

The new PMP certification examination went into effect on July 31, 2013, and is based on the *PMBOK Guide*, Fifth Edition.

The PMP Certification Process

PMP certification involves a number of steps, beginning with an application to PMI that details the prospective PMP candidate's qualifications, experience, and training. After a candidate has received approval from PMI to sit for the examination, he or she registers for the examination and must comply with various procedures set forth for the examination. The PMP certification process concludes with passage of the examination and issuance of PMP credentials by PMI.

Registering for the PMP Certification Exam

Prior to actually taking a PMP certification examination, you must submit an application to PMI for approval, including detailed documentation supporting your professional project management experience and training in specific areas of expertise.

Application Submission

PMI provides an online application, as well as a downloadable application form on its website. You can find valuable information about the PMP application process in the *PMP Handbook* that is also available on PMI's website. This handbook provides detailed information on every step of the application process. If you believe you meet the requirements for applying for PMP certification, you are ready to apply to PMI.

> **Note**
>
> Read the *PMP Handbook* prior to applying for PMP certification. Much of the information in this section can be found in this handbook, which is available at www.pmi.org/Certification/~/media/PDF/Certifications/pdc_pmphandbook.ashx.

Candidates for PMP certification must meet both the educational and experience requirements for one of two categories. You must submit verification forms showing compliance with these criteria with your application for either category. The two categories are detailed in Tables I.1 and I.2.

Category One, shown in Table I.1, is for applicants possessing a bachelor's degree or equivalent. In this category, less personal project management experience is necessary, although you must possess a minimum of 4,500 hours of hands-on project management activity. Category Two, shown in Table I.2, is ideal for candidates with longer work histories who do not hold a bachelor's degree. In this category, you can use 7,500 hours of project management performance to substitute for a college degree.

TABLE I.1 **Category One Applicants**

Criteria	Minimum	Explanation
Bachelor's degree or equivalent from a university		
Personal project management	4,500 hours	Within the past three years from the date of application.
Nonoverlapping months of personal project management experience	36 months	Individual months count toward the 36 months requirement once, even if you worked on multiple projects during the same month.
Specific instruction that addresses learning objectives in project management	35 contact hours	Must include instruction on project quality, scope, time, cost, human resources, communications, risk, procurement, and integration management.

TABLE I.2 **Category Two Applicants**

Criteria	Minimum	Explanation
Personal project management experience within five process groups	7,500 hours	Within the past five years from the date of application.
Nonoverlapping months of personal project management experience	60 months	Individual months count toward the 60 months requirement once, even if you worked on multiple projects during the same month.
Specific instruction that addresses learning objectives in project management	35 contact hours	Must include instruction on project quality, scope, time, cost, human resources, communications, risk, procurement, and integration management.

Additional information related to the educational and experience requirements for PMP certification eligibility are provided in the PMP Handbook.

Application Fee and PMI Membership

The application also requires an application fee, tiered for PMI members and non-PMI members, with the latter paying a higher rate. For computer-based testing (CBT), members of PMI pay $405 for the examination, while non-members pay $555. The prices for paper-based testing (PBT) are $250 for PMI members and $400 for non-members. The annual cost for PMI membership is $129, which means that membership is actually cheaper than the difference between the examination cost for non-members and members. The total cost for joining PMI and sitting for the PMI examination is $534. (This does not include chapter, special interest groups, and college memberships, which require additional fees.)

Audit

A random sample of applicants are chosen for audit prior to issuing eligibility letters. If you are selected for an audit, you are asked to provide additional information supporting your work experience, including supporting documentation from your supervisors that details your work on specific projects.

Examination Administration

The PMP certification examination is offered globally. CBT is the standard method used to administer the PMP exam. PMI administers CBT through Prometric. A complete list of testing sites and vendors is available on the PMI website. PBT is available if a candidate lives more than 300 km (186.5 miles) from a Prometric CBT site or if a corporate sponsor wishes to administer the exam to its own employees.

Prometric requires a PMI Eligibility ID code to register. PMI provides this code to a PMP candidate when approval is granted to sit for an examination. After you've been approved to sit for the exam, you can register online or use Prometric's interactive voice-response telephone registration system.

Specific instructions for registering are also included in your approval letter from PMI.

To learn more about Prometric and its administration of the PMP certification examination, visit Prometric's website, at www.prometric.com.

After your application has been approved by PMI, passing the PMP certification examination is your final step in becoming a PMP.

Re-Examination

Candidates who do not pass the PMP certification examination on their first attempt may take the exam up to two more times within one year from the original eligibility date.

Cancellation

Candidates can cancel and reschedule an examination at any time more than two business days prior to the scheduled testing. Cancellations within 30 days of the scheduled test date will carry a fee of $70. There are no refunds for any tests cancelled within two days of the scheduled test date.

Candidates unable to appear for a scheduled examination due to a medical emergency must submit written notification to the PMI Certification Program Department within 72 hours of the scheduled exam. A rescheduling fee is charged. All circumstances are reviewed on a case-by-case basis.

Refund

You have one year from the date of your eligibility letter in which to take the PMP certification examination. A refund can be obtained by written request to PMI one month before your exam eligibility expires. A $100 processing fee will be retained from your original application fee.

Arriving at the Exam Site

To be admitted into the test site, you are required to present a current form of government-issued identification that includes a picture and a signature. If your government-issued identification does not display a photograph or a signature, you may use a secondary form of identification with your government-issued identification. The *PMP Handbook* contains a list of acceptable identification types. Your approval letter from PMI and your registration confirmation from Prometric also detail what forms of identification are acceptable. You are not allowed to bring anything to the exam. An examiner provides you with a calculator and scrap paper.

Wear comfortable clothing and layer your clothing. You will spend up to four hours in the examination room, and your ability to concentrate and focus on the task at hand can be dramatically affected by the room temperature and your sense of comfort.

Get to your exam site early so you can review the PMP Cram Sheet provided in this book and any additional notes you create to quickly focus your mind on specific topics prior to the test. An early arrival ensures that you have ample time to relax and mentally prepare for the examination.

In the Exam Room

Do not start the examination immediately. Sit down at your computer terminal and acclimate to the examination room and your immediate environment. Organize your peripherals for your comfort. Are the mouse and keyboard set correctly? Does your chair need to be adjusted? Is the monitor at the correct eye level for you? A few minor corrections can make a big difference during the next few hours.

Prior to the start of the examination, the test administrator will review any specific instructions and tell you what is and is not allowed during the examination period. You are allowed to take breaks and use the restrooms as necessary.

Pretest Tutorial

Prior to beginning the examination, you are provided with a briefing and 15-minute online tutorial designed to familiarize you with the computer and operational procedures for the test. If you have taken a computer-based test previously or have participated in computer-based training, you will feel comfortable in this environment. The pretest tutorial will show you how to navigate through the test using your computer mouse. You'll be shown how to select an answer to a question, move forward to a new question, return to a previous question, and similar functions. The clock begins after you've completed the tutorial, so if you feel comfortable with the information presented, move forward to the actual examination.

Time Allotted for the Test

You have up to four hours to complete the examination. Pace yourself. There are 200 multiple-choice questions, which breaks down to 50 questions per hour, so you have a little more than 1 minute per question. But not all questions require equal time. Don't agonize over every question; do read the question and each possible answer in its entirety prior to selecting an answer.

Answer the PMI Way

More than one answer can seem plausible and correct. You are not asked to select the correct answer but rather the *best* answer from those provided. Attempt to rule out any obviously wrong choices immediately to narrow your field of best answers. You should strive to select the best answer based on how you believe PMI and the PMBOK would respond, given the question, and not necessarily from your own project management experience.

> ### ExamAlert
>
> It cannot be emphasized enough that the PMI answer is the correct answer. You might do a task a certain way in real practice, and that method might even be one of the answer choices, but for purposes of the PMP certification examination, the PMBOK answer is the only correct answer. Don't get caught off guard here!

The best answer as determined by PMI is provided as one of the four possible responses. Be suspicious of answers offering definitive responses like *never* and *always*. Some answers might tout non-PMI methods and reflect common project management misconceptions. Some answers might offer correct information, but the information is not pertinent to the question at hand. Similarly, some questions might contain factually correct information that has no bearing on the possible answers.

Pace Yourself During the Exam

After the first hour, you will be able to determine your speed and make adjustments as necessary. It is important to be aware of your time so you won't have to rush at the end to complete the examination. You should leave adequate time to review any responses you were unsure of and to return to unanswered questions. If you are spending more than one minute on a question, it is better to skip over the question and mark it for review later than to agonize over the question and lose the opportunity to answer other questions whose answers you know.

The examination allows you to mark questions for later review and make multiple passes through the exam. Mark every question you are unsure of, even if you have selected an answer. This approach saves you time when you review your responses because you will not need to review any unmarked questions. If, on a second review, you determine an answer, unmark the question. Continue this process of going through all the marked questions until you have answered all the questions or are nearing the end of the allotted time period.

Save the last 20 minutes or so of the test to finalize any unmarked answers and ensure that you have provided an answer to each question. Try to make a best guess by ruling out definitely wrong answers, as discussed earlier, but do not give up. Select an answer for each question—even if you have to guess. There is no penalty for guessing.

> **ExamAlert**
>
> Remember, there is no penalty for guessing. So be sure all questions have been answered—even if you have to guess. You at least give yourself an opportunity to get it right if you have an answer marked!

Throughout the testing period, keep an eye on the clock or use your watch timer to remind you at discreet intervals to take a break. It is amazing what simply standing up and stretching for a few minutes can do for your concentration.

At the conclusion of the test, candidates can opt to complete a satisfaction survey.

Exam Room Surveillance

You might be under surveillance during the examination. Some testing centers use both video and human monitors to ensure the validity of the test. After you get under way with your examination and start to concentrate on the task at hand, you will be unaware of any other activity. Any monitoring by the testing center will be unobtrusive.

Grading Your Exam

At the end of the examination period, you will receive a printed copy of your results indicating your status—either pass or fail. The scores are submitted to PMI by the end of the business day. If you have passed the examination, PMI will mail a PMP credential packet to you within six to eight weeks.

If you are taking a PBT, answer sheets are scored when they are returned to the test administrator. You can request that your exam be hand scored for an additional $45 fee.

Any questions regarding your score from either the CBT or PBT should be addressed to PMI's exam supervisor.

About This Book

This book offers you tools, techniques, tips, and other information to assist you in passing the PMP certification examination and becoming PMP certified. The emphasis is on reconciling your approach to the exam with PMI's viewpoint and perspective on the examination. This book is not a guide to general project management but rather a specific study tool aimed at distilling PMI's approach to project management as set forth in the *PMBOK Guide*, Fifth Edition. Project initiation, planning, execution, control, and closing are the core topics in this book and are parallel to those same key areas in the PMBOK.

Using This Book and CD

This book and CD prepare you to pass the PMP certification examination by highlighting important project management principles, providing insight into proven test-taking strategies, emphasizing key information you can expect to see on the examination, and providing exam practice questions. You get guidance and clarification on PMBOK concepts and understand their relationship to other project management methodologies. You have many opportunities to apply your knowledge through practice examinations and test questions.

This book provides a practice examination as well as practice questions at the beginning and end of each section. The Cram Saver questions before each section help you decide how well you already know the material. If you answer all of the Cram Saver questions correctly, you can choose to skim a section before going to its Cram Quiz at the end. After you complete a section, answer the Cram Quiz questions to determine how well you comprehended the information in the section. If you missed more than one or two questions, work your way through the section again, focusing on the concepts that you missed.

Similarly, you can test your knowledge and evaluate your level of preparation for the PMP certification examination by taking the practice exam under real conditions. After you've worked your way through this book, take the practice exam. Evaluate your results and then reread the chapters of this book related to any areas of the practice examination where you were less certain or did not select the correct answer.

Finally, the Cram Sheet condenses all the concepts, knowledge areas, processes groups, terminology, and formulas presented throughout this book into a tear-out sheet you can take with you to the exam site for quick review prior to entering the testing facility. The Cram Sheet is also a valuable tool for use in quick daily reviews after you have completed this book. Review the Cram Sheet every day; if any terms seem vague, go to the appropriate topic in the book for a refresher.

Pearson IT Certification Practice Test Engine and Questions on the CD

The CD in the back of the book includes the Pearson IT Certification Practice Test engine, software that displays and grades a set of exam-realistic multiple-choice questions. This book comes with three practice exams for use with the Pearson IT Certification Practice Test engine. Using the Pearson IT Certification Practice Test engine, you can either study by going through the questions in Study Mode or take a simulated exam that mimics real exam conditions.

The installation process requires two major steps: installing the software and activating the exam. The CD in the back of this book has a recent copy of the Pearson IT Certification Practice Test engine. The practice exam—the database of exam questions—is not on the CD.

> **Note**
>
> The cardboard CD case in the back of this book includes the CD and a piece of paper. The paper lists the activation code for the practice exams associated with this book. Do not lose the activation code. On the opposite side of the paper from the activation code is a unique, one-time-use coupon code for the purchase of the Premium Edition eBook and Practice Test.

Installing the Software from the CD

The Pearson IT Certification Practice Test is a Windows-only desktop application. You can run it on a Mac using a Windows virtual machine, but it was built specifically for the PC platform. The minimum system requirements are as follows:

▶ Windows XP (SP3), Windows Vista (SP2), Windows 7, or Windows 8

▶ Microsoft .NET Framework 4.0 client

▶ Pentium-class 1-GHz processor (or equivalent)

▶ 512 MB RAM

▶ 650 MB hard disk space plus 50 MB for each downloaded practice exam

▶ Access to the Internet to register and download exam databases

The software installation process is relatively routine. If you have already installed the Pearson IT Certification Practice Test software from another Pearson product, there is no need for you to reinstall the software. Simply launch the software on your desktop and proceed to activate the practice exam from this book by using the activation code included in the CD sleeve.

The following steps outline the installation process:

1. Insert the CD into your PC.

2. The software that automatically runs is the Pearson software to access and use all CD-based features, including the exam engine and the CD-only appendixes. From the Practice Exam tab, click the option Install Practice Exam.

3. Respond to the prompts as you would with any typical software installation process. The installation process gives you the option to activate your exam with the activation code supplied on the paper in the CD sleeve. This process requires that you establish a Pearson website login. You need this login to activate the exam, so please do register when prompted. If you already have a Pearson website login, there is no need to register again. Just use your existing login.

Activating and Downloading the Practice Exam

After the exam engine is installed, you should then activate the exam associated with this book (if you did not do so during the installation process) as follows:

1. Start the Pearson IT Certification Practice Test software from the Windows Start menu or from your desktop shortcut icon.

2. To activate and download the exam associated with this book, from the My Products or Tools tab, click the Activate button.

3. At the next screen, enter the activation key from the paper inside the cardboard CD holder in the back of the book. Then click the Activate button.

4. After the activation process downloads the practice exam, click Next and then click Finish.

When the activation process is complete, the My Products tab should list your new exam. If you do not see the exam, make sure you have selected the My Products tab on the menu. At this point, the software and practice exam are ready to use. Simply select the exam and click the Open Exam button.

To update a particular exam you have already activated and downloaded, simply click the Tools tab and click the Update Products button. Updating your exams ensures that you have the latest changes and updates to the exam data.

If you want to check for updates to the Pearson IT Certification Practice Test software, simply click the Tools tab and click the Update Engine button. You can then ensure that you are running the latest version of the software engine.

Activating Other Exams

You must complete the exam software installation process and the registration process only once. Then, for each new exam, you have to follow only a few steps. For instance, if you buy another new Pearson IT Cert Guide or Cisco Press Official Cert Guide, extract the activation code from the CD sleeve in the back of that book. From there, all you have to do is start the exam engine (if it's not still up and running) and perform steps 2 through 4 from the previous list.

Chapter Formats

Each chapter follows a regular structure and provides graphical cues about especially important or useful material. The structure of a typical chapter is as follows:

▶ **Topical coverage**—Each chapter begins by listing the exam topics covered in that chapter.

▶ **Cram Saver questions**—You get a short list of questions related to the specific section topic. Each question is followed by explanations of both correct and incorrect answers. The Cram Saver questions help you decide how well you already know the material covered in the section.

▶ **Exam Alerts**—Throughout the topical coverage section, Exam Alerts highlight material most likely to appear on the exam by using a special exam alert layout that looks like this:

ExamAlert

This is what an Exam Alert looks like. An Exam Alert stresses concepts, terms, or activities that are likely to appear in one or more exam questions. For that reason, any information offset in Exam Alert format is worthy of extra attention on your part.

Even if material isn't flagged as an Exam Alert, all the content in this book is associated in some way with test-related material. What appears in the chapter content is critical knowledge.

▶ **Cram Quiz questions**—Each section ends with a short list of test questions related to the specific topics of that section. Each question is followed by explanations of both correct and incorrect answers. These practice questions highlight the most important areas on the exam.

The bulk of the book follows this chapter structure, but there are a few other important elements:

▶ **PMP Practice Exam**—There is a full practice test at the end of this book. The questions are designed to challenge your knowledge and readiness for the PMP exam.

▶ **Answers to the PMP Practice Exam**—This book provides the answers to the practice exam, complete with explanations of both the correct responses and the incorrect ones.

▶ **Cram Sheet**—This tear-out sheet inside the front cover is a valuable tool that represents a collection of the most critical items you should memorize before taking the test. Remember, you can dump this information out of your head onto the margins of your test booklet or scratch paper as soon as you enter the testing room.

You might want to look at the Cram Sheet in your car or in the lobby of the testing center just before you walk into the testing center. The Cram Sheet's information is grouped together under headings, so you can review the appropriate parts just before the test.

Using the CD

The CD contains two elements that help you prepare for the PMP exam:

▶ **Exam Practice Engine**—This exam engine software includes all the questions from the book's practice exam in electronic format. You can take a full, timed exam or choose to focus on particular topics in study mode. Use your feedback and the topics listed in the book to zero in on the areas where you need more study.

▶ **Cram Quizzes**—All of the book's Cram Quizzes and their answers have been compiled into one convenient document on the CD for you to have another portable practice option.

About the PMP Exam

The PMP certification examination consists of 200 four-option, multiple-choice questions developed by PMPs. According to the *PMP Handbook*, "The passing score for all PMI credential examinations is determined by sound psychometric analysis" and is not based on a fixed number of correct answers.

There are no prescribed guidelines for a course of study because the examination is objective in scope and intended to test your knowledge of the project management field; however, emphasis is strongly placed on the PMBOK.

Do note that the PMP exam includes a performance requirement specific to professional responsibility in the practice of project management. The PMI Code of Ethics and Professional Conduct is not a component of the PMBOK; rather, it is a standalone document available on the PMI website that you will be tested on as part of the examination. The PMI Code of Ethics and Professional Conduct can also be found in the *PMP Handbook*.

The PMP certification examination tests for professional responsibility and five process groups:

- ▶ Initiating

- ▶ Planning

- ▶ Executing

- ▶ Monitoring and Controlling

- ▶ Closing

The most significant knowledge areas are

- ▶ **Planning**—This knowledge area accounts for 24% of the test material.

- ▶ **Executing**—This knowledge area accounts for 30% of the test material.

- ▶ **Monitoring and Controlling**—This knowledge area accounts for 25% of the test material.

Overall, 79% of the examination deals exclusively with planning, executing, and monitoring and controlling projects.

Initiating accounts for 13% of the exam, and closing accounts for 8%.

A new PMP certification examination went into effect on July 31, 2013, based on the *PMBOK Guide*, Fifth Edition.

PMP Exam Topics

Table I.3 lists all the PMP exam topics covered in this book. Use this table to find where a topic is covered in the book. For example, if your CD exam feedback indicates that you scored poorly in a particular topic, find that topic in this table so you can find where it is covered in the book.

In general, the chapters are organized by process group. Within each process group, the sections are organized by knowledge area. As much as possible, the flow is consistent with the project flow defined in the PMBOK. The section references in the following table and throughout the book refer to the specific sections in the *PMBOK Guide*, Fifth Edition. At any time you can go directly to the PMBOK to see the section that corresponds to the topic in this book that you are reading.

TABLE I.3 **PMP Exam Topics**

Topic	Chapter
Understand the Project Management Framework	1
Explain Organizational and Environmental Factors	1
Describe the Project Life Cycle	1
PMI Code of Ethics and Professional Conduct	2
Responsibility	2
Respect	2
Fairness	2
Honesty	2
Initiating Process Group—3.3	3
Develop Project Charter—4.1	3
Identify Stakeholders—13.1	3
Planning Process Group—3.4	4
Develop Project Management Plan—4.2	4
Plan Scope Management—5.1	4
Collect Requirements—5.2	4
Define Scope—5.3	4
Create WBS—5.4	4
Plan Schedule Management—6.1	4
Define Activities—6.2	4
Sequence Activities—6.3	4
Estimate Activity Resources—6.4	4
Estimate Activity Durations—6.5	4
Develop Schedule—6.6	4
Plan Cost Management—7.1	4
Estimate Costs—7.2	4
Determine Budget—7.3	4
Plan Quality Management—8.1	5
Plan Human Resource Management—9.1	5
Plan Communication Management—10.1	5
Plan Risk Management—11.1	5
Identify Risks—11.2	5

Topic	Chapter
Perform Qualitative Risk Assessment—11.3	5
Perform Quantitative Risk Assessment—11.4	5
Plan Risk Responses—11.5	5
Plan Procurement Management—12.1	5
Plan Stakeholder Management—13.2	5
Executing Process Group—3.5	6
Direct and Manage Project Work—4.3	6
Perform Quality Assurance—8.2	6
Acquire Project Team—9.2	6
Develop Project Team—9.3	6
Manage Project Team—9.4	6
Manage Communications—10.2	6
Conduct Procurements—12.2	6
Manage Stakeholder Engagement—13.3	6
Monitoring and Controlling Process Group—3.6	7
Monitor and Control Project—4.4	7
Perform Integrated Change Control—4.5	7
Validate Scope—5.5	7
Control Scope—5.6	7
Control Schedule—6.7	7
Control Costs—7.4	7
Control Quality—8.3	7
Control Communications—10.3	7
Control Risks—11.6	7
Control Procurements—12.3	7
Control Stakeholder Engagement—13.4	7
Close Project or Phase—4.6	8
Close Procurements—12.4	8

CHAPTER 1

Project Management Framework Fundamentals

This chapter covers the following PMP exam topics:

▶ Understand the Project Management Framework

▶ Explain Organizational and Environmental Factors

▶ Describe the Project Life Cycle

(For more information on the PMP exam topics, see "About the PMP Exam" in the Introduction.)

This chapter introduces the basic terminology and topics that the Project Management Body of Knowledge (PMBOK) covers and provides a general outline for the PMP exam material. The Project Management Institute (PMI) was formed in 1969 as a group dedicated to the discipline of project management. PMI published the first draft of the PMBOK in 1986 as a study guide for the PMP certification exam and a standard collection of project management best practices. The current PMBOK version is the result of changes in the project management discipline, as well as standardization of project management concepts. The topics in this chapter correspond to the first three chapters of the PMBOK, including project introduction, project life cycle, and project processes.

The Project Management Framework

▶ **Understand the Project Management Framework**

CramSaver

If you can correctly answer these questions before going through this section, save time by skimming the Exam Alerts in this section and then completing the Cram Quiz at the end of the section.

1. What are the two most important attributes that describe a project?

2. What is the relationship between a project, a program, and a portfolio?

Answers

1. According to the PMBOK, a project is "a temporary endeavor undertaken to create a unique product, service, or result."

2. A group of related projects is called a *program*. A *portfolio* is a collection of projects and programs that satisfy the strategic needs of an organization.

The Project Management framework is the first section of the PMBOK and serves as the foundation for the document. Briefly stated, it presents the structure used to discuss and organize projects. The PMBOK uses this structure to document all facets of a project on which consensus has been reached among a broadly diverse group of project managers. The PMBOK is not only the document that defines the methods to manage projects; it is also the most widely accepted project management foundation. This document provides a frame of reference for managing projects and teaching the fundamental concepts of project management.

Note that the PMBOK does not address every area of project management in all industries. It does, however, address the recognized best practices for the management of a single project. Most organizations have developed their own practices that are specific to their organization.

It is important that you read the PMBOK. Although many good references and test preparation sources can help prepare for the PMP exam, they are not substitutes for the PMBOK itself.

ExamAlert

The PMP exam tests your knowledge of project management in the context of the PMBOK and PMI philosophy. Regardless of the experience you might have in project management, your answers will be correct only if they concur with PMI philosophy. If the PMBOK presents a method that differs from your experience, go with the PMBOK's approach. That being said, the PMP exam will also contain questions that are not specifically addressed in the PMBOK. It is important that you coordinate your understanding of project management with that of PMI. This book will help you do that.

What a Project Is and What It Is Not

The starting point in discussing how projects should be properly managed is to first understand what a project is (and what it is not). According to the PMBOK, a *project* has two main characteristics that differentiate it from regular, day-to-day operation. Know these two characteristics of projects.

A Project Is Temporary

Unlike day-to-day operation, a project has specific starting and ending dates. Of the two dates, the ending date is the more important. A project ends either when its objectives have been met or when the project is terminated due to its objectives not being met. If you can't tell when an endeavor starts or ends, it's not a project. This characteristic is important because projects are, by definition, constrained by a schedule.

A Project Is an Endeavor Undertaken to Produce a Unique Product or Service

In addition to having a discrete time frame, a project must also produce one or more specific products or services. A project must "do" something. A project that terminates on schedule might still not be successful; it must also produce something unique.

ExamAlert

The PMP exam contains a few questions on the definition of *project*. Simply put, if an endeavor fails to meet both of the project criteria, it is an operational activity. Remember this: Projects exist to achieve a goal. When the goal is met, the project is complete. Operations conduct activities that sustain processes, often indefinitely.

Programs, Portfolios, and the PMO

It is common practice for an organization to have more than one project active at a time. In fact, several projects that share common characteristics or are related in some way are often grouped together to make management of the projects more efficient. A group of related projects is called a *program*. If there are multiple projects and programs in an organization, they can further be grouped into one or more portfolios. A *portfolio* is a collection of projects and programs that satisfy the strategic needs of an organization.

> **ExamAlert**
>
> The PMP exam and the PMBOK only cover techniques to manage single projects. You need to be aware of what programs and portfolios are, but you will only address single project management topics in regard to the exam.

Many organizations have found that project management is so effective that they maintain an organizational unit with the primary responsibility of managing projects and programs. The unit is commonly called the *project management office (PMO)*. The PMO is responsible for coordinating projects and, in some cases, providing resources for managing projects. A PMO can make the project manager's job easier by maintaining project management standards and implementing policies and procedures that are common within the organization. According to the PMBOK, the PMO supports project managers by

- ▶ "Managing shared resources across all projects administered by the PMO."

- ▶ "Identifying and developing project management methodology, best practices, and standards."

- ▶ "Coaching, mentoring, training, and oversight."

- ▶ "Monitoring compliance with project management standards policies, procedures, and templates via project audits."

- ▶ "Developing and managing project policies, procedures, templates, and other shared documentation (organizational process assets)."

- ▶ "Coordinating communication across projects."

The PMBOK defines three types of PMO structures, depending on the amount of influence and control the PMO has over projects. These are the three types of PMO structures:

▶ **Supportive**—The PMO supplies technical and administrative support and provides input to project managers, as needed. This type of PMO provides low control.

▶ **Controlling**—The PMO does not directly manage projects but does require compliance with organizational methodologies, frameworks, and tools. This type of PMO provides medium control.

▶ **Directive**—The PMO manages projects directly. This type of PMO provides a high level of control.

What Project Management Is

According to the PMBOK, "Project management is the application of knowledge, skills, tools, and techniques to project activities to meet project requirements." In other words, project management is taking what you know and proactively applying that knowledge to effectively guide your project through its life cycle.

The purpose of applying this knowledge is to help the project meet its objectives. Sounds pretty straightforward, doesn't it? The PMP exam tests your project management knowledge, but it's more than that. It is also a test that evaluates your ability to apply your knowledge through the use of skills, tools, and techniques. The application of project management knowledge is what makes the exam challenging. Understanding project management is more than just memorization. You do have to memorize some things (and we'll let you know what those are), but it's more important to know how to apply what you know. Some of the hardest questions on the exam look like they have two, or even three, correct answers. You really have to understand the PMBOK to choose the most correct answer.

ExamAlert

Did you notice I said the *most correct answer*? The PMP exam throws several questions at you that seem to have more than one correct answer. In fact, many questions on the exam have multiple answers that can be considered correct. You need to be able to choose the one that best satisfies the question as asked. Read each question carefully and always remember that the PMBOK rules.

Changes in the *PMBOK Guide*, Fifth Edition

PMI is constantly reviewing its documents and exams for currency and applicability to today's project management practices. The *PMBOK Guide*,

Fifth Edition, was released in December 2012 as an update to the previous edition, the *PMBOK Guide*, Fourth Edition. There are several changes in the new edition. None of the changes are major, although the PMBOK has been slightly reorganized to better reflect current project management practices. The changes from the Fourth Edition focus on increasing the consistency and clarity of the guide and on harmonizing with other PMI standards and ISO 21500. Here is a summary of the changes that are included in the *PMBOK Guide*, Fifth Edition:

▶ Established business rules to promote clarity and consistency within the inputs, tools and techniques, and outputs for all processes.

▶ Ensured that terms in the PMBOK align with the PMI Lexicon of Project Management Terms.

▶ Improved consistency by defining and using standard terms throughout the PMBOK, including work performance data, work performance information, and work performance reports.

▶ Added five new processes, moved one to a different knowledge area, and added a new knowledge area. The *PMBOK Guide*, Fifth Edition, defines a total of 47 processes (up from 42 defined in the *PMBOK Guide*, Fourth Edition).

▶ Clarified the differences between the Project Management Plan and the Project *Documents*.

▶ Moved the Standard for Project Management of a Project from Section 3 to Appendix A1 and replaced Section 3 with an overview of the process groups and knowledge areas.

ExamAlert

PMI transitioned to the *PMBOK Guide*, Fifth Edition exam on July 31, 2013. All PMP exams after the transition date are based on the *PMBOK Guide*, Fifth Edition. If you have been studying another reference that is based on the *PMBOK Guide*, Fourth Edition, make sure you review the newer PMBOK before taking the exam. (Of course, this reference covers the new PMBOK material.)

To summarize the process additions, deletions, and name changes, Table 1.1 lists the processes that have changed in the *PMBOK Guide*, Fifth Edition. (Some processes only change the section number where they appear in the document. We highlight just name changes here.)

TABLE 1.1 **Process Name Changes in the *PMBOK Guide*, Fifth Edition**

Process Name, Fourth Edition	Process Name, Fifth Edition
4.3 Direct and Manage Project Execution	4.3 Direct and Manage Project Work
Not in this edition	5.1 Plan Scope Management
5.5 Verify Scope	5.5 Validate Scope
Not in this edition	6.1 Plan Schedule Management
Not in this edition	7.1 Plan Cost Management
8.1 Plan Quality	8.1 Plan Quality Management
8.3 Perform Quality Control	8.3 Control Quality
9.1 Develop Human Resources Plan	9.1 Plan Human Resource Management
10.2 Plan Communications	10.1 Plan Communications Management
10.3 Distribute Information	10.2 Manage Communications
10.4 Manage Stakeholder Expectations	13.3 Manage Stakeholder Engagement
10.5 Report Performance	10.3 Control Communications
11.6 Monitor and Control Risks	11.6 Control Risks
12.1 Plan Procurements	12.1 Plan Procurement Management
12.3 Administer Procurements	12.3 Control Procurements
Not in this edition	13.2 Plan Stakeholder Management
Not in this edition	13.4 Control Stakeholder Engagement

In addition to the process name changes, each knowledge area incorporates changes from the *PMBOK Guide*, Fourth Edition, that help to clarify the document and make the various sections more cohesive. The *PMBOK Guide*, Fifth Edition, also separates stakeholder activities from the Project Communications Management knowledge area to create a new knowledge area, Project Stakeholder Management. Be sure you focus on the changed material as you study for the exam if you are already comfortable with a previous PMBOK edition.

Project Management Knowledge Areas

The PMBOK organizes all the activities that define a project's life cycle into 47 processes. These processes represent content from 10 knowledge areas. It is extremely important to have a good understanding of each of the project processes and how they relate to one another. We'll go into more details of each process in a later section. For now, understand the 10 knowledge areas and what purposes they serve for the project. The PMBOK itself is organized by knowledge areas, and there is a separate chapter for each knowledge area.

Table 1.2 shows the 10 knowledge areas and gives a brief description of each.

TABLE 1.2 **Project Management Knowledge Areas**

Knowledge Area	Description
Project Integration Management	Processes and activities that pull together the various elements of project management, including developing plans, managing project execution, monitoring work and changes, and closing the project.
Project Scope Management	Processes that ensure the project includes the work required to successfully complete the project, and no more. This includes scope planning, definition, verification, and control. This area also includes work breakdown structure creation.
Project Time Management	Processes that ensure the project completes in a timely manner. Activity sequencing and scheduling activities occur in this area.
Project Cost Management	Processes that ensure the project completes within the approved budget. Basically, any cost management activity goes here.
Project Quality Management	Processes that ensure the project will meet its objectives. This area includes quality planning, assurance, and control.
Project Human Resource Management	Processes that organize and manage the project team.
Project Communications Management	Processes that specify how and when team members communicate and share information with one another and others not on the team.
Project Risk Management	Processes that conduct risk management activities for the project. These activities include risk analysis, response planning, monitoring, and control.
Project Procurement Management	Processes that manage the acquisition of products and services for the project, along with seller and contract management.
Project Stakeholder Management	Processes that identify the parties that could impact, or be impacted by, the project and develop strategies to manage their engagement in the project.

Figure 1.1 shows each of the project management knowledge areas and the specific processes contained in each one.

4. Integration Management	5. Scope Management	6. Time Management
4.1 Develop Project Charter 4.2 Develop Project Management Plan 4.3 Direct and Manage Project Work 4.4 Monitor and Control Project Work 4.5 Perform Integrated Change Control 4.6 Close Project or Phase	5.1 Plan Scope Management 5.2 Collect Requirements 5.3 Define Scope 5.4 Create WBS 5.5 Validate Scope 5.6 Control Scope	6.1 Plan Schedule Management 6.2 Define Activities 6.3 Sequence Activities 6.4 Estimate Activity Resources 6.5 Estimate Activity Durations 6.6 Develop Schedule 6.7 Control Schedule

7. Cost Management	8. Quality Management	9. Human Resource Management
7.1 Plan Cost Management 7.2 Estimate Costs 7.3 Determine Budget 7.4 Control Costs	8.1 Plan Quality Management 8.2 Perform Quality Assurance 8.3 Control Quality	9.1 Plan Human Resource Management 9.2 Acquire Project Team 9.3 Develop Project Team 9.4 Manage Project Team

10. Communications Management	11. Risk Management	12. Procurement Management
10.1 Plan Communications Management 10.2 Manage Communications 10.3 Control Communications	11.1 Plan Risk Management 11.2 Identify Risks 11.3 Perform Qualitative Risk Analysis 11.4 Perform Quantitative Risk Analysis 11.5 Plan Risk Responses 11.6 Control Risks	12.1 Plan Procurement Management 12.2 Conduct Procurements 12.3 Control Procurements 12.4 Close Procurements

13. Stakeholder Management
13.1 Identify Stakeholders 13.2 Plan Stakeholder Management 13.3 Manage Stakeholder Expectations 13.4 Control Stakeholder Engagement

FIGURE 1.1 **Project management knowledge areas and processes.**

Cram Quiz

Answer these questions. The answers follow the last question. If you cannot answer these questions correctly, consider reading this section again until you can.

1. You are a project manager working for a large utility company. You have been assigned the responsibility to manage a project that performs monthly security vulnerability assessments and addresses any identified vulnerabilities. You question the assignment because

   ○ **A.** Security vulnerability assessments do not materially contribute to your organization's products and should not be considered important enough to be classified as a project.

   ○ **B.** This endeavor cannot be considered a project because no start date is specified.

   ○ **C.** The recurring nature of the assessment in addition to the lack of ending date means that this endeavor is not a project at all.

   ○ **D.** A security vulnerability assessment produces no specific product, so it is not a project.

2. Which project knowledge area contains the processes that ensure the project includes the work required to successfully complete the project, and no more?

   ○ **A.** Project Scope Management

   ○ **B.** Project Quality Management

   ○ **C.** Project Integration Management

   ○ **D.** Project Risk Management

Cram Quiz Answers

1. Answer C is the best answer. As explained in this question, recurring security vulnerability assessments with no ending date cannot be considered a project. Projects must have time boundaries. Answer A is incorrect because the project product does not have to be directly related to an organization's main product(s). Answer B is incorrect because the lack of a specific start date in the question description would not automatically disqualify the assessment as a project. Answer D is incorrect because a security vulnerability assessment does create at least one product—the vulnerability assessment report.

2. Answer A is the best answer. Project scope management is mainly concerned with defining the work a project needs to accomplish. This definition is used to ensure all the necessary work is done and no unnecessary work is done. Answers B, C, and D are incorrect because these knowledge areas focus on areas of a project other than scope.

Organizational Frameworks

▶ **Explain Organizational and Environmental Factors**

CramSaver

If you can correctly answer these questions before going through this section, save time by skimming the Exam Alerts in this section and then completing the Cram Quiz at the end of the section.

1. What are the three main types of organizational structures?

2. What are some of the resources often included in the organizational process assets, which are used as inputs to many project processes?

Answers

1. The PMBOK defines the *functional*, *matrix*, and *projectized* organizational structures.

2. Common Organizational Process Assets include

   ▶ Organizational policies

   ▶ Operational guidelines

   ▶ Templates used to create many project process outputs

   ▶ Project closure procedures

   ▶ Communication requirements and procedures

   ▶ Change control procedures

   ▶ Financial control procedures

   ▶ Quality control procedures

   ▶ Project historical files

   ▶ Pertinent organizational knowledge bases

In nearly all cases, a project exists within a larger organization. Some group or organization creates each project, and the project team must operate within the larger organization's environment. Simply put, no project exists in a vacuum. Every process within every project is affected to some degree by organizational culture and practices. Let's explore some of the most common organizational effects on projects.

Working with Organizational Politics and Influences

In many cases, the extent to which the initiating organization derives revenue from projects affects how projects are regarded. In an organization where the primary stream of revenue comes from various projects, the project manager generally enjoys more authority and access to resources. On the other hand, organizations that create projects only due to outside demands will likely make it more difficult for the project manager to acquire resources. If a particular resource is needed to perform both operational and project work, many functional managers will resist requests to assign that resource to a project.

Another factor that influences how projects operate with respect to sponsoring organizations is the level of sponsorship from the project's origin. A project that has a sponsor who is at the director level typically encounters far less resistance than one with a sponsor who is a functional manager. The reason for this is simple: Many managers tend to protect their own resources and are not willing to share them unless they have sufficient motivation to do so. The more authority a project sponsor possesses, the easier time the project manager has when requesting resources from various sources.

In addition to the previous issues, the sponsoring organization's maturity and project orientation can have a substantial effect on each project. More mature organizations tend to have more general management practices in place that allow projects to operate in a stable environment. Projects in less mature organizations might find that they must compete for resources and management attention due to having fewer established policies. There can also be many issues related to the culture of an organization, such as values, beliefs, and expectations that can affect projects.

The last major factor that has a material impact on how projects exist within the larger organization is the management style of the organization. The next section introduces the main types of project management organizations and their relative strengths and weaknesses.

Differentiating Functional, Matrix, and Projectized Organizational Structures

Each organization approaches the relationship between operations and projects differently. The PMBOK defines three main organizational structures that affect many aspects of a project, including

▶ The project manager's authority

▶ Resource availability

▶ Control of the project budget

▶ The project manager and administrative staff roles

Functional Organizational Structure

A *functional* organizational structure is a classical hierarchy in which each employee has a single superior. Employees are then organized by specialty, and work accomplished is generally specific to that specialty. Communication with other groups generally occurs by passing information requests up the hierarchy and over to the desired group or manager. Of all the organizational structures, this one tends to be the most difficult for the project manager. The project manager lacks the authority to assign resources and must acquire people and other resources from multiple functional managers. In many cases, the project's priority is considered to be lower than operations for which the functional manager is directly responsible. In these organizations, it is common for the project manager to appeal to the senior management to resolve resource issues.

Matrix Organizational Structure

A *matrix* organization is a blended organizational structure. Although a functional hierarchy is still in place, the project manager is recognized as a valuable position and is given more authority to manage the project and assign resources. Matrix organizations can be further divided into weak, balanced, and strong matrix organizations. The difference between the three is the level of authority given to the project manager (PM). A *weak* matrix gives more authority to the functional manager (FM), whereas the *strong* matrix gives more power to the PM. As the name suggests, the *balanced* matrix balances power between the FM and the PM.

Projectized Organizational Structure

In a *projectized* organization, there is no defined hierarchy. Resources are brought together specifically for the purpose of a project. The necessary resources are acquired for the project, and the people assigned to the project work for the PM only for the duration of the project. At the end of each project, resources are either reassigned to another project or returned to a resource pool.

There are many subtle differences between the types of structures. Table 1.3 compares the various organizational structures and the roles of the project manager and the functional manager.

TABLE 1.3 **Organizational Structures**

	Functional	Weak Matrix	Balanced Matrix	Strong Matrix	Projectized
Description	Traditional organization with a direct supervisor.	The PM and FM share responsibility, with the FM having more authority.	The PM and FM share responsibility, with each having equal authority.	The PM and FM share responsibility, with the PM having more authority.	Projects do not exist under functional departments. The PM generally has sole management authority.
Authority of project manager	Very low	Low	Low to medium	Medium to high	High
Resource availability	Very low	Low	Low to medium	Medium to high	High
Project manager involvement	Part-time	Part-time	Full-time	Full-time	Full-time
Staff involvement	Part-time	Part-time	Part-time	Full-time	Full-time
Advantages	The FM holds accountability for the project.	The PM gets some authority to manage the project.	The PM and FM share the responsibility for the project.	The PM gets more authority to assign resources and manage the project.	The PM has full, or almost full, authority to staff and manage the project.
Disadvantages	The PM holds little or no authority.	The FM can see the PM as a threat and cause conflict.	The PM and FM can be confused about who manages what.	The FM may feel out of the loop.	The PM holds accountability for the project.

Understanding Enterprise Environmental Factors

It is the responsibility of a project manager to understand the project environment. All projects operate within a specific environment or blend of environments. In addition to understanding the organizational structure, a project manager needs to understand the effects that enterprise environmental factors play in managing projects. The most obvious enterprise environmental factors for projects are

▶ Organizational culture and structure

▶ Human resources currently in place

▶ Political climate

▶ Government or industry standards and regulations

▶ Infrastructure

▶ Marketplace conditions

▶ Stakeholder risk tolerances

Organizational Process Assets

Two of the goals of project management are to make projects repeatable and to do a better job with each new project. To this end, organizations that are committed to effective project management develop shared, and often standardized, resources to help project managers do their jobs well. These resources are called *organizational process assets* and include formal and informal plans, policies, procedures, and guidelines.

These assets might begin as a simple set of templates and project-related documents. As these assets are put to use, they tend to be altered and refined. New documents often become necessary or useful as well. All lessons learned from previous projects should be examined to apply any necessary changes to the process assets. This continuous process of improvement encourages the base of assets to become a critical core of resources for any project. You will see organizational process assets mentioned in many of the project management processes. The assets can include many types of documents, including

▶ Organizational policies

▶ Operational guidelines

▶ Templates used to create many project process outputs

▶ Project closure procedures

▶ Communication requirements and procedures

▶ Change control procedures

▶ Financial control procedures

▶ Quality control procedures

▶ Project historical files

▶ Pertinent organizational knowledge bases

Cram Quiz

Answer these questions. The answers follow the last question. If you cannot answer these questions correctly, consider reading this section again until you can.

1. You are managing a project that will implement a new accounting software package. You have assigned the resources, both personnel and equipment, and want to keep the IT manager in the loop by informing her of your decisions. Which type of organizational structure are you working in?

   O **A.** Projectized

   O **B.** Strong matrix

   O **C.** Weak matrix

   O **D.** Functional

2. During your accounting software implementation project, two project team members have difficulty working together. They come to you, the project manager, for help with resolving the issues. You immediately set up a meeting that includes the functional manager. After the meeting, you and the functional manager discuss the issues and agree on a solution. This type of management probably indicates you are working in what type of organizational structure?

   O **A.** Functional

   O **B.** Weak matrix

   O **C.** Balanced matrix

   O **D.** Projectized

Cram Quiz Answers

1. **Answer B is correct.** In a strong matrix, the project manager has the preeminent position of authority. Because the functional manager does still have authority, a good project manager will keep the functional manager in the loop as much as possible. Answer A is incorrect because projectized organizations do not have functional managers. Answers C and D are incorrect because in a weak matrix in a functional organization, the project manager does not have greater authority than the functional manager. The project manager would have to defer to the functional manager, not just keep her in the loop.

2. **Answer C is correct.** In a balanced matrix, the project manager and functional manager work together to meet the needs of the department and the project. Answers A and B are incorrect because the functional manager has greater authority and would likely handle problems directly in a functional or weak matrix structure. Answer D is incorrect because the project manager would handle such issues directly in a projectized organization.

Project Life Cycle and Organization

▶ **Describe the Project Life Cycle**

CramSaver

If you can correctly answer these questions before going through this section, save time by skimming the Exam Alerts in this section and then completing the Cram Quiz at the end of the section.

1. At what point in a project's life cycle is the level of uncertainty and risk the highest?

2. What is a project stakeholder?

3. List some common project constraints that a project manager must balance.

Answers

1. The level of uncertainty and risk is the highest at the beginning of a project because the least is known about the project at that point.

2. A stakeholder is any person or entity with an interest in a project or its outcome. Stakeholders can include the project manager, customers, project team members, the performing organization, the project management team, influencers, and the PMO.

3. Common project constraints include scope, quality, schedule, budget, resources, and risk.

Projects occur in the context of an organization that is larger than the project itself. It is important to understand the structure of a project and how it matures from beginning to end to properly manage the work of the project. This section examines the life cycle of projects and how they are organized to be effective and repeatable.

Understanding Project Life Cycles

The project manager and project team have one shared goal: to carry out the work of the project for the purpose of meeting the project's objectives. Every project has an inception, a period during which activities move the project toward completion, and a termination (either successful or unsuccessful). Taken together, these phases represent the path a project takes from the beginning to its end and are generally referred to as the project *life cycle*.

The project life cycle is often formally divided into phases that describe common activities as the project matures. The activities near the beginning of a project look different from activities closer to the end of the project. Most projects share activity characteristics as the project moves through its life cycle. You might see several questions on the exam that ask you to compare different phases in a project's life cycle. In general, here are the common comparisons of early and late project life cycle activities:

▶ **The least is known about the project near its beginning**—As the project matures, more is learned about the project and the product it produces. This process is called *progressive elaboration*. As you learn more about the project, all plans and projections become more accurate.

▶ **The level of uncertainty and risk is the highest at the beginning of a project**—As more is learned about the project and more of the project's work is completed, uncertainty and risk decrease.

▶ **Stakeholders assert the greatest influence on the outcome of a project at the beginning**—After the project starts, the stakeholders' influence continually declines. Their influence to affect the project's outcome is at its lowest point at the end of the project.

▶ **Costs and personnel activity vary throughout a project**—Costs and personnel activity are both low at the beginning of a project, are high near the middle of the project, and tend to taper off to a low level as the project nears completion.

▶ **The cost associated with project changes is at its lowest point at the project's beginning**—No work has been done, so changing is easy. As more and more work is completed, the cost of any changes rises.

One of the most important relationships to understand throughout the project life cycle is the relationship between project knowledge and risk. As stated earlier, knowledge of a project increases as more work is done due to progressive elaboration, and risk decreases as the project moves toward completion. Figure 1.2 depicts the relationship between knowledge and risk.

Another important relationship present in a project's life cycle is the relationship between the declining influence of stakeholders on the outcome of a project and the cost of changes and error corrections. Because little or no work has been accomplished near the beginning of a project, changes require few adjustments and are generally low in cost. At the same time, stakeholders can assert their authority and make changes to the project's direction. As more work is accomplished, the impact and cost of changes increase and leave stakeholders with fewer and fewer viable options to affect the project's product. Figure 1.3 shows how the influences of stakeholders and cost of changes are related to the project life cycle.

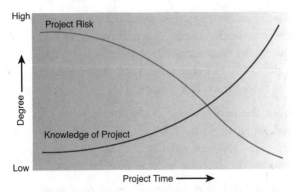

FIGURE 1.2   **Project risk versus knowledge of project.**

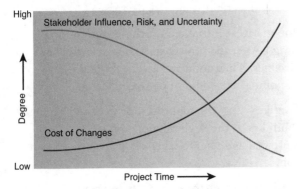

FIGURE 1.3   **Stakeholder influence and cost change impact through the life of a project.**

Although all projects are unique, they do share common components or processes that are normally grouped together. Here are the generally accepted process groups defined in the PMBOK:

▶ Initiating

▶ Planning

▶ Executing

▶ Controlling

▶ Closing

Moving from one phase in the life cycle to another is generally accompanied by a transfer of technical material or control from one group to another. Most phases officially end when the work from one phase is accepted as sufficient to meet that phase's objectives and is passed onto the next phase. The work from one phase could be documentation, plans, components necessary for a subsequent phase, or any work product that contributes to the project's objectives.

Who Are the Stakeholders?

A project exists to satisfy a need. (Remember that a project produces a unique product or service.) Without a need of some sort, a project is not necessary. Needs originate with one or more people; someone has to state a need. As a result, a project fills the need and likely affects some people or organizations. All people and organizations that have an interest in the project or its outcome are called project *stakeholders*. The stakeholders provide input to the requirements of the project and the direction the project should take throughout its life cycle.

The list of stakeholders can be large and can change as the project matures. One of the first requirements to properly manage a project is the creation of a key stakeholder list. Be very careful to include all key stakeholders. Many projects have been derailed due to the political fallout of excluding a key stakeholder. Every potential stakeholder cannot be included in all aspects of a project, so it is important to identify the stakeholders who represent all other stakeholders.

Although it sounds easy to create a list of stakeholders, in reality they are not always easy to identify. You often need to ask many questions of many people to ensure that you create a complete stakeholder list. Because stakeholders provide input for the project requirements and mold the image of the project and its expectations, it is vitally important that you be as persistent as necessary to identify all potential stakeholders. Key stakeholders can include

- ▶ **Project manager**—The person responsible for managing the project.

- ▶ **Customer or user**—The person or organization that will receive and use the project's product or service.

- ▶ **Performing organization**—The organization that performs the work of the project.

- ▶ **Project team members**—The members of the team who are directly involved in performing the work of the project.

- ▶ **Project management team**—Project team members who are directly involved in managing the project.

- ▶ **Sponsor**—The person or organization that provides the authority and financial resources for the project.

▶ **Influencers**—People or groups not directly related to the project's product but with the ability to affect the project in a positive or negative way.

▶ **Project management office (PMO)**—If a PMO exists, it can be a stakeholder if it has responsibility for the project's outcome.

The Project Manager

One of the most visible stakeholders is the *project manager*, the person responsible for managing the project and a key stakeholder. Although the project manager is the most visible stakeholder, he or she does not have the ultimate authority or responsibility for any project. Senior management— specifically the project sponsor—has the ultimate authority over the project. Senior management issues the project charter (discussed in Chapter 3, "Understand Project Initiating") and is responsible for the project. Senior management grants the project manager the authority to get the job done and to resolve many issues. The project manager is also in charge of the project but often does not control the resources.

Look at these sections and chapters in the *PMBOK Guide*, Fifth Edition, for more detailed information on the project manager's roles and responsibilities:

▶ "Introduction," Chapter 1

▶ "Organizational Influences on Project Management," Chapter 2

▶ "Project Human Resource Management," Chapter 9

▶ "Project Stakeholder Management," Chapter 13

▶ "Interpersonal Skills," Appendix X3

ExamAlert

You must have a clear understanding of the project manager's roles and responsibilities for this exam. Go through the PMBOK, search for "project manager," and look at all the responsibilities defined. Know what a project manager must do, should do, and should not do.

The PDF version of the PMBOK enables you to easily search for terms. Use it to search for any terms you are unsure of.

Managing Project Constraints

Managing projects is a continual process of balancing the various competing project variables, or constraints. Historically, project managers have focused on the three common constraints of scope, time, and cost. But in reality, there are more than just three constraints. Each of the project constraints is related and has an effect on the outcome of a project. The project manager must manage the competing constraints to successfully complete a project. Too much attention on one generally means one or more of the others suffer. A major concern of a project manager is to ensure that each of these variables is balanced with the others at all times. The project constraints include, but are not limited to,

▶ **Scope**—The amount of work to be done. Increasing the scope causes more work to be done and vice versa.

▶ **Quality**—The quality standards that the project must fulfill. Higher quality standards often require more work, impacting other constraints.

▶ **Schedule**—The time required to complete the project. Modifying the schedule alters the start and end dates for tasks in the project and can alter the project's overall end date.

▶ **Budget**—The cost required to accomplish the project's objectives. Modifying the cost of the project generally has an impact on the scope, time, or quality of the project.

▶ **Resources**—Resources that are available to conduct the work of the project.

▶ **Risk**—The trade-off that comes with each decision made in the planning and execution of a project. Riskier decisions might have consequences that affect other constraints.

Any change to one of the variables has some effect on one or several of the remaining variables. Likewise, a change to any of the variables has an impact on the overall outcome of the project. The key to understanding the project constraints is that they are all interrelated. For example, if you decrease the cost of your project, it is likely that you decrease the quality and perhaps even increase the risk. With less money, less work gets done. Or you might find that it takes more time to produce the same result with less money. Either way, a change to cost affects other variables.

Even though this concept is fairly straightforward, a project manager must stay on top of each variable to ensure that they are all balanced. In addition to managing the project constraints, the project manager also is responsible for explaining the need for balance to the stakeholders. All too often, stakeholders favor one constraint over another. You have to ensure that the stakeholders understand the need for balancing all constraints.

Project Management Process Groups

As we discussed earlier in this chapter, work executed during a project can be expressed in specific groups of processes. Each project moves through each of the groups of processes, some more than once. These common collections of processes that the PMBOK defines are called *process groups*. Process groups serve to group processes in a project that represent related tasks and mark a project's migration toward completion.

Remember that the PMBOK defines these five process groups:

▶ **Initiating**—Defines the project objectives and grants authority to the project manager.

▶ **Planning**—Refines the project objectives and scope and plans the steps necessary to meet the project's objectives.

▶ **Executing**—Puts the project plan into motion and performs the work of the project.

▶ **Monitoring and Controlling**—Measures the performance of the executing activities and compares the results with the project plan.

▶ **Closing**—Documents the formal acceptance of the project's product and brings all aspects of the project to a close.

Figure 1.4 depicts how the five process groups provide a framework for the project.

All the process groups are discussed in detail throughout the rest of this book. Be sure you are comfortable with how a project flows from inception through each of the process groups. The *PMBOK Guide*, Fifth Edition, has added new figures that depict process flows, inputs and outputs, and interaction between process groups. Look at the *PMBOK Guide*, Fifth Edition, Chapter 3 for these figures. Use them: They will help you remember how the processes flow throughout the project.

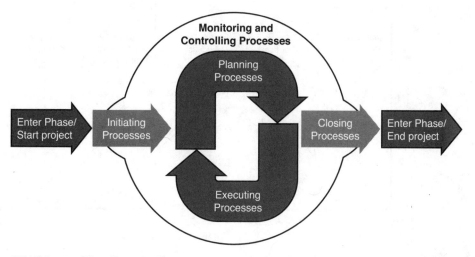

FIGURE 1.4   **Process groups flow.**

Understanding Project Life Cycle and Project Management Processes Relationships

The PMBOK defines 47 project processes, grouped into five process groups. These processes define the path a project takes through its life cycle. The processes are not linear; some overlap others. In fact, some processes are iterative and are executed multiple times in a single project. It is important to become comfortable with the process flow and how it defines the project life cycle.

Throughout the life of a project, different processes are needed at different times. A project starts with little activity. As the project comes to life, more tasks are executed and more processes are active at the same time. This high level of activity increases until near the completion of the project (or project phase). As the end nears, activity starts to diminish until the termination point is reached.

Figure 1.5 shows how the process groups interact in a project.

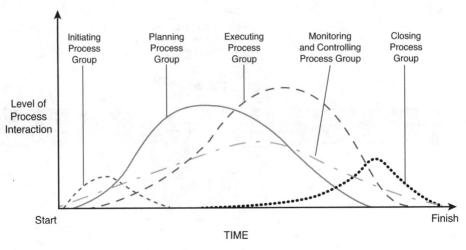

FIGURE 1.5 **Process group interactions.**

Processes, Process Groups, and Knowledge Areas

The best way to prepare for questions that test your knowledge of the project management processes is to know and understand each of the processes, along with its process group and knowledge area assignment.

> **Note**
>
> You might notice that the process numbering starts with 4.1. The numbers refer to the sections in the PMBOK where each process is defined. The first three chapters in the PMBOK cover introductory material, the project life cycle, and a high-level overview of project processes. Chapters 4 through 13 cover each of the project processes in detail, organized by knowledge area. So, the first chapter in which you will find project process details is Chapter 4.

Table 1.4 shows how all 47 processes are grouped by process group and are related to the knowledge areas.

TABLE 1.4 Grouping Processes by Group and Knowledge Areas

Knowledge Areas	Project Management Process Groups				
	Initiating Process Group	Planning Process Group	Executing Process Group	Monitoring and Controlling Process Group	Closing Process Group
Project Integration Management	4.1 Develop Project Charter	4.2 Develop Project Management Plan	4.3 Direct and Manage Project Work	4.4 Monitor and Control Project Work 4.5 Perform Integrated Change Control	4.6 Close Project or Phase
Project Scope Management		5.1 Plan Scope Management 5.2 Collect Requirements 5.3 Define Scope 5.4 Create WBS		5.5 Validate Scope 5.6 Control Scope	
Project Time Management		6.1 Plan Schedule Management 6.2 Define Activities 6.3 Sequence Activities 6.4 Estimate Activity Resources 6.5 Estimate Activity Durations 6.6 Develop Schedule		6.7 Control Schedule	
Project Cost Management		7.1 Plan Cost Management 7.2 Estimate Costs 7.3 Determine Budget		7.4 Control Costs	

Knowledge Areas	Project Management Process Groups				
	Initiating Process Group	Planning Process Group	Executing Process Group	Monitoring and Controlling Process Group	Closing Process Group
Project Quality Management		8.1 Plan Quality Management	8.2 Perform Quality Assurance	8.3 Control Quality	
Project Human Resource Management		9.1 Plan Human Resource Management	9.2 Acquire Project Team 9.3 Develop Project Team 9.4 Manage Project Team		
Project Communications Management		10.1 Plan Communications Management	10.2 Manage Communications	10.3 Control Communications	
Project Risk Management		11.1 Plan Risk Management 11.2 Identify Risks 11.3 Perform Qualitative Risk Analysis 11.4 Perform Quantitative Risk Analysis 11.5 Plan Risk Responses		11.6 Control Risks	
Project Procurement Management		12.1 Plan Procurement Management	12.2 Conduct Procurements	12.3 Control Procurements	12.4 Close Procurements
Project Stakeholder Management	13.1 Identify Stakeholders	13.2 Plan Stakeholder Management	13.3 Manage Stakeholder Engagement	13.4 Control Stakeholder Engagement	

Understanding Process Interaction Customization

The five process groups defined in the PMBOK are general in nature and common to projects. However, all projects are unique, and some do not require all 47 individual project processes. The processes defined in the PMBOK are there for use when needed. You should need the majority of the processes to properly manage a project, but in some cases you will not require each process.

Because projects differ from one another, a specific process can differ dramatically between projects. For example, the process of developing a communication plan is simple and straightforward for a small project with local team members. However, the process is much more involved and complicated if the team is large and located in several countries.

Understand the five process groups and 47 processes as defined in the PMBOK. But, more importantly, understand when and how to use each process. The exam focuses more on process implementation than on process memorization. Be prepared to really think about which processes you need for a particular project.

Cram Quiz

Answer these questions. The answers follow the last question. If you cannot answer these questions correctly, consider reading this section again until you can.

1. Which of the following statements best describes the influence of stakeholders over the life of a project?

   ○ **A.** Stakeholders ultimately direct all project activities.

   ○ **B.** Stakeholder influence is low at the beginning and tends to grow throughout the project.

   ○ **C.** Stakeholder influence is the highest at the beginning and tends to decrease throughout the project.

   ○ **D.** Stakeholders do not directly influence the project's outcome; they only provide authority and resources.

2. During your accounting software implementation project, you find that training is not progressing as quickly as the schedule requires and the users are not well trained after the sessions are over. After investigating the cause, you find that the trainers you have retained do not have the proper experience and knowledge to effectively train your users. Which statement best describes the effect on the project and the effect of the action required to fix the problem?

   ○ **A.** The schedule is suffering. To fix the situation, you have to hire more experienced trainers and schedule extra training sessions. Your schedule returns to planned values while cost increases.

   ○ **B.** The quality and schedule are being negatively impacted. To fix the situation, you likely have to hire more experienced trainers at a higher rate and schedule extra training sessions. Quality and schedule return to planned values while cost increases.

   ○ **C.** This problem is the responsibility of the organization that provided the trainers. They provide replacement trainers who are qualified at the same price to continue the training required.

   ○ **D.** Although your training looks like it is behind schedule, you wisely built in enough slack time to cover such a problem. You simply find replacement trainers and continue the training.

3. You have just completed the defining activities, estimating activity resources, and estimating activity durations processes. Which process have you left out?

   ○ **A.** Sequence Activities

   ○ **B.** Develop Schedule

   ○ **C.** Control Schedule

   ○ **D.** Create WBS

Cram Quiz Answers

1. Answer C is the best answer. Stakeholder influence is greatest at the beginning of a project. When the initial objectives are being developed, the stakeholders have a lot of input. After the main project parameters are agreed upon, the project manager and project team start working on those objectives, and the stakeholder involvement decreases. Answer A is incorrect because the project manager, not the stakeholders, directs project activities. Answers B and D are incorrect because they do not reflect the stakeholder involvement.

2. Answer B is correct. The question states that training is not meeting the schedule, and the result is that the training is not getting people properly trained. This means both schedule and quality are suffering. Of all the solutions, Answer B provides the best description of the effects on your project. Answer A is incorrect because it does not mention the impact on project quality. Answer C is incorrect for several reasons. The problem might be the responsibility of the organization that supplied the trainers, but the responsibility for the impact on the project is the project manager's. Answer C also ignores the quality issue. Answer D is incorrect because it implies that the project manager padded the schedule. This is not an ethical practice. Your estimates should be realistic. If you expect such problems to occur, you should address them in the beginning of the project, along with appropriate recovery methods. By padding the schedule, you hide a real risk to the project.

3. Answer A is correct. The PMBOK places sequencing activities between defining activities and estimating activity resources. Answers B, C, and D are incorrect because they do not follow the PMBOK flow. You will see questions similar to this one on the PMP exam. Know your process flows.

What Next?

If you want more practice on this chapter's exam topics before you move on, remember that you can access all of the Cram Quiz questions on the CD. You can also create a custom exam by topic with the practice exam software. Note any topic you struggle with and go to that topic's material in this chapter.

CHAPTER 2

Professional and Social Responsibility

This chapter covers the following PMP exam topics:

▶ PMI Code of Ethics and Professional Conduct

▶ Responsibility

▶ Respect

▶ Fairness

▶ Honesty

(For more information on the PMP exam topics, see "About the PMP Exam" in the Introduction.)

The PMP certification examination changed several times to include additional performance requirements specific to professional and social responsibility in the practice of project management. With the news media routinely reporting ethical lapses and abuses of professional judgment in various industries and companies, PMI chose to clearly establish what is and is not appropriate in the performance of professional project management services. Previous PMP exam versions separated questions regarding ethics and PMP conduct into a distinct section. The latest version of the PMP exam is different. Although you will learn about professional and social responsibility in this chapter, PMI has chosen to incorporate the topic into questions throughout the exam. You must understand PMI's view of social and professional responsibility and be able to apply those concepts to all knowledge areas in the PMBOK.

The PMI Code of Ethics and Professional Conduct

▶ **PMI Code of Ethics and Professional Conduct**

CramSaver

If you can correctly answer these questions before going through this section, save time by skimming the Exam Alerts in this section and then completing the Cram Quiz at the end of the section.

1. How many pages is the PMI Code of Ethics and Professional Conduct?

2. What are the four core values for project managers that are specifically addressed in the PMI Code of Ethics and Professional Conduct?

Answers

1. The PMI Code of Ethics and Professional Conduct is eight pages in length. This might sound like a strange question, but if you answered anything else, you have the incorrect version. The older versions of the Code were shorter.

2. The four core values addressed in the PMI Code of Ethics and Professional Conduct are

   ▶ Responsibility

   ▶ Respect

   ▶ Fairness

   ▶ Honesty

The PMI Code of Ethics and Professional Conduct focuses on conflicts of interest, truthful representation, and your responsibility to the profession, the customers, and the public. Most of the information contained in the PMI Code of Ethics and Professional Conduct will seem obvious and intuitive upon your initial read, but the Code ensures that all project manager practitioners have an equal understanding of the responsibilities for honesty and integrity in the profession.

The PMI Code of Ethics and Professional Conduct is not a component of the PMBOK; rather, it is an eight-page standalone document available on the PMI website. You should read it carefully and thoroughly.

Where Do I Find the PMI Code of Ethics and Professional Conduct?

The PMI Code of Ethics and Professional Conduct is available in the *PMP Handbook* on the PMI website, http://www.pmi.org/Certification/~/media/PDF/Certifications/pdc_pmphandbook.ashx.

If this URL is inactive or no longer works, visit the PMI website and select "Certification." Then select "Project Management Professional (PMP)" in the quick links on the right side of the window. The updated quick links window will contain a link to download the *PMP Handbook*.

ExamAlert

The PMI Code of Ethics and Professional Conduct is part of most of the questions you will see on the PMP exam. This small document is the basis for a significant number of exam questions.

Core Values

The PMI Code of Professional Conduct comprises five chapters:

► Vision and Applicability

► Responsibility

► Respect

► Fairness

► Honesty

Each section challenges all practitioners of project management to apply ethical standards to work efforts, acting in an accurate, trustworthy, honest manner while acknowledging and minimizing conflicts of interest.

The first chapter sets the overall tone of the call for high standards in professional and social behavior. This initial chapter also increases the scope from previous Codes of Conduct to include all project management practitioners. Prior to the release of the current version of the Code, several Codes of Professional Conduct existed. Membership status in PMI and the particular certification held dictated the specific Code(s) that applied to you. The current unified Code of Ethics and Professional Conduct applies to all project management practitioners, regardless of credentials held.

Taken together, these core values provide the basis of the project manager standards of conduct. These standards exist to both promote confidence in the field of project management and to challenge each project manager to strive for excellence. Don't take the code lightly! PMI views the code as an integral part of the continued development of the project management profession.

Aspirational and Mandatory Conduct

Each chapter in the PMI Code of Ethics and Professional Conduct contains two sets of standards. First are the aspirational standards. These are the behaviors to which we aspire. In other words, these are the behaviors all project managers would exhibit in the best of situations. Some of these take work to achieve, but they give us good goals that strengthen each project manager and the profession as a whole. There are no specific consequences for violating the aspirational standards.

Second, the PMI Code of Ethics and Professional Conduct presents the mandatory standards. These standards provide the minimum acceptable behavior for project managers. Violation of any of the mandatory standards carries consequences. Such consequences can result in loss of credentials or worse.

ExamAlert

Exam questions from this topic are almost exclusively application questions. PMI doesn't care that you have memorized the Code of Ethics and Professional Conduct. It wants to see that you can apply the Code to specific situations. As you study, consider how you will apply the Code to your projects.

Cram Quiz

Answer these questions. The answers follow the last question. If you cannot answer these questions correctly, consider reading this section again until you can.

1. To whom does the PMI Code of Ethics and Professional Conduct apply?

   O **A.** PMPs and PMP candidates

   O **B.** All project managers

   O **C.** All persons who are PMI members or hold a PMI certification

   O **D.** All PMI members

2. What is the most important goal of the PMI Code of Ethics and Professional Conduct?

- O **A.** To advance the profession of project management
- O **B.** To weed out unethical project managers
- O **C.** To address known ethical weaknesses of inexperienced project managers
- O **D.** To help project managers increase their skill levels

Cram Quiz Answers

1. Answer C is the best answer. The PMI Code of Ethics and Professional Conduct applies to all PMI members, all persons who are not PMI members but hold a PMI certification, and anyone who serves in a volunteer capacity for PMI.

2. Answer A is correct. The main goal of the PMI Code of Ethics and Professional Conduct is to advance the profession as a whole. While the other goals are part of the Code, they are only parts of the overall goal of advancing the profession.

Responsibility

▶ **Responsibility**

CramSaver

If you can correctly answer these questions before going through this section, save time by skimming the Exam Alerts in this section and then completing the Cram Quiz at the end of the section.

1. A colleague overstates her qualifications in her application for PMP certification. PMI selected her application for audit, and you have been asked to sign off on her Experience Verification Form. What do you do?

    ○ **A.** Explain that the project occurred a few years back, and you simply cannot recall the details.

    ○ **B.** Ask the colleague what she wants you to do.

    ○ **C.** Ask your colleague to submit a new Experience Verification Form that accurately states her experience.

    ○ **D.** Do not respond to PMI's request.

2. As the project manager recently assigned to a project in execution, you're asked to rescope the existing project. The project sponsor believes the current scope is unattainable, given the budget and scheduled end date. The project is over budget and not meeting schedule milestones. Project cost estimates and timelines were created under the previous project manager. Your analysis of the original project assumptions and constraints shows that scope reduction will not enable you to meet the originally estimated end date or budget. What do you do?

    ○ **A.** Inform the project sponsor that a scope reduction will not allow the project to meet the original timeline or budget and await further instruction.

    ○ **B.** Re-estimate the entire project in terms of scope, timeline, and budget and then present the project sponsor with each available option, given the project assumptions and constraints.

    ○ **C.** Reduce the scope and proceed with the direction given by the project sponsor.

    ○ **D.** None of the above.

Answers

1. Answer C is the best response. You have a responsibility to cooperate with PMI concerning ethics violations and the collection of related information. You have a further responsibility to support and disseminate the PMI Code of Ethics and Professional Conduct. You must provide accurate, truthful representations concerning qualifications, experience, and performance of services. Answers A, B, and D conflict with these responsibilities.

2. Answer B is the best response. You have a responsibility to provide accurate and truthful representations in the preparation of estimates concerning costs, services, and expected results. It is your responsibility as a project management professional to give the project sponsor all the information pertinent to make informed decisions regarding the viability and continuation of a project.

Taking responsibility simply means that the project manager takes ownership for the decisions and actions made, as well as the consequences of the results. This responsibility also addresses decisions and actions that should have been made but were not. The position of project manager carries a lot of responsibility, and we, as project management practitioners, must treat that responsibility with care. In a nutshell, this section says that the project manager will honor the commitments of the project and take responsibility for the result of the project.

Aspirational Standards for Responsibility

The aspirational standards for responsibility include the decisions and the approach to the decision-making process that lead to a transparent method of managing projects that instills confidence in the process. Remember that the aspirational standards are things we *should* do. The aspirational standards for responsibility include

- ▶ Upholding the best interests of society, public safety, and the environment in all decisions and actions
- ▶ Only accepting assignments for which you are prepared, based on your background, experience, skill, and qualifications
- ▶ Doing what you say you will do—fulfilling your commitments
- ▶ In making a mistake, owning up to it and correcting it promptly
- ▶ Protecting proprietary and confidential information
- ▶ Upholding this Code and holding others accountable to it

Mandatory Standards for Responsibility

In all categories of the Code of Ethics and Professional Conduct, the mandatory standards are the things we *must* do. Failure to comply with the mandatory standards will likely tarnish the overall perception of project managers. The mandatory standards for responsibility include

- ▶ Knowing and upholding all policies, rules, regulations, and laws that are applicable to work, professional, and volunteer activities
- ▶ Reporting any unethical or illegal activity
- ▶ Reporting Code violations for resolution

▶ Only filing ethics violations that are substantiated by facts

▶ Pursuing disciplinary action against any individual who retaliates against anyone who raises an ethics issue

---

ExamAlert

It should go without saying that a project manager should obey all the rules. However, pay attention to the fact that obeying all the rules is clearly stated in the Code of Ethics and Professional Conduct. You very well might see a question on the exam based on this simple premise.

Ethics Complaints

As a project management professional, you have a professional responsibility to report possible violations of professional conduct within the project management professional community. This is a self-policing provision. However, before you bring any accusations to the appropriate authorities, you must ensure that you have the facts. If you cannot substantiate your claims, do more research or drop the complaint.

In accordance with your charge to report professional conduct violations, you are also required to cooperate with PMI in its investigation of ethics violations and the collection of pertinent information. An investigation requiring your cooperation might arise independently of you actually reporting a possible ethics violation. Further, you are required to pursue disciplinary action against any individual who retaliates against a person raising ethics concerns.

Responsible Conduct

In performing professional project management services for customers, it is imperative that you meet your customer's expectations and complete all work in accordance with the agreed-upon scope and objectives. Your customer should approve any deviations from or changes to the work plan.

Confidentiality should be maintained at all times. This applies in the case of intellectual property and also in the context of all professional activities performed.

Cram Quiz

Answer these questions. The answers follow the last question. If you cannot answer these questions correctly, consider reading this section again until you can.

1. You have access to proprietary information a vendor included as part of a bid proposal. The information was marked confidential and was included to show that the vendor would be issued a patent by the end of the month, which makes this company's bid the best candidate for your company and significantly improves the market share of the vendor. What do you do with this information?

   - ○ **A.** Invest in the company immediately

   - ○ **B.** Tell your friends to invest in this company

   - ○ **C.** Wait until the information becomes public knowledge and then decide if you want to invest in the company

   - ○ **D.** Provide the proprietary information to a competing vendor

2. You are a project manager working on a project that has had numerous change requests from the customer that have resulted in scope creep. The project is over schedule and over budget. The remaining scope entails preferred user requirements that do not affect the operation of the application. You can complete the project this month if you reduce the scope and remove these preferred user requirements. What do you do?

   - ○ **A.** Continue with the project and complete the remaining scope

   - ○ **B.** Explain to the customer the benefits of reducing scope and make the customer sign off on this final change request

   - ○ **C.** Reduce the scope, do not document this change, and tell the customer the project has been completed

   - ○ **D.** Explain to the customer that the preferred user requirements are not possible and get the customer to sign off on this final change request reducing the project scope

Cram Quiz Answers

1. Answer C is the best response. You have a responsibility to maintain and respect the confidentiality of sensitive information obtained in the course of professional activities. This responsibility makes Answers A and B incorrect. You have a responsibility to recognize and respect intellectual property developed and owned by others, which makes Answer D an incorrect choice.

2. Answer A is the best response. You have a responsibility to maintain and satisfy the scope and objectives of professional services, unless otherwise directed by your customer. Answers B, C, and D require manipulation of your customer and/or falsification of information, which is not in compliance with professional conduct.

Respect

▶ **Respect**

CramSaver

If you can correctly answer these questions before going through this section, save time by skimming the Exam Alerts in this section and then completing the Cram Quiz at the end of the section.

1. Why should project managers discourage any racial jokes from circulating among team members?

2. What is wrong with avoiding a difficult team member and venting your frustrations with a friend?

Answers

1. There are many obvious answers to this question, but in terms of the PMI Code of Ethics and Professional Conduct, racial jokes or slurs of any kind violate the respect value and are not permitted by ethical project managers. As with much of the rest of the PMI Code of Ethics and Professional Conduct, this is just common sense.

2. According to the PMI Code of Ethics and Professional Conduct, one aspect of respect is agreeing to directly approach anyone with whom you have conflict. In other words, don't talk about people behind their backs.

The manner in which we treat people and things is based on the value we place on them. The standard of respect states that we should treat people and resources as though we value them. In the context of project management, these might include people, money, reputation, safety, and environmental resources. These resources are entrusted to the project manager and must be treated with the utmost respect.

Aspirational Standards for Respect

The aspirational standards for respect include developing an environment that promotes trust, confidence, and excellence for all who are engaged in the project. The aspirational standards for respect include

▶ Learning the norms and customs of others and avoiding behaviors that could be disrespectful

▶ Listening to and attempting to understand others' points of view

- ▶ Dealing with conflict and disagreement directly with the other person
- ▶ Conducting yourself in a professional manner, even when not everyone else does so

Mandatory Standards for Respect

The mandatory standards for respect include

- ▶ Negotiating in good faith
- ▶ Not using your authority to influence others to your personal benefit
- ▶ Never acting in an abusive manner toward others
- ▶ Respecting others' property rights

ExamAlert

Remember that respect includes showing a high regard to more than just other people. There might be questions on the exam that require you to understand that respect also applies to money, reputation, the safety of others, and natural or environmental resources.

The Impact of Respect

An overwhelming number of conflicts among any group of people boil down to one simple issue: a lack of respect. Failing to show respect or actively showing disrespect will cause a conflict faster than nearly any other single action (or omission). Every person has a set of expectations about how to act. Trying to react to different behavioral standards can be tricky, but it is an important skill for a project manager.

There are many different issues related to respect, but the most important areas in which most people have well-developed respect expectations include

- ▶ Religious beliefs
- ▶ Political beliefs
- ▶ Allegiance to other people and/or organizations
- ▶ Perceived or actual rank or status
- ▶ Cultural practices

The preceding list is only a partial listing of areas in which certain levels of respect are expected. If a person, through intent or ignorance, shows disrespect to something or someone, conflict might result. Examples of a disrespectful act can be as simple as a comment about a revered sports team or as egregious as a religious slur. You should avoid all forms of disrespect, and you must treat all people equally with respect in all cases.

Cram Quiz

Answer these questions. The answers follow the last question. If you cannot answer these questions correctly, consider reading this section again until you can.

1. You are a project manager who has noticed that one of your team members is visibly agitated. The team member is upset because of pictures displayed in another team member's cubicle. The pictures are clearly visible and do not appear objectionable to you. What should you do?

   O **A.** Encourage the upset team member to stop making a big deal over nothing.

   O **B.** Meet with the team member who has displayed the pictures, make a few jokes to keep it light, then suggest that the pictures be displayed in a less obvious place.

   O **C.** Meet with the team member who is upset to try and understand the basis for the concern. Work with the team member to find an acceptable solution.

   O **D.** Notify human resources that there is a personnel problem that needs attention.

2. While leading a project status meeting, a functional manager disagrees with a decision you have made and makes it a point to be very vocal about it. He uses the meeting to express his doubts about your skills and even goes so far as to suggest that your race plays a part in the way you make decisions. How should you react?

   O **A.** Do nothing. File a complaint with the manager's boss after the meeting.

   O **B.** Use your authority as the meeting leader to take control of the discussion and present your rebuttal.

   O **C.** Suggest an immediate meeting between the two of you to discuss your differences.

   O **D.** Bring the manager's boss into the meeting and ask for assistance in addressing his comments.

Cram Quiz Answers

1. Answer C is the best choice. One aspect of respect is listening to others and trying to understand them. Your best option is to start with the team member who is agitated and try to understand the cause of the agitation. You might find that the objection is valid after you have heard the other person's point of view. Answers A and B do not show respect to your team member, and Answer D just attempts to pass the responsibility to someone else.

2. Answer C is the correct answer. The PMI Code of Ethics and Professional Conduct requires that you act in a professional manner even when others do not. Answer A is incorrect because doing nothing solves nothing. Going to the manager's boss is likely to make the situation worse, not better. Answer B is incorrect because it is an emotional response, not a professional one. Answer D is incorrect because you should always first attempt to solve differences one-on-one.

Fairness

▶ **Fairness**

CramSaver

If you can correctly answer these questions before going through this section, save time by skimming the Exam Alerts in this section and then completing the Cram Quiz at the end of the section.

1. A vendor sends you a holiday greeting card signed by the company's staff using digital signatures. Included in the card is a gift certificate for $100 at a local steakhouse, addressed to recipient. You know that your company has a policy against accepting compensation for personal gain. What do you do?

   ○ **A.** Use the certificate to go out to dinner with a friend

   ○ **B.** Return the gift certificate and explain your company's policy on gift acceptance

   ○ **C.** Donate the gift certificate to a 503(c) charity

   ○ **D.** Give the gift certificate to your boss

2. A meeting with a vendor runs late, and a suggestion is made that the meeting should be continued over dinner. When the bill arrives, the vendor offers to pay for your meal. How do you respond?

   ○ **A.** You accept and thank him for the meal.

   ○ **B.** You accept and tell him you will pay for the next meal.

   ○ **C.** You counter and offer to pay for his meal on your expense account.

   ○ **D.** You decline and pay for your own meal.

Answers

1. Answer B is the best response. You have a responsibility to refrain from accepting inappropriate payments, gifts, or other forms of compensation for personal gain, according to the PMI Code of Ethics and Professional Conduct. You might have additional responsibilities in accordance with your company's policies and procedures. Answer A is not correct because accepting the gift would be a violation of the PMI Code of Ethics and Professional Conduct. Answer C is not correct because the vendor might be led to believe the gift was accepted and the appearance of impropriety might still exist. Although Answer D might seem acceptable, it is not the best response of the choices given.

2. Answer D is the best response. You have a responsibility to refrain from accepting inappropriate forms of compensation for personal gain. Answer A is incorrect for this reason. You have a responsibility to refrain from offering inappropriate forms of compensation for personal gain, making Answer C incorrect. Answer B is a poor choice because the appearance of impropriety is present.

As a project manager, you are responsible for managing the project and moving toward a successful outcome of the project. Because all projects are initiated to meet some need of the sponsoring organization, it is your responsibility to ensure that the goal is fulfilled. The only way to ensure that the needs of the sponsoring organization are being met is to manage the project fairly. An unfair decision is one that puts the project manager's desire above the stated goals of the project. All your decisions should be made impartially and fairly. The tangible and intangible effects of transparent fairness strengthen your project team and increase your ability to meet your project's goals.

Aspirational Standards for Fairness

The aspirational standards for fairness affect how project managers make decisions. Fair decisions are those made impartially and objectively. It is important that a project manager not render decisions that involve competing self-interests, prejudice, or favoritism. In short, your decisions as a project manager should benefit the project, not yourself. The aspirational standards for fairness include

- ▶ Demonstrating transparency in your decision-making process

- ▶ Reexamining your impartiality and objectivity on a continual basis

- ▶ Providing equal access to information for authorized personnel

- ▶ Making opportunities available to all qualified candidates without favoring one over another

Mandatory Standards for Fairness

The mandatory standards for fairness include

- ▶ Fully disclosing any real or potential conflicts of interest to the appropriate stakeholders

- ▶ Not participating in the decision-making process any time you identify a conflict of interest until the conflict of interest has been addressed by the stakeholders and you are authorized to re-engage

- ▶ Not allowing personal considerations to enter into any decisions related to personnel decisions

- ▶ Not discriminating against others for any reason

- ▶ Not allowing favoritism or prejudice to influence how you apply the rules of your organization

Conflict of Interest

Full disclosure of any conflicts of interest, either real or perceived, to all stakeholders is crucial in complying with the PMI Code of Ethics and Professional Conduct. You are responsible for informing clients, customers, owners, contractors, and/or vendors of even the appearance of impropriety.

Conflicts of interest can arise if you are related to a vendor performing services for your company or have previous unacknowledged relationships with contractors who are bidding on work you are responsible for managing. This applies to your entire project team. In an ideal situation, you would address any potential conflicts of interest prior to project initiation.

Identifying conflicts of interest is a best practice for all business transactions and ensures that all business associates are acting in good faith. If an actual conflict of interest is determined, all stakeholders can decide the best course of action for resolution of the conflict. By disclosing any perceived conflicts of interest, you avoid the appearance of impropriety.

As a project manager with decision-making responsibility that affects a project, you must take the high moral ground. Your judgments and decisions must be beyond reproach. If a conflict of interest arises that is not disclosed, this potential conflict can impair your ability to successfully lead the project. Your client, your fellow team members, and your professional colleagues might question your choices regarding any conflict of interest as well as all other decisions you are responsible for making.

As a project manager, your truthfulness, reputation, and integrity are paramount. PMI believes these are obligations to the profession as well as to the stakeholders. The concept of a conflict of interest being tied to your responsibilities as a project management professional is addressed in all of the four core values in the PMI Code of Ethics and Professional Conduct but is most strongly identified with fairness.

> **ExamAlert**
>
> Conflict of interest is a key concept. Understanding this concept and its implications to a project is key to truly understanding fairness. Expect the exam to include questions related to conflict of interest.

You have an obligation to acknowledge a conflict of interest, but you must also ensure that a conflict of interest does not compromise the legitimate business interests of your customer. You cannot allow a conflict of interest to influence nor interfere with your judgment or the fulfillment of your professional project management responsibilities. This is particularly important when you are accountable for decision making as the project manager.

You have a responsibility to your client to be forthright. If you engage in behavior that is questionable, or even improper, you are compromising your credibility as a project management professional. Your decisions regarding the specific incident can be tainted, as can your behavior and judgment regarding all facets of the project. Every decision becomes suspect.

Inappropriate payments, gifts, or other forms of compensation for personal gain must be declined. Examples of inappropriate compensation can vary from the seemingly innocuous, such as theater tickets or lunch paid for by a vendor, to the more extreme, such as cash payments or vacation packages.

Similarly, you should refrain from offering inappropriate payments, gifts, or other forms of compensation to another party for personal gain. You might be familiar with the term *kickback*, which has been used to describe this activity in various industries. The PMI Code of Ethics and Professional Conduct is explicit in condemning this activity.

PMI makes exceptions in cases where offering or accepting payments, gifts, or other forms of compensation for personal gain conforms with applicable laws or customs of the country where project management services are being performed. In instances where you believe this exception might be valid, consult a legal professional. This practice is not acceptable for companies incorporated within the United States, regardless of where they are doing business.

Your obligation to be trustworthy and exemplify a high standard of integrity is implicit within the PMI Code of Ethics and Professional Conduct. Inflating the number of project hours worked by team members to appear ahead of schedule or even on schedule is inappropriate. Overstating your hourly rates to make the project appear to be operating within budget when you are funneling those funds to other project costs, tinkering with progress/ status reports, and manipulating project milestones to appear on time and on budget are simply wrong. Such actions are insults to the profession of project management and are not ethical.

More often than not, you know if your actions are creating a conflict of interest or if you are engaging in questionable behavior. If you cannot be completely honest with all parties regarding your actions, they are suspect. If you catch yourself thinking "What the client doesn't know won't hurt them" or not fully disclosing information to your own project team, your actions are improper. You might have the greater good of the project at heart when you claim that Phase I of the project completed on schedule because you plan to use more resources in Phase II to make up the gap, but this is false reporting. You must be honest with your client regarding the true status of the project and then work with the affected parties to develop strategies for mitigating the problem.

You must also be honest with your project team. Your responsibility in this regard is two-fold: You have an obligation to communicate openly with your fellow team workers; furthermore, as the project manager, you are the team lead for the project and must lead by example.

Communicating honestly, openly, and effectively with your client and your project team can be difficult. It is hard to tell a paying client that a project is facing severe setbacks and obstacles, particularly when the client might (rightly or wrongly) hold you accountable for the problems. A client might continue to make change requests late into development or place unrealistic demands on you and your team in terms of the project budget, scope, and timeline.

Similarly, it can be tough to deal with a project team during a stressful implementation. You might have team members you do not personally like and whom you did not select for your team. There might be interpersonal conflicts. Such situations can lead to breakdowns in communication and are normal scenarios you might face during a project. These problems are compounded when a conflict of interest, real or perceived, is present.

As the project manager, you do not want to compound your workload by ignoring or discounting potential conflicts of interest, regardless of when they arise during the project. Address as many issues as possible at the beginning of the project, during the planning process. You set the tone for the entire project by how you broach issues up front. If your client and project team see you minimizing or negating issues, the die is cast for other team members to do the same. Furthermore, your integrity is compromised.

You must also be vigilant throughout the project, actively identifying and mitigating issues regarding conflict of interest. Sometimes a potential conflict of interest does not make itself known until midway through a project. Always recognize conflicts of interest at their earliest point of origin. This ensures your client and project team that you are above board. If situations arise that were unknown and for some reason were not immediately addressed and rectified, make the conflict of interest transparent to all parties as soon as possible. This is essential to maintaining your credibility as a project management professional with your client, your team, and the public.

In summary, avoid conflicts of interest. If this is not a viable option, identify and acknowledge conflicts of interest, both real and potential, as soon as possible. Avoid all situations where your honesty and integrity as a project manager can be questioned or condemned. If you question the ethical consequences of an action or feel a decision should be hidden from your project team, you should not engage in the behavior.

ExamAlert

Expect scenario-based questions on the exam that are related to conflict of interest. These questions ask you to determine what you would do in a given situation. Be careful to select the best response, in accordance with the PMI Code of Ethics and Professional Conduct. There might be multiple answers that appear to be correct. In these instances, narrow your choices by determining the clearly incorrect answers and then select the best response from the remaining choices.

Cram Quiz

Answer these questions. The answers follow the last question. If you cannot answer these questions correctly, consider reading this section again until you can.

1. Your spouse works for a vendor that is bidding on a project at your company. You are not affiliated with the specific project team that is evaluating bids, but you are part of the executive project management team. What do you do?

   - A. Inform your company of the relationship
   - B. Inform the vendor of the relationship
   - C. Both A and B
   - D. Disqualify the vendor

2. You work for a U.S.-based company hired to perform project management services in a foreign country. Other companies that have done business in this country inform you that gifts must be made to the government to obtain the necessary project approvals. What do you do?

   - A. Offer the recommended gifts to obtain project approvals
   - B. Do not offer gifts to obtain project approvals
   - C. Ignore the need for project approvals
   - D. Both B and C

Cram Quiz Answers

1. Answer C is the best response. You have a responsibility to disclose to both the vendor and your company significant circumstances that could be construed as a conflict of interest or an appearance of impropriety. Answers A and B are both correct but are not the best responses. Answer D is not correct. You have an obligation to disclose the information. Your company and the vendor can decide the best course of action, given the information.

2. Answer B is the best response. Answer A is not correct because you have a responsibility to refrain from offering inappropriate gifts for personal gain. The exemption regarding conformity with applicable laws or customs of the country where project management services are being performed does not apply because you are working for a U.S.-based company and are subject to U.S. law. Answers C and D are incorrect because you have a responsibility to comply with laws and regulations in the country where providing project management services requires project approvals.

Honesty

▶ **Honesty**

CramSaver

If you can correctly answer this question before going through this section, save time by skimming the Exam Alerts in this section and then completing the Cram Quiz at the end of the section.

1. You apply for a position at a company and list PMI membership on your resume. The company wants to hire a PMP. You are scheduled to take the PMP exam in a few days. At your interview, a comment is made implying that you are PMP certified. What do you do?

   ○ **A.** Provide no clarification. Your resume states that you are a member of PMI. An assumption that you are PMP certified is not your responsibility to correct, and you will be certified soon if you pass the exam.

   ○ **B.** Clarify that you are a member of PMI and are scheduled to take your PMP certification exam soon but are not yet PMP certified.

   ○ **C.** Confirm that you are a member of PMI but do not address PMP status.

   ○ **D.** Confirm that you are a member of PMI and are PMP certified. You will be certified soon if you pass the exam.

Answer

1. Answer B is the best response. You have a responsibility to provide accurate, truthful representations concerning your qualifications, experience, and performance of services. Answers A and C are lies of omission. You are misleading the hiring company about your qualifications. Answer D is a lie of fact, which could result in revocation of your PMI membership and your PMP certification.

The final value in the four core values for project managers is honesty. In some perspectives, it is the most basic and elemental of the four. Without honesty, the other values have virtually no impact. In an environment lacking trust, no one believes they are being treated fairly or with respect. Honesty lays the foundation for all project activities and interaction.

Aspirational Standards for Honesty

The aspirational standards for honesty are pretty basic and straightforward. In short, you should understand the truth and always act in a truthful manner. The aspirational standards for honesty include

- ▶ Earnestly seeking to understand the truth

- ▶ Being truthful in all that you do and say

- ▶ Providing accurate and timely information

- ▶ Making all commitments in good faith

- ▶ Making every effort to create an environment where everyone feels safe to tell the truth

Mandatory Standards for Honesty

The mandatory standards for honesty include

- ▶ Never engaging in, nor condoning, any behavior that knowingly deceives others

- ▶ Not engaging in dishonest activity designed to benefit one person at the expense of another

Qualifications, Experience, and Performance of Professional Services

As a project manager, you are required to be accurate and truthful in your representations to PMI as well in your professional undertakings. You have a duty to properly represent your qualifications, experience, and performance of professional services when soliciting work and advertising. Estimates of costs, services, and expected results should be justly presented. You are accountable for providing accurate, trustworthy information to customers and the public.

ExamAlert

You are responsible for accurate and truthful representations in the information you present to PMI and to the public. The concept appears throughout the PMI Code of Ethics and Professional Conduct. Expect questions on the exam regarding this concept.

Cram Quiz

Answer these questions. The answers follow the last question. If you cannot answer these questions correctly, consider reading this section again until you can.

1. Falsification of information at any point during the PMI certification program can result in

   ○ **A.** Revocation of your PMI membership

   ○ **B.** Revocation of your PMP certification

   ○ **C.** Notification of your employer

   ○ **D.** Both A and B

2. You are responsible for developing a cost estimate to bid on a government contract. The scope was set by the government. Your supervisor says the cost estimate is too high and should be reduced by one-third to ensure that your company wins the contract. Your analysis shows that any reduction to the proposed cost estimate makes the project unable to meet the specified scope. What do you do?

   ○ **A.** Reduce the cost estimate and submit the proposal

   ○ **B.** Submit your initial cost estimate without reducing the cost

   ○ **C.** Explain to your supervisor in writing that your analysis shows that a reduction in the cost estimate makes the project unable to meet the specified scope

   ○ **D.** Both A and C

Cram Quiz Answers

1. Answer D is the best response. Falsification of any information directly or indirectly related to all aspects of the PMI certification program can result in both revocation of your PMI membership and your PMP certification. Although Answers A and B are both correct, they are not the best responses. Answer C is not correct. PMI will not notify your employer if you falsify information at any point during the PMI certification program.

2. Answer C is the best response. You have a responsibility to provide accurate and truthful representations in the preparation of estimates concerning costs, services, and expected results. This responsibility makes Answers A and D inappropriate. You have accountability to your management, and Answer B is not appropriate because you are usurping your manager's authority and undermining your own professional conduct by doing so.

What Next?

If you want more practice on this chapter's exam topics before you move on, remember that you can access all of the Cram Quiz questions on the CD. You can also create a custom exam by topic with the practice exam software. Note any topic you struggle with and go to that topic's material in this chapter.

CHAPTER 3

Understand Project Initiating

This chapter covers the following PMP exam topics:

▶ Initiating Process Group—3.3

▶ Develop Project Charter—4.1

▶ Identify Stakeholders—13.1

(For more information on the PMP exam topics, see "About the PMP Exam" in the Introduction.)

The first process group you will encounter in the project life cycle is the *initiating process group*. Although initiating is a relatively small topic that represents only 13% of the questions on the PMP exam, it is an important topic. In addition to being a small topic, it is also one with which most project managers have little experience. In spite of clear PMI definitions of activities that should be carried out during initiating, many organizations approach the initial steps of projects differently. As a result, your firsthand experience might differ from the PMI recommendations in this process group. Don't trivialize the material in this chapter. Ensure that you understand initiating before moving on to tackle some of the larger topics.

Initiating Process Group

▶ **Initiating Process Group—3.3**

CramSaver

If you can correctly answer these questions before going through this section, save time by skimming the Exam Alerts in this section and then completing the Cram Quiz at the end of the section.

1. At what points in a project might you perform the processes of initiating a project?

   ○ **A.** Initiating is the first process group and occurs only at the beginning of a project.

   ○ **B.** Initiating should actually be named "phase initiation" and really only occurs during execution between major project phases.

   ○ **C.** Initiating must occur at the beginning of a project and before any major milestone to authorize the project to continue toward the next milestone.

   ○ **D.** Initiating can occur at the beginning of a project and again at any point when authorization to continue the project is either required or desired.

2. Which document formally authorizes a project?

   ○ **A.** The project sponsor/initiator charter

   ○ **B.** The project charter

   ○ **C.** The preliminary project scope statement

   ○ **D.** The project contract

Answers

1. Answer D is correct. Initiating a project or phase generally occurs at the beginning of a project and can also optionally be included multiple times throughout the project. There are no absolute requirements for conducting initiating processes during a project. Because initiating can occur during a project but is not required, Answers A, B, and C are incorrect.

2. Answer B is correct. Answer A mentions a document that is not defined in the PMBOK. The preliminary scope statement is a document that is not defined in the *PMBOK Guide*, Fifth Edition, so Answer C is incorrect. The project contract is one of the inputs to both processes in the initiating process group and does not convey project authorization, which means Answer D is incorrect. The contract commits the organization to perform action but does not authorize the project itself.

The initiating process group is the first step in the project life cycle. In fact, much of the work performed in this process group is actually outside the scope of the project. The main purpose of initiating is to authorize a project to begin or continue. Notice that the initiating process group serves two potential roles. It generally occurs at the beginning of a project but can also occur several more times throughout the life of a project. Some larger projects define specific milestones that require revisiting the initiating processes to continue the project. Invoking the initiating processes at the start of each phase helps keep the project focused on the business need the project was undertaken to address.

The Purpose of Initiating a Project

Initiating commonly occurs at the beginning of a project and can also be required at certain points throughout the project. For example, a large project with the goal of producing a prototype of a commercial jet will likely encounter several points along the project life cycle at which important decisions must be made. After the fuselage and airfoil have been produced and joined together, they must be tested to evaluate performance against project goals. If the performance does not meet certain standards, the components must be reworked to meet standards before continuing. The whole project could be terminated if the product is deemed to be unable to effectively meet the project standards. This phase in the project is a crucial go/no-go decision point and constitutes activities in the initiating process group.

ExamAlert

It bears repeating that the initiating process group activities can be required more than once in the project life cycle. Although the most common time for these activities to occur is at the beginning of a project, don't overlook the fact that they can be called for during the project at any point in time.

It is not uncommon for large projects to call for initiating processes several times throughout the project life cycle. Any time you need to assess the progress of a project, reevaluate its merit, and request approval to continue, initiating processes are executed.

In all cases, initiating processes require input from preceding activities. The entities charged with deciding whether to proceed require substantiating information on which to base a decision. When initiating occurs at the beginning of a project, at least some of the input must be created in tasks that are not part of the project. This work predates the project initiation date and can make the project start point fuzzy. The points in time at which a project begins and ends are referred to as the *project boundaries*. Because a substantial amount of the inputs to the initiating processes is created outside the scope of the project, the starting boundary can be unclear. A project always starts as a result of a business need, and the business need develops before the project commences. Likewise, any documentation of the need for the project is developed before the actual project starts.

ExamAlert

You need to know the inputs and outputs of each process defined in the PMBOK. That's 47 separate input and output sets! The exam includes several questions that require you to know process inputs, outputs, and general information flow. Start now by rationalizing the inputs and outputs of each process.

Think: "For this process, what information do I need before I start (inputs), and what information or deliverables will I produce (outputs)?"

Subsequent initiating iterations (within the project life cycle) use inputs from preceding activities. It is important to understand that the activities in the initiating process group always result in a critical project decision. The end of the initiating process group is represented by a decision to continue the project, go back and redo some of the work, or terminate the project altogether.

In most projects, you should include any customers and other stakeholders in many of the activities in the initiating process group. Including as many stakeholders as possible in the early project activities fosters a sense of pride and shared ownership of the project. Any stakeholder who feels a sense of ownership is apt to be more diligent about ensuring that the project succeeds. Stakeholder participation increases the success of setting the project scope, gathering project requirements, and defining the overall criteria for project success.

Project Manager Assignment

PMI requires that the project manager be assigned prior to any project planning taking place. The project manager doesn't have to be assigned until the end of the initiating process group. However, it can be beneficial to assign the project manager earlier. A project manager who helped create the project charter is more comfortable with a project and has an easier time planning the project.

It is the responsibility of the project initiator, or project sponsor, to officially assign the project manager. After the project managers are assigned, the project charter identifies the project managers and provides them the authority to carry out project management tasks.

The Project Charter and Its Purpose

The initiating process group consists of two processes. The first process is the development of the project charter, and the second process is identifying stakeholders. The *project charter* is the initial document that describes the project at a high level and formally authorizes the project. PMI requires that a project charter be created and accepted before a project is considered official. As a PMP, you are required to insist on a project charter before proceeding in the role of project manager.

> **ExamAlert**
>
> The PMBOK requires a project charter for every project. The lack of a project charter is a project stopper.

Authorization from the project sponsor, the project management office (PMO), or portfolio steering committee is necessary for the project manager to allocate resources and actually perform the work of the project. Even before bestowing authorization, the stakeholders must assign the project manager to the project. The project charter provides the framework for carrying out these actions. It is also the first deliverable of the project and sets the stage for the whole project.

There is no standard format for a project charter, but each project charter should address these areas:

- ▶ Purpose or justification
- ▶ Project objectives
- ▶ High-level requirements
- ▶ Project description
- ▶ Risks

- ▶ Summary milestone schedule
- ▶ Summary budget
- ▶ Approval requirements
- ▶ Project manager
- ▶ Authorizing party

ExamAlert

The PMP exam asks a few questions about the roles of the project initiator, or sponsor, and the project manager. The project initiator starts the official project process. All of the project manager's authority comes from the project initiator and the initial stakeholders. For this reason, the project charter must be issued by someone with the authority to fund the project and assign resources to it. The project initiator's role is to describe and authorize the project, assign the project manager, and fund the project. The project manager's role is to plan and execute the project.

Cram Quiz

Answer these questions. The answers follow the last question. If you cannot answer these questions correctly, consider reading this section again until you can.

1. You are a project manager newly assigned to a project to implement new manufacturing management software. The project sponsor tells you he has chosen you because he is impressed with your record of completing projects. He tells you that work must start immediately, and there is not enough time to go through all of the formal documentation process. He asks for a quick list of tasks to start now. What do you do?

   ○ **A.** Put together a quick list of the most important tasks, per the sponsor's request.

   ○ **B.** Start working on the project tasks and develop a general plan as soon as you can.

   ○ **C.** Refuse to start on the project until you develop a project charter and get it approved.

   ○ **D.** Explain to the sponsor the need for a project charter and project plan.

2. What is the main purpose for initiating a project?

   ○ **A.** Produce the project charter

   ○ **B.** Formally describe the project

   ○ **C.** Formally authorize the project

   ○ **D.** Assign the project manager to the project

Cram Quiz Answers

1. Answer D is correct. Answers A and B ignore the PMBOK requirement that a project manager insist on proper project management techniques. It is crucial that a PMP candidate understand the need for properly obtaining authorization for a project (initiating) and then planning a project before starting actual work. Answer C is too extreme for the initial response. The sponsor might have made the request to immediately begin work out of a lack of understanding of project management. Always start by getting as much information as you can and educating others on the benefits of good project management.

2. Answer C is correct. Answer A mentions one of the outputs of a process in initiating, but the project charter is not the main purpose of project initiation. Answer B is incorrect as well because describing the project is not the primary purpose of initiating. Answer D is incorrect because assigning a project manager is a task carried out during initiating but is not the primary purpose.

Integration Management

▶ **Develop Project Charter—4.1**

CramSaver

If you can correctly answer these questions before going through this section, save time by skimming the Exam Alerts in this section and then completing the Cram Quiz at the end of the section.

1. What is the purpose of the project charter?

2. Which of the following sections would NOT appear in a project charter?

   ○ **A.** Project purpose

   ○ **B.** Project objectives

   ○ **C.** Project team

   ○ **D.** Project risks

Answers

1. The project charter is a document that formally authorizes either a project or a project phase and lists the initial requirements that meet the stakeholders' expectations.

2. Answer C is correct. The project team is not identified and assembled in the initiating process group. All other sections identified should be present in a project charter.

After a decision is made to initiate a project, the collection of input information begins. This is where the project boundaries can be a little unclear, but it is generally accepted that activities starting with the collection of inputs for initiating are part of the project. Remember that the project has not yet been authorized, so all resources required for the initiating processes must be funded explicitly by the project initiator. In other words, someone has to pay for the time required to produce the project charter.

It is entirely possible that the organization will decide not to pursue a project after it sees the project charter. The project charter might show that the project will not be worth the resource expenditures. In such a case, the resources already expended to produce the project charter have actually saved the organization from wasting many more resources. Therein lies part of the value of the initiating processes.

The specific project management process that results in the project charter is the develop project charter process. Remembering the output of this process is easy because the only output is the project charter document. The inputs are more numerous, however. Table 3.1 lists the inputs, the tools and techniques, and the output for the develop project charter process.

TABLE 3.1 **Develop Project Charter Process: Inputs, Tools and Techniques, and Output**

Inputs	Tools and Techniques	Output
Project statement of work	Expert judgment	Project charter
Business case	Facilitation techniques	
Agreements		
Enterprise environmental factors		
Organizational process assets		

As you study for the PMP exam, don't just memorize each of the inputs, tools and techniques, and outputs for each process. Really think about why PMI put them where they are. In the case of the develop project charter process, ask yourself what you need before you start. Each piece of information you need to start the process of creating the project charter is represented in the input section. You need some sort of document that specifies the need for the project (agreement, or statement of work). You also need to understand the policies and procedures governing projects for your organization. Once you have all the information needed to begin, you can start the process of developing the project charter.

During the project charter development, you use your own expert judgment—as well as the expert judgment of subject matter experts in various areas—to create the output or deliverable. Expert judgment involves using all the project selection techniques in your project manager bag of tricks. You will also employ various facilitation techniques to ensure that you have the best available input from the beginning of the project. (We discuss some of the project selection and related accounting topics later in this chapter.)

In the case of the project charter, the only output is the project charter itself. The main point of listing each of the inputs, tools and techniques, and outputs for each process is to understand each component of each process. Don't just memorize the tables! Really think through why each element is included.

Because the development of the project charter is the first project activity, much of the work to produce the input for this process occurs either before project initiation or within the scope of another project. Most of the input for this process serves to define the project and the environment in which it exists.

After the input information has been collected, the project initiator compiles and issues the project charter. The initiator must be someone who holds the authority to fund the project. Although it is desirable to assign a project manager early in the process, the project manager is not absolutely necessary to issue the project charter. It is important that the stakeholders have a material role in the creation of the project charter. The project manager, if one has been assigned at this point, can be the one to actually do the work of compiling the stakeholders' needs, but the actual input for the project charter and the authority to issue it comes from the project initiator. The main reason so much emphasis is put on the project charter is that it provides the first and best opportunity for the stakeholders to really think through a project before the work begins, and it gives everyone a chance to consider the project before committing to it.

Project Selection Methods

PMI encourages organizations to employ formal methods to select projects. Formal methods make it possible to compare multiple projects and select the one(s) that will produce the most benefit for an organization without being persuaded by emotional ties to certain projects. In addition, organizations can set specific standards that potential projects must meet to be accepted. There are two main selection method categories you need to know for the PMP exam. It is not important that you have in-depth knowledge of these methods, but you need to be able to identify each type of method and understand their basic differences.

Benefit Measurement Methods

Benefit measurement methods document the relative benefits of completing each project. This approach enables organizations to compare projects by comparing their impact. Each specific method uses different measurements and results in different types of output. You don't need to understand how to assess the relative measurements for the exam. Just know that these methods produce relative output that an organization can use to compare projects.

Mathematical Models

Mathematical models analyze project description data to result in a more standardized set of output values. For example, a mathematical model can rate a project on a scale from 1 to 100. The organization then decides how desirable a single project is based on its rating.

Project Management Methodology

An organization's standard practices when conducting project activities along with the project management standards make up the project management methodology. Any standards, guidelines, procedures, or common practices work together to form the general way of managing projects within any organization. The particular methodology you use depends on the culture of your organization, and all these factors affect the content of the project charter.

Project Management Information System

The project management information system (PMIS) is the collection of computerized tools used to collect, store, analyze, and interpret project information. Although most project managers use software to schedule projects, the PMIS often consists of far more than just project management software. When managing a project, learn which tools are available and use them to support the project throughout its life cycle.

Expert Judgment

The first tool and technique referenced in creating the project charter is tapping into the expert judgment of others. Expert judgment of the project manager is included here if the project manager has been assigned. Some technical or procedural details might require input from an expert in a specific area. Such experts can be stakeholders or customers of the project, or they can be totally unrelated to the project. PMI encourages use of any available source for project information input. When considering input sources for the project charter, or any needed expert input, consider any of these alternatives:

- ▶ Internal organization assets with specific expertise
- ▶ External consultants
- ▶ Stakeholders, including customers
- ▶ Professional or trade associations
- ▶ Industry or user groups

Facilitation Techniques

One of the primary responsibilities of a project manager is to bring together various resources to accomplish project goals. Effective project managers must rely on techniques to ensure that the process of collaboration and cooperation move toward meeting project goals. Facilitation techniques are useful in many project processes and are introduced in the PMBOK. These techniques include encouraging team members to contribute ideas and input, resolving conflicts, solving problems, and managing efficient meetings. In fact, any techniques that promote positive team interaction and outcomes can be considered facilitation techniques.

Cram Quiz

Answer these questions. The answers follow the last question. If you cannot answer these questions correctly, consider reading this section again until you can.

1. Which of the following statements does NOT apply to the project charter?

   ○ **A.** The project charter formally authorizes the project.

   ○ **B.** The project charter provides the project manager with authority to devote organizational resources to project activities.

   ○ **C.** The project charter identifies an external project sponsor.

   ○ **D.** The project charter includes a work breakdown structure (WBS) and associated WBS dictionary.

2. Who is responsible for creating the project charter?

   ○ **A.** The project manager

   ○ **B.** The project sponsor

   ○ **C.** The project team

   ○ **D.** The project management office (PMO)

Cram Quiz Answers

1. Answer D is the correct response. A work breakdown structure (WBS) is not a component of the project charter. Answers A, B, and C are all components of the project charter.

2. Answer B is correct. The project sponsor creates the project charter. Answers A, C, and D list groups that can assist in creating the project charter but do not have the responsibility for creating the project charter.

Stakeholder Management

▶ **Identify Stakeholders—13.1**

CramSaver

If you can correctly answer these questions before going through this section, save time by skimming the Exam Alerts in this section and then completing the Cram Quiz at the end of the section.

1. Who are the stakeholders of a project?

2. The ability for project stakeholders to influence the project scope and cost is greatest during which phase of a project?

- ○ **A.** Initiating
- ○ **B.** Planning
- ○ **C.** Executing
- ○ **D.** Monitoring and controlling

Answers

1. Project stakeholders are entities or people who are actively involved in a project or whose interests are affected by the outcome of the project.

2. Answer A is the correct response. Stakeholders have the ability to influence the project scope and project cost to the greatest extent during the initiating phase of the project. This influence decreases during the life cycle of the project.

The only other process in the initiating process group is the identify stakeholders process. Although you might have a preliminary list of interested parties during the development of the project charter, the official identification of stakeholders does not occur until after the project charter is complete. You are prepared to identify all of the parties affected by the project only after reviewing a complete project charter.

Identifying stakeholders is a crucial part of any project. As a project manager, you spend much of your time during a project communicating with stakeholders. It is important that you include every necessary stakeholder and no one else. The identify stakeholders process results in an effective list of stakeholders and a description of how each one is involved in your project. Table 3.2 lists the inputs, the tools and techniques, and the output for the identify stakeholders process.

TABLE 3.2 **Identify Stakeholders Process: Inputs, Tools and Techniques, and Outputs**

Inputs	Tools and Techniques	Outputs
Project charter	Stakeholder analysis	Stakeholder register
Procurement documents	Expert judgment	
Enterprise environmental factors	Meetings	
Organizational process assets		

There is a lot of duplication in the process requirements. The important point is that you understand what each process does and how its inputs and outputs connect with other processes.

The most noteworthy point for the identify stakeholders process is the stakeholder analysis. This process is far more than just writing down a list of names. In addition to creating a list of stakeholders, you also need to know how much each stakeholder is involved in the project and how much influence each stakeholder can, and will, assert on the project.

> **ExamAlert**
>
> Do not underestimate the importance of the stakeholder analysis. The exam might have a question that asks you to decide on a course of action that requires knowledge of stakeholder interest and influence. That information comes directly from the identify stakeholder process.

A stakeholder who is very interested in the project and has a lot of influence is apt to demand substantial attention. A stakeholder with little interest or influence should not require as much of your time. You always want to provide full disclosure of project activities to all of the stakeholders, but knowing who's who among your stakeholders allows you to manage the project more efficiently.

Cram Quiz

Answer these questions. The answers follow the last question. If you cannot answer these questions correctly, consider reading this section again until you can.

1. How much do stakeholders influence a project after the initiating and planning process groups?

○ **A.** None at all. Stakeholders only influence a project during the initiating and planning process groups.

○ **B.** Very little. Stakeholders only occasionally monitor a project's progress after the planning process group.

○ **C.** Substantially. Stakeholders can potentially influence all aspects of a project throughout its life cycle.

○ **D.** It depends entirely on the project manager.

2. Which of the following are generally NOT project stakeholders?

○ **A.** Vendors

○ **B.** Customers

○ **C.** Functional managers

○ **D.** Project management office (PMO)

Cram Quiz Answers

1. Answer C is correct. Since stakeholders all have an interest in the outcome of the project, they generally use their influence to ensure that the project proceeds in a manner with which they are comfortable. The project manager must ensure that stakeholders do not interfere with the overall goal of the project by protecting their own interests.

2. Answer A is correct. Although a vendor might be a stakeholder in some cases, vendors generally do not appear on the common stakeholders list. All other entities listed are generally considered stakeholders.

What the Project Manager Needs to Know

▶ **Develop Project Charter—4.1**

CramSaver

If you can correctly answer these questions before going through this section, save time by skimming the Exam Alerts in this section and then completing the Cram Quiz at the end of the section.

1. Which is the only process that must occur after a project manager has been assigned to the project?

   ○ **A.** Develop the project charter

   ○ **B.** Identify stakeholders

   ○ **C.** Develop the project statement of work

   ○ **D.** Scope planning

2. Who applies project selection methods to decide whether to accept or reject a project?

   ○ **A.** The project sponsor

   ○ **B.** The project manager

   ○ **C.** The project team

   ○ **D.** The project accountant

Answers

1. Answer D is correct. The scope planning process occurs during project planning. Answers A, B, and C occur during project initiation. Even though a project manager should be assigned as early as possible, the project manager is not required until project planning.

2. Answer A is correct. All the other answers list project team members who lack the authority to select (or reject) a project. The project sponsor must have the authority to select and fund the project.

The project manager is responsible for all activity that takes place during the project life cycle. In addition, the project manager is responsible for properly managing all the resources associated with the project. These resources can include people, equipment, money, supplies, and even influence. An important aspect of project manager responsibilities is the ability to measure the effectiveness and impact of project decisions and compare various options. Project managers need to be able to assess the potential impact of various options and select the option that makes the most sense for the project and the organization. Let's look at a general management approach and a few specific techniques to measure and assess decisions.

Using Management by Objectives

Many organizations use a common management technique called management by objectives (MBO). MBO is not covered directly in the PMBOK, but it is helpful to understand this concept for the PMP exam. In very simple terms, MBO helps ensure that objectives in various areas or levels within an organization agree, or harmonize, with objectives from other areas and levels. In short, MBO gets everyone thinking with an enterprisewide perspective.

The initiating process group is really a set of activities that directly support MBO techniques. The main purpose of initiating a project is to ensure that the project is understood, provides value to the organization, and is fully authorized by the organization.

MBO is closely related to solid project management practices for several reasons:

▶ MBO implements goal setting and recurring reviews and suggests activities similar to the project control process.

▶ MBO is concerned with ensuring that goals are consistent across an organization, and one task of the project charter is to state how the project supports an organization's overall goals.

▶ Both MBO and sound project management work only if management supports them at a high level.

Implementing MBO is relatively simple. Here are the basic MBO process steps:

1. Establish clear and achievable objectives.

2. Periodically check whether objectives are being met.

3. Take corrective actions on any discovered discrepancies.

Accounting Concepts Used with Initiating Processes

It is important for project managers to have a good general understanding of the basic accounting principles that apply to their projects. Nearly all phases of the project life cycle require some type of accounting processes and valuation. Even initiating requires projects to be evaluated for the benefit to the organization. We discussed the two general categories of project selection methods earlier in this chapter. Both benefit measurement methods and constrained optimization methods require the application of some accounting methods.

For the PMP exam, you need to understand several cost accounting concepts that are frequently used during the project selection process. Of the two main project selection methods, benefit measurement methods requires more cost calculations. You are not expected to be an expert at cost methods for the PMP exam. However, you need to understand all these accounting concepts and know how to use them during the project selection activity. Table 3.3 lists the main accounting concepts you need to know and how they relate to project selection.

TABLE 3.3 **Project Selection Accounting Concepts**

Accounting Concept	Description	Keys for Project Selection	Notes
Present value	The value today of future cash flow	The higher the present value, the better.	Present value = $FV/(1 + r)n^*$
Net present value (NPV)	The present value of cash inflow less the present value of cash outflow	A negative NPV is unfavorable; the higher the NPV, the better.	Accounts for different project durations
Internal rate of return (IRR)	The interest rate that makes the net present value of all cash flow equal zero	The higher the IRR, the better.	The return that a company would earn if it invested in the project
Payback period	The number of time periods required until inflows equal, or exceed, costs	The lower the payback period, the better.	
Benefit cost ratio (BCR)	A ratio describing the relationship between the cost and benefits of a proposed project	A BCR less than 1 is unfavorable; the higher the BCR, the better.	
Opportunity cost	The difference in benefit received between a project that was chosen and a project that was not chosen		

Accounting Concept	Description	Keys for Project Selection	Notes
Sunk costs	Money that has already been spent and cannot be recovered	This should not be a factor in project decisions.	

* In the present value calculation, *FV* is the future value, *r* is the interest rate, and *n* is the number of time periods.

PMI also expects a project manager to understand other accounting concepts. Table 3.4 lists some of the most common accounting concepts you need to know for the PMP exam.

TABLE 3.4 **General Accounting Concepts**

Accounting Concept	Description	Notes
Variable costs	Costs that change based on an organization's activity	For example, fuel costs
Fixed costs	Costs that remain constant, regardless of activity level	For example, rent and lease payments
Direct costs	Costs that can be directly associated with the production of specific goods or services	For example, labor and material costs
Indirect costs	Costs that cannot be directly associated with the production of specific goods or services	For example, legal costs, administration, and insurance
Working capital	Total assets less total liabilities	
Straight-line depreciation	A depreciation method that evenly divides the difference between an asset's cost and its expected salvage value by the number of years it is expected to be in service	The simplest method
Accumulated depreciation	A depreciation method that allows greater deductions in the earlier years of the life of an asset	Also called double declining balance (DDB)
Life cycle costing	Includes costs from each phase of a project's life cycle when total investment costs are calculated	

ExamAlert

These accounting principles represent one area of project management (and general management) that a project manager must understand. There are several general management concepts on the PMP exam, but you just need to understand the basic concepts presented here.

Cram Quiz

Answer these questions. The answers follow the last question. If you cannot answer these questions correctly, consider reading this section again until you can.

1. When should a project manager be assigned to a project?

   ○ **A.** Prior to the start of project planning

   ○ **B.** After the project charter is approved

   ○ **C.** During project planning

   ○ **D.** During project execution

2. Which accounting concept refers to the value today of future cash flow?

   ○ **A.** Present value

   ○ **B.** Net present value (NPV)

   ○ **C.** Opportunity cost

   ○ **D.** Sunk cost

Cram Quiz Answers

1. Answer A is the best response. A project manager should be assigned prior to the start of project planning. Answer B is incorrect because the project manager should be assigned prior to the creation of a project charter. Answer C is incorrect because a project manager should be assigned prior to, not during, project planning. Similarly, Answer D is incorrect because a project manager should be in place before project execution.

2. Answer A is correct. Answers B, C, and D refer to other accounting concepts. Refer to Table 3.3 for more information.

What Next?

If you want more practice on this chapter's exam topics before you move on, remember that you can access all of the Cram Quiz questions on the CD. You can also create a custom exam by topic with the practice exam software. Note any topic you struggle with and go to that topic's material in this chapter.

CHAPTER 4

Examine Project Planning

In Chapter 1, "Project Management Framework Fundamentals," we introduced the PMI concepts of processes, process groups, and knowledge areas. Recall that PMI defines a total of 47 project processes that describe activities throughout a project's life cycle. These processes are organized into 10 knowledge areas and represent 5 process groups. One of the most prominent of the process groups is project planning. Over half of the processes occur in this group; 24 of the 47 processes are in this group. You might think that planning processes are localized to a particular area of your project, but note that processes in the planning group span all 10 knowledge areas. Let's look at project planning in more detail.

Understanding PMI's Planning Process Group

▶ **Planning Process—3.4**

CramSaver

If you can correctly answer these questions before going through this section, save time by skimming the Exam Alerts in this section and then completing the Cram Quiz at the end of the section.

1. What are the two main inputs (outputs from processes in the initiating process group) that you need to start planning a project? (Remember that you can't start planning a project from scratch; planning is not the starting point.)

2. Which planning process group process output is the result of project deliverable decomposition into manageable components called work packages?

Answers

1. The two outputs from initiating process group processes necessary to start planning are the project charter and the stakeholder register. These two documents provide the starting point for planning a project.

2. The work breakdown structure (WBS) is the result of decomposing work into smaller, more manageable components until the work and deliverables are defined to the work package level.

After you have completed the *initiating processes*, you are ready to start planning your project. Remember what that means? It means that you possess formal authorization to conduct the work of the project. But you don't know what to do without a plan. Planning answers a few very important questions, such as What work will you do? and What exactly are you trying to accomplish?

To answer these questions, start from what you know. There are two outputs from the initiating process group processes. Always start with the information necessary to proceed. Recall that PMI refers to this initial information for each process as the process's inputs. There are two outputs from the initiating processes:

▶ The project charter

▶ The stakeholder register

Armed with these initiating documents, you can start the planning processes. In a nutshell, you follow each of the planning processes to refine the project documents from these outputs. As you develop the planning documents, always remember how the various processes are related.

Think of the initiating process group as the processes that answer the "what" and "why" questions. The planning processes answer the "how" questions. The planning processes result in outputs that explain how the project will progress toward reaching its goals.

Figure 4.1 shows how the processes in the planning group are related in the *PMBOK Guide*, Fifth Edition.

ExamAlert

Planning includes many processes, so be prepared to answer many questions in this area on the exam. Planning process group questions make up 24% of the PMP exam. As with all other process groups, make sure you know the inputs, tools and techniques, and outputs of each process. It helps to draw your own process flow. Just the act of physically drawing the process flow in each process group helps you remember how the processes relate to one another.

PMI is explicit in stressing the importance of planning. Far too many projects suffer from the poor practice of starting work before anyone really knows what needs to be done. This almost always results in wasted effort and lost time. Proper planning requires good communication among the team and sound leadership from the project manager. The result of solid planning is a project team that is more informed and prepared to carry out the work required to meet the project's goals. You should expect to see several questions on the exam that require you to understand the importance of fully planning before starting work.

Because planning is such a large process group, the material is divided into two separate chapters. This chapter covers the general concepts of planning and the processes that relate to the development of project baselines, including the following topics:

▶ Integration

▶ Scope

▶ Time

▶ Cost

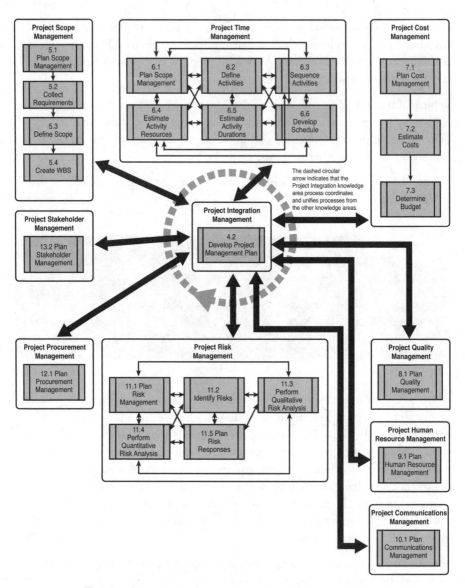

FIGURE 4.1 **The planning process group process interactions.**

Chapter 5, "Explore More Elements of Project Planning," covers the remaining project planning processes that support project planning by applying more details to the baselines. Topics covered in Chapter 5 include these:

▶ Communications

▶ Risk

▶ Quality

▶ Procurement

▶ Human resources

▶ Stakeholders

The main purpose of planning is to provide a framework to gather information to produce a project management plan. In fact, the plan itself is really a collection of other plans. The majority of activities in the planning group center around developing the supporting documents that comprise the final project management plan. As more detailed information is learned about the project, the overall plan becomes more complete, and the stakeholders' confidence in the project increases.

Planning is an iterative group of processes. As a project progresses, it often becomes necessary to modify the plan for a number of reasons. Unexpected results, delays, outside factors, and internal factors can all require additional planning. Any scope changes are likely to require one or more planning processes to be revisited. Don't assume that planning is accomplished only once. The exam requires that you understand how planning is iterative throughout a project.

The following are some fundamental planning process items you need to understand for the exam:

▶ **Project management plan**—One process in the planning group addresses the project management plan. The develop project management plan process is the high-level process that provides direction for developing subsidiary plans and compiling their information into the final project plan.

▶ **Scope**—Four processes address scope planning. These direct the refinement of the preliminary scope statement and break down the high-level goals of the project into smaller, more manageable chunks.

▶ **Activity**—Six processes deal with activity planning. After the work of the project is expressed in small, manageable chunks, the activity-related processes focus on defining the activity details, integrating with project resources, and sequencing the project activities.

▶ **Cost**—Three processes address cost planning. These processes collect estimates and organize them into a project budget.

We examine each of these processes in the next section.

Cram Quiz

Answer these questions. The answers follow the last question. If you cannot answer these questions correctly, consider reading this section again until you can.

1. What is a common result of poor project planning?

    ○ **A.** Wasted effort

    ○ **B.** Lost time

    ○ **C.** Increased cost

    ○ **D.** All of the above

2. Which of the following aspects of planning has the most processes and is concerned with decomposing the work of a project into manageable chunks?

    ○ **A.** Scope

    ○ **B.** Time

    ○ **C.** Cost

    ○ **D.** Quality

Cram Quiz Answers

1. Answer D is correct. Poor project planning almost always results in wasted effort, lost time, and increased cost.

2. Answer B is correct. There are six time-related planning processes. Time management processes provide the mechanism to decompose work into small, manageable chunks.

Integration Management

▶ **Develop Project Management Plan—4.2**

CramSaver

If you can correctly answer these questions before going through this section, save time by skimming the Exam Alerts in this section and then completing the Cram Quiz at the end of the section.

1. According to the PMBOK, what is the basic purpose of the project management plan?

2. Name three of the subsidiary plans to the project management plan.

Answers

1. The project management plan is the result (output) of the develop project management plan process that documents the actions necessary to define, prepare, integrate, and coordinate all subsidiary plans.

2. The subsidiary project management plans could include

   ▶ Project scope management plan

   ▶ Requirements management plan

   ▶ Schedule management plan

   ▶ Cost management plan

   ▶ Quality management plan

   ▶ Process improvement plan

   ▶ Human resource plan

   ▶ Communication management plan

   ▶ Risk management plan

   ▶ Procurement management plan

The *project management plan process* covers all activities that identify and direct the actions of many other processes in the planning process group. Developing the project management plan includes coordinating the development of the subsidiary plans and incorporating them into the complete project plan. The main purpose of the project management plan is to define how the project is to progress from its beginning to completion.

In short, the project management plan provides the high-level game plan for how the project moves through its life cycle. PMI defines many potential subsidiary plans that make up the overall project management plan. These subsidiary plans provide the specific details for managing each aspect of the project from initiation through closure. The subsidiary project management plans could include

▶ Project scope management plan

▶ Requirements management plan

▶ Schedule management plan

▶ Cost management plan

▶ Quality management plan

▶ Process improvement plan

▶ Human resource plan

▶ Communication management plan

▶ Risk management plan

▶ Procurement management plan

Note

This list of subsidiary plans is a great outline of a project. Use the list as a table of contents when you consider what should be in a project management plan.

One of the most common mistakes inexperienced project managers make is to confuse a project plan with a project schedule. The output from many common project management software packages does not qualify as a project plan. This output is a good start, but a true project plan is made up of much more information than just scheduling information. This process requires a focused effort to create a plan that incorporates all known information about a project. Table 4.1 shows the inputs, tools and techniques, and outputs for the develop project management plan process.

TABLE 4.1 **Develop Project Management Plan Inputs, Tools and Techniques, and Outputs**

Inputs	Tools and Techniques	Outputs
Project charter	Expert judgment	Project management plan
Outputs from planning processes	Facilitation techniques	
Enterprise environmental factors		
Organizational process assets		

ExamAlert

You will see expert judgment listed as a tool and technique for several processes. The meaning of *expert judgment* is specific to each process. In the context of the develop the project management plan process, expert judgment includes

▶ Tailoring the process to meet the project needs

▶ Developing technical and management details to be included in the project management plan

▶ Determining resources and skill levels needed to perform project work

▶ Defining the level of configuration management to apply to the project

▶ Determining which project documents are subject to the formal change control process

Cram Quiz

Answer these questions. The answers follow the last question. If you cannot answer these questions correctly, consider reading this section again until you can.

1. You are a project manager newly assigned to a large project for your organization. The project charter has been signed, and the stakeholders have been identified. What should you do next?

   ○ **A.** Ask appropriate team members to submit WBS input

   ○ **B.** Initiate the scope planning process

   ○ **C.** Start the develop project management plan process

   ○ **D.** Begin the activity definition process

2. Which of the following is NOT part of the expert judgment tool and technique for the develop project management plan process?

   ○ **A.** Tailor the process to meet the project needs

   ○ **B.** Hold planning meetings to develop the risk management plan

   ○ **C.** Determine resources and skill levels needed to perform project work

   ○ **D.** Define the level of configuration management to apply to the project

Cram Quiz Answers

1. Answer C is correct. The first process in the planning group is develop project management plan. Answers A, B, and D skip the first process and start subsequent processes prematurely.

2. Answer B is correct. Holding planning meetings to develop the risk management plan is a tool and technique for the plan risk management process. Answers A, B, and D all refer to valid components of the expert judgment tool and technique for the develop project management plan process.

Scope Management

▶ **Plan Scope Management—5.1**

▶ **Collect Requirements—5.2**

▶ **Define Scope—5.3**

▶ **Create WBS—5.4**

CramSaver

If you can correctly answer these questions before going through this section, save time by skimming the Exam Alerts in this section and then completing the Cram Quiz at the end of the section.

1. The project scope management plan, as a component of the project management plan, includes which of the following?

   ○ **A.** Preparation of a detailed project scope statement

   ○ **B.** Creation of the work breakdown structure (WBS)

   ○ **C.** Specifications for formal verification and acceptance of completed project deliverables

   ○ **D.** All of the above

2. You are creating your WBS and find that you keep decomposing tasks into smaller and smaller units. How can you tell when you are done?

   ○ **A.** Keep decomposing tasks until you reach an amount of work that is small enough to reliably estimate required resources and duration.

   ○ **B.** Keep decomposing tasks until you reach an amount of work that can be accomplished in one hour.

   ○ **C.** Keep decomposing work until you reach an amount of work that can be accomplished in your organization's basic work unit.

   ○ **D.** Keep decomposing work until you reach a predetermined number of hierarchy levels to keep the WBS balanced.

3. Which of the following is a valid input to the collect requirements process?

   ○ **A.** Project charter

   ○ **B.** Requirements traceability matrix

   ○ **C.** Validated deliverables

   ○ **D.** Work performance information

1. Answer D is the best response. The project scope management plan includes preparation of a detailed project scope statement, creation of the WBS, and a process specifying how formal verification and acceptance of the completed project deliverables will be obtained.

2. Answer A is correct. A properly sized work package is one that is small enough to allow for reliable estimates for required resources and duration. Answers B, C, and D are incorrect because they assume that you are working toward some artificial target that does not contribute to appropriately sized work packages.

3. Answer A is correct. The project charter is one of two defined inputs for the collect requirements process. (The other input is the stakeholder register.) Answer B is incorrect because the requirements traceability matrix is an output for the collect requirements process. Answers C and D are incorrect because they refer to inputs from other processes.

Scope management is the set of processes which ensures that the requirements of the customer are captured in a specification of work that ensures the delivery of the project's deliverables, that all the project work is done, and that only the work required to complete the project is done. In other words, scope management makes sure that the project is completed without expending any unnecessary effort.

Plan Scope Management

The first process in scope management is a new process, plan scope management. The *PMBOK Guide*, Fifth Edition, adds several processes to separate the initial planning activities from other activities. While all the processes you will learn about in this chapter relate to planning, the new initial processes in scope management and three other process groups bring attention to the importance PMI places on proper planning. The plan scope management process creates the scope management plan. The scope management plan describes the project scope and documents how it will be further defined, validated, and controlled. This process results in a plan that gives the project team guidance on how to manage the scope throughout the project life cycle. Table 4.2 shows the inputs, tools and techniques, and outputs for the plan scope management process.

TABLE 4.2 **Plan Scope Management Inputs, Tools and Techniques, and Outputs**

Inputs	Tools and Techniques	Outputs
Project management plan	Expert judgment	Scope management plan
Project charter	Meetings	Requirements management plan
Enterprise environmental factors		
Organizational process assets		

Collect Requirements

The second process in the scope management process group is the collect requirements process. This process seeks to use multiple tools and techniques to collect all the project requirements from all the stakeholders. This process attempts to leave no stone unturned and results in a complete list of project requirements. When properly performed, the collect requirements process dramatically reduces surprises as the project moves toward completion.

Table 4.3 shows the inputs, tools and techniques, and outputs for the collect requirements process. Pay particular attention to the various creative methods you can employ to develop a list of project requirements.

TABLE 4.3 **Collect Requirements Inputs, Tools and Techniques, and Outputs**

Inputs	Tools and Techniques	Outputs
Scope management plan	Interviews	Requirements documentation
Requirements management plan	Focus groups	Requirements traceability matrix
Stakeholder management plan	Facilitated workshops	
Project charter	Group creativity techniques	
Stakeholder register	Group decision-making techniques	
	Questionnaires and surveys	
	Observations	
	Prototypes	
	Benchmarking	
	Context diagrams	
	Document analysis	

Define Scope

The next process, *define scope*, is a process that clearly states what the project will and will not accomplish. The supporting documents are reviewed to ensure that the project will satisfy the stated goals, and the resulting scope should state the stakeholders' needs and clearly communicate the expectations for the performance of the project. Table 4.4 shows the inputs, tools and techniques, and outputs for the define scope process.

TABLE 4.4 Define Scope Inputs, Tools and Techniques, and Outputs

Inputs	Tools and Techniques	Outputs
Scope management plan	Expert judgment	Project scope statement
Project charter	Product analysis	Project document updates
Requirements documentation	Alternatives identification	
Organizational process assets	Facilitated workshops	

Work Breakdown Structure: A Common and Dangerous Omission

Many inexperienced project managers move too quickly from the scope statement to the activity sequencing processes. This practice is a mistake and often leads to activity omissions and inaccurate plans. PMI stresses the importance of creating a *work breakdown structure (WBS)* before moving to activity management processes.

A WBS provides the project manager and project team with the opportunity to decompose the high-level scope statement into much smaller, more manageable units of work, called *work packages*. The resulting WBS should provide a complete list of all work packages required to complete the project (and nothing more). Table 4.5 shows the inputs, tools and techniques, and outputs for the create WBS process.

TABLE 4.5 Create WBS Inputs, Tools and Techniques, and Outputs

Inputs	Tools and Techniques	Outputs
Scope management plan	Decomposition	Scope baseline (project scope statement, WBS, and WBS dictionary)
Project scope statement	Expert judgment	Project document updates
Requirements documentation		

Inputs	Tools and Techniques	Outputs
Enterprise environmental factors		
Organizational process assets		

ExamAlert

The *PMI Practice Standard for Work Breakdown Structures* is the guide you need to use for the PMP exam. This is an example of information on the exam that goes beyond the PMBOK. You can find this document in the publications section of the PMI website (http://www.pmi.org/en/PMBOK-Guide-and-Standards/Standards-Library-of-PMI-Global-Standards.aspx).

In creating the WBS, the project team repeatedly decomposes the work of the project into smaller and smaller units of work, and the result is a collection of small work packages. The process continues until the resulting work packages are simple enough to reliably estimate duration and required resources. Don't go overboard, though. When you have work packages that are manageable and each represent a single work effort, stop the process. Each project is different, so this process results in different levels of detail for each project.

ExamAlert

The term *work package* refers to an individual project activity. The work package is the lowest-level WBS component. According to the PMBOK, "A work package can be scheduled, cost estimated, monitored, and controlled."

The last main feature of the WBS is that it is organized in a hierarchical fashion. The highest level is the project. The children that represent project phases, divisions, or main deliverables are listed under the project. Each child process or task is divided into further levels of detail until the lowest level, the work package, is reached. Figure 4.2 depicts a sample WBS with multiple levels.

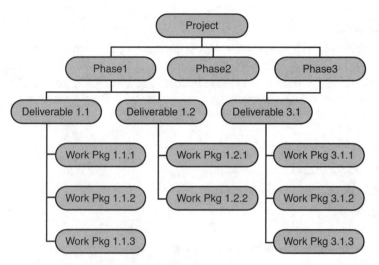

FIGURE 4.2 **Sample work breakdown structure.**

In addition to the WBS itself, another output of the create WBS process is the WBS dictionary. The *WBS dictionary* is a document that supports the WBS by providing detailed information for each work package. The WBS dictionary can contain many types of information, including

- ► Work package name or identifier
- ► Accounting code identifier
- ► Description of work
- ► Technical specifications
- ► Quality requirements
- ► Owner or responsible party assignment
- ► Required resources
- ► List of schedule milestones
- ► Associated schedule activities
- ► Cost estimates
- ► Acceptance criteria
- ► Contract information

Cram Quiz

Answer these questions. The answers follow the last question. If you cannot answer these questions correctly, consider reading this section again until you can.

1. As project manager, you are about to start the define scope process. You have the project charter and the organizational process assets list. Because there are no change requests in your project at this point, what must you have before you begin?

   - ○ **A.** Product analysis
   - ○ **B.** Requirements documentation
   - ○ **C.** Updates to project documents
   - ○ **D.** WBS

2. What does a project scope statement document?

   - ○ **A.** What work is to be completed during the project
   - ○ **B.** What deliverables need to be produced by the project
   - ○ **C.** Both A and B
   - ○ **D.** Neither A nor B

3. The work breakdown structure (WBS) does all of the following except

   - ○ **A.** Organizes and defines the entire scope of the project
   - ○ **B.** Divides the project into smaller, more manageable tasks
   - ○ **C.** Serves as a high-level planning tool for work planned but not yet approved
   - ○ **D.** Both A and B

4. Which of the following is an output of the collect requirements process?

   - ○ **A.** Scope management plan
   - ○ **B.** Requirements management plan
   - ○ **C.** Requirements risk breakdown
   - ○ **D.** Requirements traceability matrix

Cram Quiz Answers

1. Answer B is correct. The requirements documentation is an input you need before starting the define scope process. Answer A is incorrect because product analysis is a tool and technique of define scope, not an input. Answer C is incorrect because project document updates are an output, not an input. Answer D is incorrect because the WBS is created in a subsequent process and is not available at this point. Know your inputs, tools and techniques, and outputs of all processes.

2. Answer C is the best response. A project scope statement documents what work is to be accomplished and which deliverables need to be produced. Answers A and B are both individually correct, but Answer C is the better response. Answer D is incorrect.

3. Answer C is the correct response. The WBS provides a detailed definition of work specified in the current, approved project scope statement. Both Answers A and B describe the WBS and are therefore incorrect responses to the question.

4. Answer D is the correct response. Answers A and B are incorrect because these are outputs of the plan scope management process. Answer C is incorrect because there is no such defined output as a requirements risk breakdown.

Activity Planning—From WBS to Project Schedule

▶ **Plan Schedule Management—6.1**

▶ **Define Activities—6.2**

▶ **Sequence Activities—6.3**

▶ **Estimate Activity Resources—6.4**

▶ **Estimate Activity Durations—6.5**

▶ **Develop Schedule—6.6**

CramSaver

If you can correctly answer these questions before going through this section, save time by skimming the Exam Alerts in this section and then completing the Cram Quiz at the end of the section.

1. Which type of network diagram method allows you to depict four types of dependencies?

   ○ **A.** Precedence diagramming method (PDM)

   ○ **B.** Arrow diagramming method (ADM)

   ○ **C.** Dependency diagramming method (DDM)

   ○ **D.** Gantt chart diagram (GCD)

2. What term is defined as the practice of planning activities based on how soon the tasks are scheduled to start, such that activities that are close to their start date are planned at a more detailed level than those farther in the future? This term also implies that more detailed plans are required as activities approach their start date.

   ○ **A.** Progressive elaboration

   ○ **B.** Rolling wave planning

   ○ **C.** Planning component elaboration

   ○ **D.** Milestone detail planning

3. Which of the following statements best describes the estimate activity resources process?

   ○ **A.** Identifying and documenting relationships among the project activities

   ○ **B.** Identifying the specific actions to be performed to produce the project deliverables

   ○ **C.** Estimating the number of work periods needed to complete individual activities

   ○ **D.** Estimating the type and quantities of material, people, equipment, or supplies to perform each activity

DAC1

4. Which estimating technique is best to use if you know the standard usage rate for a resource (such as an installer can pull 40 feet of cable per hour) to estimate the duration of an activity?

   ○ **A.** Analogous estimating

   ○ **B.** Parametric estimating

   ○ **C.** Three-point estimates

   ○ **D.** Reserve analysis

5. Which of the following is NOT a tool and technique for the develop schedule process?

   ○ **A.** Critical path method

   ○ **B.** Alternatives analysis

   ○ **C.** Schedule network analysis

   ○ **D.** Leads and lags

Answers

1. Answer A is correct. The precedence diagramming method (PDM), also called activity-on-node (AON) diagramming, supports finish-to-start, finish-to-finish, start-to-start, and start-to-finish dependencies. PDM is often used in critical path methodology (CPM). Answer B is incorrect because the arrow diagramming method (ADM) only allows for finish-to-start dependencies. Answers C and D are incorrect because they are not real diagramming methods.

2. Answer B is the best answer. Rolling wave planning is providing detailed plans for tasks that are starting in the near future by using the most current information and revisiting future activities as their starting dates approach. Although rolling wave planning is a type of progressive elaboration, it is mainly concerned with near-term activities. Answer A is not the best answer because progressive elaboration is the process of continuously improving a project plan as more is learned about the project. Answers C and D are incorrect because they are not valid project planning terms.

3. Answer D is correct. Estimate activity resources is the process of estimating the type and quantities of material, people, equipment, or supplies to perform each activity. Answer A is incorrect because it describes the sequence activities process. Answer B is incorrect because it describes the define activities process. Answer C is incorrect because it describes the estimate activity durations process.

4. Answer B is correct. Parametric estimating uses known historical data, such as production rates, to estimate duration. Answer A is incorrect because analogous estimating uses comparison with other, similar project work. Answer C is incorrect because three-point estimates use best, worst, and most likely estimates to calculate duration. Answer D is incorrect because it refers to the process of including contingency reserves into estimates, not actually calculating estimate durations.

> 5. Answer B is correct. Alternative analysis is a tool and technique for the estimate activity resources process. Estimate activity resources is the process of estimating the type and quantities of material, people, equipment, or supplies to perform each activity. Answers A, C, and D are all tools and techniques for the develop schedule process.

The next section of the planning processes address the steps required to develop the project schedule. This is the part of the project plan that might be most familiar to new project managers. Many automated project management tools help create schedules by keeping track of activities, resources, durations, sequencing, and constraints. Although the schedule is an integral part of the project plan, it is only one part. Don't start working on the schedule until you have a proper WBS. Starting to work before completing the WBS nearly always results in doing more work than is necessary. A good WBS reduces task redundancy and helps ensure that all work performed is in the scope of the project.

Plan Schedule Management

The first process in the time management knowledge area is *plan schedule management*. This process defines the policies and procedures for planning, managing, and controlling the project schedule. This process provides guidance on how the schedule will be managed throughout the project. All the subsequent processes in the time management knowledge area depend on the plan developed in this process. Table 4.6 shows the inputs, tools and techniques, and outputs for the plan schedule management process.

TABLE 4.6 **Plan Schedule Management Inputs, Tools and Techniques, and Outputs**

Inputs	Tools and Techniques	Outputs
Project management plan	Expert judgment	Schedule management plan
Project charter	Analytical techniques	
Enterprise environmental factors	Meetings	
Organizational process assets		

Define Activities

The first process in the activity planning section is *define activities*. This process starts with the WBS and identifies the activities required to produce the various project deliverables. Activities are viewed from the perspective of the work packages. You ask the question, "What activities are required to satisfy this work package requirement?" Next, the resulting information from this process is used to organize the activities into a specific sequence. Table 4.7 shows the inputs, tools and techniques, and outputs for the define activities process.

TABLE 4.7 **Define Activities Inputs, Tools and Techniques, and Outputs**

Inputs	Tools and Techniques	Outputs
Schedule management plan	Decomposition	Activity list
Scope baseline	Rolling wave planning	Activity attributes
Enterprise environmental factors	Expert judgment	Milestone list
Organizational process assets		

Sometimes it is difficult to know everything about a project during the planning stage. It is common to learn more about the project as you work through the project life cycle. This is called *progressive elaboration* and affects the planning process. If you don't know everything about a project, you can't plan the whole project to the necessary level of detail.

For a large project, it is common to plan the entire project at a high level. The project starts with detailed plans in place for the work packages that are near the beginning of the project. As the time draws near to begin additional work, the more detailed, low-level plans for those work packages are added to the project plan. The planning process is revisited multiple times to ensure that the detailed plans contain the latest information known about the project. This practice is called *rolling wave planning* because the planning wave always moves to stay ahead of the work execution wave.

Sequence Activities

The next process is arranging the activities list from activity definition into a discrete sequence. Some activities can be accomplished at any time throughout the project. Other activities depend on input from another activity or are constrained by time or resources. Any requirement that restricts the start or end time of an activity is a *dependency*. This process identifies all relationships between activities and notes restrictions imposed by these relationships.

For example, when building a car, you cannot install the engine until the engine has been built and delivered to the main assembly line. This is just one example of how activities can be dependent on one another. The sequence activities process is one that can benefit from the use of computer software to assist in noting and keeping track of inter-activity dependencies. Table 4.8 shows the inputs, tools and techniques, and outputs for the sequence activities process.

TABLE 4.8 Sequence Activities Inputs, Tools and Techniques, and Outputs

Inputs	Tools and Techniques	Outputs
Schedule management plan	Precedence diagramming method (PDM)	Project schedule
Activity list	Dependency determination	Project documents updates
Activity attributes	Leads and lags	
Milestone list		
Project scope statement		
Enterprise environmental factors		
Organizational process assets		

Network Diagrams

One of the most important topics to understand when planning project activities is how to create network diagrams. A *network diagram* provides a graphical view of activities and how they are related to one another. The PMP exam tests your ability to recognize and understand the most common type of network diagramming method: the *precedence diagramming method (PDM)*. Make sure you can read a PDM diagram and use the information it presents.

Figure 4.3 shows an example of a PDM diagram.

Precedence Diagramming Method (PDM)

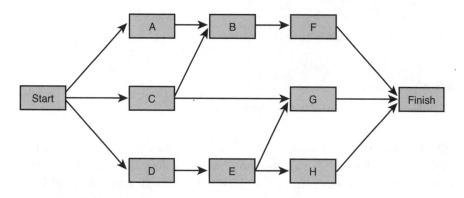

8 Activities with 13 Dependencies

FIGURE 4.3   **The precedence diagramming method.**

Precedence Diagramming Method

A PDM diagram shows nodes—representing activities—connected by arrows that represent dependencies. To represent that activity B is dependent on activity A (in other words, activity A must be complete before activity B starts), simply draw an arrow from A to B. PDM diagrams are also referred to as activity-on-node (AON) diagrams because the nodes contain the activity duration information. (We don't have enough information to complete all the information presented here yet. We'll fill in the duration information during activity duration estimating.) In fact, nodes generally contain several pieces of information, including

▶ **Early start**—The earliest date the activity can start

▶ **Duration**—The duration of the activity

▶ **Early finish**—The earliest date the activity can finish

▶ **Late start**—The latest date the activity can start

▶ **Late finish**—The latest date the activity can finish

▶ **Slack**—Difference between the early start and the late start dates

Figure 4.4 shows an example of a PDM node template.

Early Start	Duration	Early Finish
Task Name		
Late Start	Slack	Late Finish

FIGURE 4.4 **The sample PDM node template.**

The PDM diagram in Figure 4.3 shows eight activities, labeled A through H, with 13 dependencies. The arrows show how some activities are dependent on other activities. For example, activity B cannot start until activities A and C are complete. To show this dual dependency, we draw an arrow from A to B and another arrow from C to B.

You can represent four types of dependencies with a PDM diagram:

▶ **Finish-to-start (the most common dependency type)**—The successor activity's start depends on the completion of the predecessor activity.

▶ **Finish-to-finish**—The completion of the successor activity depends on the completion of the predecessor activity.

▶ **Start-to-start**—The start of the successor activity depends on the start of the predecessor activity.

▶ **Start-to-finish**—The completion of the successor activity depends on the start of the predecessor activity.

ExamAlert

Carefully consider the different types of dependencies. Some—especially start-to-finish—can be confusing. On the exam, you are asked to evaluate the scheduling effect of changes in start or end dates. The overall effect on the project depends on the type of relationship between activities. Don't skip over the dependencies too quickly. Take the time to really read the question before you construct diagrams.

Project Task Information

When you are comfortable with the main types of network diagrams, you need to understand how to use them. Let's talk about a few basic scheduling concepts and look at how network diagrams help you understand project schedules, starting with a few project tasks. Table 4.9 lists the tasks for a project, along with the predecessors, duration, and earliest start date.

TABLE 4.9 **Project Task Information**

Activity	Predecessor	Duration	Earliest Start Date
A	None	5	9/5/14
B	A	2	9/10/14
C	A	3	9/10/14
D	B	7	9/12/14
E	C	4	9/13/14
F	D	1	9/19/14
G	E, F	2	9/20/14

Now use the sample PDM node template shown in Figure 4.4 to create a PDM diagram for the project.

Your completed network diagram should look like the one shown in Figure 4.5.

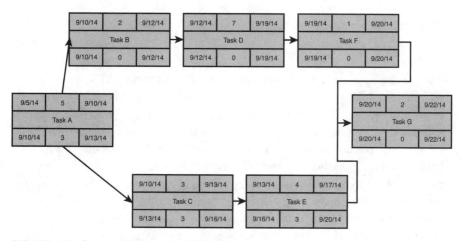

FIGURE 4.5 **A completed sample PDM diagram.**

Estimate Activity Resources

Now you have a list of activities and their relative dependencies. The next process is to associate activities with the resources required to accomplish the work. This process involves listing each type and amount, or quantity, of each required resource. Every activity requires resources of some sort. Activity resources can include

- ▶ People
- ▶ Equipment
- ▶ Materials and supplies
- ▶ Money

Table 4.10 shows the inputs, tools and techniques, and outputs for the estimate activity resources process.

TABLE 4.10 **Estimate Activity Resources Inputs, Tools and Techniques, and Outputs**

Inputs	Tools and Techniques	Outputs
Schedule management plan	Expert judgment	Activity resource requirements
Activity list	Alternative analysis	Resource breakdown structure
Activity attributes	Published estimating data	Project documents updates
Resource calendars	Bottom-up estimating	
Risk register	Project management software	
Activity cost estimates		
Enterprise environmental factors		
Organizational process assets		

Two of the tools and techniques warrant further discussion. One of the techniques you use when estimating activity resources is *alternative analysis*. Analyzing the various alternatives provides an opportunity to consider other sources or ways to achieve the desired result for an activity. Alternatives might be more desirable than the initial expected approach due to cost savings, higher quality, or earlier completion. Another important outcome of alternative analysis is that in case the primary source becomes unavailable, you might have already identified a replacement method to complete the work. Suppose your main supplier of industrial fittings suffers a catastrophic fire. If your alternative analysis identified another source, you might be able to continue the project with minimal disruption.

The second item is bottom-up estimating. Recall that one of the purposes of creating the WBS is to decompose project work into work packages that are small enough to reliably estimate for duration and resource requirements. Using the WBS, you can provide estimates for mid- and high-level work by aggregating the estimates for the work packages that make up the desired work. Because this process starts at the lowest level of work (the work package) to create the estimate, it is called *bottom-up estimating*. This type of estimating tends to be fairly accurate because the estimates come from the people doing the actual work. The alternative is *top-down estimating*. Top-down estimates generally come from management or a source that is higher up than the people actually doing the work. The estimates are really educated guesses on the amount of resources required for a collection of work packages and tend to be less reliable than bottom-up estimates.

Estimate Activity Durations

After the resource estimates are established for each of the activities, it's time to assign duration estimates. The *estimate activity durations process* approximates the number of work periods that are needed to complete scheduled activities. Each estimate assumes that the necessary resources are available to be applied to the work package when needed. Table 4.11 shows the inputs, tools and techniques, and outputs for the activity duration estimating process.

TABLE 4.11 **Estimate Activity Duration Inputs, Tools and Techniques, and Outputs**

Inputs	Tools and Techniques	Outputs
Schedule management plan	Expert judgment	Activity duration estimates
Activity list	Analogous estimating	Project documents updates
Activity attributes	Parametric estimating	
Activity resource requirements	Three-point estimating	
Resource calendars	Group decision-making techniques	
Project scope statement	Reserve analysis	
Risk register		
Resource breakdown structure		
Enterprise environmental factors		
Organizational process assets		

In addition to expert judgment and reserve analysis, four main techniques are used for project activity duration estimation. In many cases, using multiple techniques provides more accurate estimates. The four estimation techniques are

▶ **Analogous estimating**—This uses actual duration figures from similar activities. These activities can be from the same project or another project but share similarities in budget, size, weight, complexity, or other parameters.

▶ **Parametric estimating**—This calculates duration estimates by multiplying the quantity of work by the productivity rate. This type of estimate works best for standardized, and often repetitive, activities.

▶ **Three-point estimates**—This uses three estimate values for each activity:

▶ **Most likely (t_M)**—The duration most likely to occur.

▶ **Optimistic (t_O)**—The duration of the activity based on the best-case scenario.

▶ **Pessimistic (t_P)**—The duration of the activity based on the worst-case scenario.

This approach originated with the Program Evaluation and Review Technique (PERT). PERT analysis calculates the expected (t_E) activity from the three-point estimates by using the following formula:

$$t_E = (t_O + 4 * t_M + t_P) / 6$$

▶ **Triangular distribution**—This simple estimating method takes an average of the most likely, optimistic, and pessimistic values. Unlike a three-point estimate, each value receives the same weight. This estimating method assumes that risks are just as likely to be realized as the most likely estimate. You can calculate a triangular distribution by using the following formula:

$$\text{Average} = (t_O + t_M + t_P) / 3$$

Develop Schedule

The next step is to develop the actual project schedule. The *develop schedule process* pulls all the activity information together and results in the project's initial (baseline) schedule. As work is iteratively planned and accomplished and the project moves through its life cycle, changes to the schedule are likely to occur. The schedule is a dynamic document and requires constant attention on the part of the project manager to ensure that the project stays on track. Table 4.12 shows the inputs, tools and techniques, and outputs for the develop schedule process.

TABLE 4.12 Develop Schedule Inputs, Tools and Techniques, and Outputs

Inputs	Tools and Techniques	Outputs
Schedule management plan	Schedule network analysis	Schedule baseline
Activity list	Critical path method	Project schedule
Activity attributes	Critical chain method	Schedule data

Inputs	Tools and Techniques	Outputs
Project schedule network diagrams	Resource optimization techniques	Project calendars
Activity resource requirements	Modeling techniques	Project management plan updates
Resource calendars	Leads and lags	Project documents updates
Activity duration estimates	Schedule compression	
Project scope statement	Scheduling tool	
Risk register		
Project staff assignments		
Resource breakdown structure		
Enterprise environmental factors		
Organizational process assets		

An important topic to understand with respect to project schedules is the critical path. In the AON diagram in Figure 4.3, the critical path is the longest path from start to finish. It is calculated by adding all the durations along each path from start to finish. The reason it is called the *critical path* is that any delay (or increase in duration) of any activity on the critical path causes a delay in the project. It is critical that all activities on this path be completed on schedule.

Critical Path

Using the network diagram in Figure 4.5, you can calculate the project critical path. The *critical path* is the route with the longest total duration. The *critical path method* performs a forward and backward pass through the schedule network, calculating the early start and finish dates and the late start and finish dates for all activities, based on durations and relationships. The critical path method does not take into account resource limitations. The *critical chain method* does consider resource limitations. In short, the critical chain method uses the critical path method output and modifies the schedule network to account for limited resources. In this example, there are two routes from Task A to Task G:

▶ Path A–B–D–F–G will take 17 days to complete. (Just add up all the durations: $5 + 2 + 7 + 1 + 2 = 17$)

▶ Path A–C–E–G will take 14 days to complete.

From this diagram, you can see that the longest path is A–B–D–F–G, and that is the critical path. Any delays in any of these tasks delay the project.

Float

The PDM diagram in Figure 4.5 has several pieces of information filled in for each node that we have not discussed. The task name and duration are self-explanatory. What about the rest of the information? The main task of developing the project schedule is to relate each of the tasks and combine duration, resource requirements, and dependencies. You need to make several passes through the network diagram to calculate the values necessary to create a project schedule.

In general, you make two main passes through each path in your network diagram. The first pass starts with the initial project task (the project start task). A task's early start date is the earliest you can start working on that task. The late start date is the latest you can start working on the task. The difference between the early and late start dates is called *float*. The float is the schedule flexibility of a task. In Figure 4.5, the early start date for Task A is 9/5/14. To get the early finish date, just add the duration to the early start date. The duration for Task A is 5 days, so the earliest Task A can finish is 9/10/14. Now, the early finish date for Task A becomes the early start date for any tasks that are dependent on Task A (namely, Task B and Task C). Then, continue to follow each path until you reach the final task, calculating the new early end dates by adding the duration to the early start dates.

> **Note**
>
> Make sure you follow every path from the starting task to the ending task, calculating duration of each path. There are likely several paths that will get you there. Sometimes the shortest-duration path might not be immediately evident.

Now it is time for the second pass through your project to calculate the late start and late ending dates. This pass starts at the end and moves backward through the same paths you just followed in the forward pass. The first step in the backward pass is to record the late ending date. It is the same as the early ending date for the last task in the project. Then, subtract the duration to get the late start date. In Figure 4.5, the late ending date for Task G is 9/22/14, and the late start date is 9/20/14. Next, move backward to each task on which your current task depends (that is each task that has an arrow pointing to your current task). The late ending date for this predecessor task is the same as the late start date of the dependent task. In other words, the late ending date for Task F and Task E would be 9/20/14 (the late start date for Task G). Continue backward through the project, subtracting the duration to calculate a new late start date.

After completing both the forward and backward passes, you should have all of the early start times (EST), early finish times (EFT), late start times (LST), and late finish times (LFT) filled in. To complete the network diagram entries, calculate the float for each task by subtracting the early start date from the late start date. The float is the amount of time each task can be delayed without delaying the project.

Finally, add the durations for each path from the start task to the finish task. The largest total represents the critical path of your project. There could be more than one critical path. Remember that tasks on the critical path all have a float of 0, and any delay of a task on the critical path results in an overall project delay.

Allocating Resources

In addition to calculating the critical path and critical chain, it might be necessary to address resource limitations. The process of reallocating resources that have been overallocated is called *resource leveling*. This technique seeks to avoid work stoppage due to limited resources being required by multiple activities. Remember that resource leveling can often change the critical path. Because resource allocation can change the critical path it is often useful to implement another technique: *what-if scenarios*. A what-if scenario allows the project planners to explore the effect to the critical path of resource availability changes. For example, if you depend on a particular person to complete work on the critical path, what happens if that person becomes ill? Such a question would be part of a what-if scenario.

Cram Quiz

Answer these questions. The answers follow the last question. If you cannot answer these questions correctly, consider reading this section again until you can.

Use Figure 4.6 for Questions 1, 2, and 3.

1. What is the critical path for this project, and what is the duration of the critical path?

   - ○ **A.** A–B–D–F–G, 13 days
   - ○ **B.** A–C–E–G, 14 days
   - ○ **C.** A–B–D–F–G, 14 days
   - ○ **D.** A–C–E–G, 13 days

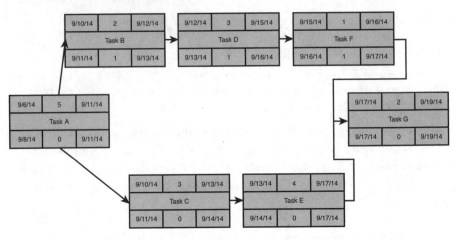

FIGURE 4.6 A sample PDM diagram.

2. How many days late can Task D start without affecting the project completion date?

   ○ **A.** One day

   ○ **B.** Two days

   ○ **C.** Zero days

   ○ **D.** Three days

3. If Task C starts two days late, what is the effect on the project end date?

   ○ **A.** The project ends one day late because there is slack of one day.

   ○ **B.** The project is still two days early because Tasks B, D, and F each have one day of slack.

   ○ **C.** The project is one day late because Task C is on the critical path.

   ○ **D.** There is no effect on the project end date.

4. When developing the estimates for project phases, you choose to add the individual estimates for the activities comprising each phase. What type of estimation method are you using?

   ○ **A.** Parametric estimating

   ○ **B.** Bottom-up estimating

   ○ **C.** Top-down estimating

   ○ **D.** Analogous estimating

5. What is the primary purpose of the define activities process?

   ○ **A.** Identify the specific actions to be performed that result in the stated project deliverables

   ○ **B.** Identify and document relationships among project activities

   ○ **C.** Analyze activity sequences, durations, resource requirements, and schedule constraints

   ○ **D.** Monitor the status of the project schedule and manage schedule changes

6. Which estimating technique is the best choice if you know the durations of similar activities from other projects?

- ○ **A.** Analogous estimating
- ○ **B.** Parametric estimating
- ○ **C.** Three-point estimating
- ○ **D.** Historical analysis estimating

7. Which of the following is NOT an output of the develop schedule process?

- ○ **A.** Project schedule
- ○ **B.** Schedule baseline
- ○ **C.** Schedule data
- ○ **D.** Resource breakdown structure

Cram Quiz Answers

1. **Answer B is correct.** The path A–C–E–G is the longest direct path from start to finish. All other answers are incorrect because they state either the incorrect path or project duration.

2. **Answer A is correct.** Because Task D is not on the critical path and has a slack of one day, it can start one day late (at most) without affecting the project end date.

3. **Answer C is correct.** Because Task C is on the critical path, any delay of the task delays the project.

4. **Answer B is correct.** Bottom-up estimating is the process of calculating estimates by aggregating the individual estimates of activities that make up the desired activity group. Answer A is incorrect because parametric estimating uses a process of multiplying quantity of work by the productivity rate. Answer C is incorrect because top-down estimating starts with an estimate and decomposes the estimate into smaller units to apply to the individual work packages. Answer D is incorrect because analogous estimating uses similar work packages, not estimate aggregation.

5. **Answer A is correct.** The stated answer is the main purpose of the define activities process. Answer B is incorrect because it states the purpose of the sequence activities process. Answer C is incorrect because it states the purpose of the develop schedule process. Answer D is incorrect because it states the purpose of the control schedule process.

6. **Answer A is correct.** Analogous estimating uses parameters from other similar activities to estimate durations. Answers B and C are incorrect because they refer to estimating techniques that do not consider similar activities. Answer D is incorrect because it refers to an estimating technique that doesn't exist.

7. **Answer D is correct.** The resource breakdown structure is an output of the estimate activity resources process. Answers A, B, and C are incorrect because they are all valid outputs of the develop schedule process.

Project Cost Estimating Factors

▶ **Plan Cost Management—7.1**

▶ **Estimate Costs—7.2**

▶ **Determine Budget—7.3**

CramSaver

If you can correctly answer these questions before going through this section, save time by skimming the Exam Alerts in this section and then completing the Cram Quiz at the end of the section.

1. Which type of cost estimation would you use to estimate the cost to finish a floor if you knew the standard cost per square foot?

   ○ **A.** Analogous estimating

   ○ **B.** Parametric estimating

   ○ **C.** Three-point estimating

   ○ **D.** Bottom-up estimating

2. Which of the following is NOT an input for the determine budget process?

   ○ **A.** Basis of estimates

   ○ **B.** Project schedule

   ○ **C.** Risk register

   ○ **D.** Agreements

Answers

1. Answer B is the best response. Parametric estimating calculates cost estimates by multiplying the quantity of work or result of work by a known rate. Answers A, C, and D are all valid estimating techniques, but they do not arrive at values based on known rates.

2. Answer C is correct. The risk register is an input to the estimate costs process, not the determine budget process. Answers A, B, and D are all valid inputs for the determine budget process.

Plan Cost Management

The first process in the cost management knowledge area is *plan cost management*. This process defines the policies and procedures for planning, managing, and controlling project costs. This process provides guidance on how costs will be managed throughout the project, taking into account stakeholder requirements for managing costs. All of the subsequent processes in the cost management knowledge area depend on the plan developed in this process. Table 4.13 shows the inputs, tools and techniques, and outputs for the plan cost management process.

TABLE 4.13 **Plan Cost Management Inputs, Tools and Techniques, and Outputs**

Inputs	Tools and Techniques	Outputs
Project management plan	Expert judgment	Cost management plan
Project charter	Analytical techniques	
Enterprise environmental factors	Meetings	
Organizational process assets		

Estimate Costs

The *estimate cost process* associates an expected cost of performing work to each activity. Cost estimates can include labor, materials, equipment, and any other direct costs for project activities. Based on the activity resource and duration estimates, the cost estimates express the cost, normally in monetary amounts, of completing the work of the project. As with all other project documents, the cost estimates can change through the project as conditions change. Different events can cause the cost for any activity to go up or down and may require the cost estimates for the project to change. Table 4.14 shows the inputs, tools and techniques, and outputs for the estimate cost process.

TABLE 4.14 **Estimate Cost Inputs, Tools and Techniques, and Outputs**

Inputs	Tools and Techniques	Outputs
Cost management plan	Expert judgment	Activity cost estimates
Human resource management plan	Analogous estimating	Basis of estimates
Scope baseline	Parametric estimating	Project documents updates
Project schedule	Bottom-up estimating	
Risk register	Three-point estimating	
Enterprise environmental factors	Reserve analysis	
Organizational process assets	Cost of quality	

Inputs	Tools and Techniques	Outputs
	Project management software	
	Vendor bid analysis	
	Group decision-making techniques	

Cost estimates are compiled into the project budget. You probably recognize several estimating techniques from other processes. Three of the techniques used in the estimate costs process are the same basic techniques used in the estimate activity durations process. The other technique, bottom-up estimating, is also used in the estimate activity resources process. Although they are the same techniques, they are applied to different criteria and bear revisiting.

▶ **Analogous estimating**—This uses actual cost values from similar activities. These activities can be from the same project or another project.

▶ **Parametric estimating**—This calculates cost estimates by multiplying the quantity of work or result of work, such as square feet or hours, by a known rate, such as $30 per square foot or $45 per hour. This type of estimate works best for standardized, and often repeated, activities.

▶ **Three-point estimating**—This uses three estimate values for each activity:

  ▶ **Most likely**—The cost most likely to occur

  ▶ **Optimistic**—The cost of the activity if everything goes as planned, or better

  ▶ **Pessimistic**—The cost of the activity in a worst-case scenario

▶ **Bottom-up estimating**—This technique calculates cost estimates by adding the costs of each individual work package. The technique starts at the most detailed level and rolls up the costs until a total cost for the project is obtained.

Determine Budget

After you know the costs to accomplish the work of the project, you can create the project budget. The *determine budget process* aggregates the activity cost estimates into a single document for the project. The resulting project budget expands on the preliminary budget from the project charter and provides far more detail. Table 4.15 shows the inputs, tools and techniques, and outputs for the determine budget process.

TABLE 4.15 **Determine Budget Inputs, Tools and Techniques, and Outputs**

Inputs	Tools and Techniques	Outputs
Cost management plan	Cost aggregation	Cost baseline
Scope baseline	Reserve analysis	Project funding requirements
Activity cost estimates	Expert judgment	Project documents updates
Basis of estimates	Historical relationships	
Project schedule	Funding limit reconciliation	
Resource calendars		
Risk register		
Agreements		
Organizational process assets		

ExamAlert

Don't confuse the estimate costs process with the determine budget process. The determine budget process aggregates all of the activity cost estimates to result in a budget baseline against which your project costs will be measured.

Cram Quiz

Answer these questions. The answers follow the last question. If you cannot answer these questions correctly, consider reading this section again until you can.

1. The project cost and schedule for deliverables can be reasonably estimated at what level of the WBS?

   ○ **A.** The highest level

   ○ **B.** The middle level

   ○ **C.** The work package level

   ○ **D.** Both A and C

2. When the cost of an activity cannot be estimated with an adequate degree of certainty, the work within the activity can be decomposed. The resource requirements for each lower, more detailed work package can be estimated and aggregated to form a basis for estimating the cost for overarching scheduled activity. What is this type of estimating called?

- ○ **A.** Bottom-up estimating
- ○ **B.** Decomposed estimating
- ○ **C.** Should-cost estimating
- ○ **D.** Three-point estimating

3. Which process results in the project funding requirements document as one of its outputs?

- ○ **A.** Estimate activity resources
- ○ **B.** Estimate activity durations
- ○ **C.** Estimate costs
- ○ **D.** Determine budget

Cram Quiz Answers

1. Answer D is the correct response. The project cost and project schedule for work can be reliably estimated at the work package, or lowest, level of the WBS using bottom-up estimating, or at the highest level using top-down estimating.

2. Answer A is the correct response. Bottom-up estimating is a technique for estimating cost through decomposition. A bottom-up estimate is based on the cost requirements for each lower work package and then is combined to estimate cost of the entire component of work. Answer B is incorrect because there is no technique called decomposed estimating. Answer C is incorrect because should-cost estimating is an activity duration estimating technique. Answer D is incorrect because three-point estimating does not incorporate decomposition.

3. Answer D is the correct response. The determine budget process produces the project funding requirements as one of its outputs, along with the cost performance baseline and project document updates. Answers A, B, and C are incorrect because these processes do not produce the project funding requirements document as an output. Make sure you know the inputs, tools and techniques, and outputs of all the project processes.

What Next?

If you want more practice on this chapter's exam topics before you move on, remember that you can access all of the Cram Quiz questions on the CD. You can also create a custom exam by topic with the practice exam software. Note any topic you struggle with and go to that topic's material in this chapter.

CHAPTER 5

Explore More Elements of Project Planning

The main components of the project management plan are the primary drivers that establish key project baselines (scope, schedule, and cost). Additional planning processes are equally important and establish the mechanisms to apply quality, stakeholder assignment, project information management (communication), reality (risk), and procurement assignment to those baselines. These plans include items such as the following:

▶ **Quality management plan**—Describes how the team will implement the quality policy. It addresses quality control, quality assurance, and continuous improvement.

▶ **Human resources management plan**—Explains when and how human resource requirements will be met, including acquisition approach, timing, training, and recognition.

▶ **Communication management plan**—Presents how communication requirements will be met, including stakeholder communication, communication responsibility, communication timing, and techniques.

▶ **Risk management plan**—Describes how risk management activities will be performed, including methodology, responsibility, cost, timing, and definitions for risk categories, probabilities, and impacts.

▶ **Procurement management plan**—Outlines how procurement activities will be performed, including contract types and responsibilities.

▶ **Stakeholder management plan**—Identifies the strategies and techniques necessary to keep stakeholders effectively engaged throughout the project.

Quality Management

▶ **Plan Quality Management—8.1**

CramSaver

If you can correctly answer these questions before going through this section, save time by skimming the Exam Alerts in this section and then completing the Cram Quiz at the end of the section.

1. Who has overall responsibility for quality planning?

- ○ **A.** Project manager
- ○ **B.** Quality manager
- ○ **C.** Senior management
- ○ **D.** Project planner

2. Which of the following best describes the plan quality management process?

- ○ **A.** Audit quality requirements and the results from quality control measurements
- ○ **B.** Monitor and record results of executing quality activities
- ○ **C.** Identify quality requirements and/or standards for the project
- ○ **D.** Identify poor process or product quality

Answers

1. Answer A is correct. The project manager has overall responsibility. All other members of the project team assist in the process.

2. Answer C is correct. The plan quality management process is the process of identifying quality requirements and/or standards for the project and product. Answer A is incorrect because it describes the perform quality assurance process. Answer B is incorrect because it describes the perform quality control process. Answer D is incorrect because it describes control quality activities.

Although the project manager has overall responsibility for quality, the entire project team plays a role in quality management. Every member of the project team must understand the importance of contributions, accept ownership for problems, be committed to monitoring and improving performance, and be willing to openly discuss issues among team members.

Although specific techniques and measures apply to the product being produced, the overall project quality management approach applies to any project and is relevant to the project as well as the product being produced.

ExamAlert

Understand the difference between *quality* and *grade*. Quality is a measure of how well characteristics match requirements. Grade is assigned based on the characteristics that a product or service might have. So a product might be of low grade, meaning it has limited features, but might still be acceptable. Low quality is never acceptable.

Also understand the difference between *precision* and *accuracy*. According to the PMBOK, "Precision means the values of repeated measurements are clustered and have little scatter. Accuracy means that the measured value is very close to the true value. Precise measurements are not necessarily accurate. A very accurate measurement is not necessarily precise."

The terms *quality* and *grade* are often confused. They are separate concepts, and the PMBOK clearly notes their differences. Table 5.1 compares low and high values of quality and grade.

TABLE 5.1 **Quality and Grade**

	Quality	Grade
Low	Errors or defects that affect the usability of a product	Few options or features
High	No obvious defects; usable product	Many options and features

The plan quality management process has a number of key inputs, many of which originate from other initiating and planning processes. Table 5.2 shows the inputs, tools and techniques, and outputs for the plan quality management process.

TABLE 5.2 **Plan Quality Management Inputs, Tools and Techniques, and Outputs**

Inputs	Tools and Techniques	Outputs
Project management plan	Cost–benefit analysis	Quality management plan
Stakeholder register	Cost of quality	Process improvement plan
Risk register	Seven basic quality tools	Quality metrics

Inputs	Tools and Techniques	Outputs
Requirements documentation	Benchmarking	Quality checklists
Enterprise environmental factors	Design of experiments	Project documents updates
Organizational process assets	Statistical sampling	
	Additional quality planning tools	
	Meetings	

The plan quality management process incorporates various quality concepts with which you should be familiar. The following list highlights important key concepts in PMI's quality management:

▶ The cost of preventing mistakes is generally less than the cost of repairing them.

▶ To be successful, management support for the quality program must exist.

▶ Quality is tied closely to the scope, cost, and time constraints; without quality, these objectives cannot be met successfully.

▶ The cost of quality refers to the cost to implement a quality program.

▶ Understanding and managing customer expectations is important to a successful quality program.

▶ The quality program should emphasize continuous improvement.

▶ There is a close alignment between the quality approach and the overall project management approach on a project.

> ### ExamAlert
>
> Memorize PMI's definition of quality: "The degree to which a set of inherent characteristics fulfill requirements."

Quality Theories and PMI Quality Management Approach

The quality management approach presented in the PMBOK is intended to be compatible with other quality standards, including those of the

International Organization for Standardization (ISO), total quality management (TQM), and Six Sigma.

Exam questions on this topic are frequently taken from sources other than the PMBOK. Table 5.3 identifies some of the most popular quality theories.

TABLE 5.3 **Common Quality Theories**

Theory Name	Pioneers	Description
Continuous improvement, or kaizen	Masaaki Imai, F.W. Taylor, and others	Processes are improved, mastered, and then further improvement. Includes quality circles as a group-oriented means of developing ideas.
The Deming cycle or Plan–Do–Check–Act	Dr. W. Edwards Deming	Very much as with kaizen, an improvement is planned, completed, measured, and then further improvement acted upon.
Six Sigma	Based on statistical work by Joseph Juran	A statistical measure of quality equating to 3.4 defects per million items. If defects can be measured, a process can be put into place to eliminate them.
Total quality management (TQM)	Dr. W. Edwards Deming	Fourteen points of management call for awareness of quality in all processes.
Malcolm Baldrige Award	Howard Malcolm Baldrige	This award was established by U.S. Congress to promote quality awareness.
OPM3 (Organizational Project Management Maturity Model)	Project Management Institute (PMI)	Assess an organization's project management maturity level against general best practices.
CMM (capability maturity model)	Software Engineering Institute (SEI)	Five levels of capability exist: initial, repeatable, defined, managed, and optimized.

The Plan–Do–Check–Act Cycle

PMI identifies the Plan–Do–Check–Act (PDCA) cycle, also referred to as the Deming cycle, as both a quality tool and the underlying concept for interaction among project management processes. First, an improvement is planned. Next, the improvement is carried out and measured. The results are checked and finally acted upon. Acting upon an improvement might mean making the improvement a standard, further modification to the improvement, or abandoning the improvement. Figure 5.1 demonstrates the PDCA cycle.

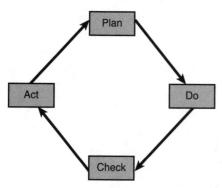

FIGURE 5.1 **The PDCA cycle.**

Quality Approaches and Project Management

Quality approaches align with project management approaches in a number of areas, including achieving customer satisfaction, preventing defects instead of inspecting for them, management support for quality, and continuous improvement. Table 5.4 provides additional detail.

TABLE 5.4 **Principles Common to Quality Management and Project Management**

Alignment Area	Description
Customer satisfaction	Customer requirements are met through a thorough understanding and management of expectations.
Prevention over inspection	It is cheaper to prevent defects than repair ones that are identified in inspections.
Management responsibility	Management must provide the support and resources for a quality program to be successful.
Continuous improvement	Processes are improved, mastered, and then further improvement is identified. Includes quality circles as a group-oriented means of developing ideas.

The Cost of Quality

Cost of quality (COQ) is a term that refers to the cost to produce a product or service that meets requirements. Part of the cost is rework when requirements aren't met. An effective quality program reduces cost related to rework.

The three primary types of cost associated with the cost of quality are

▶ Prevention costs

▶ Inspection costs

▶ Failure costs (internal and external)

Addressing prevention and inspection can be viewed as addressing the cost of conformance. This includes training, prototyping, design reviews, and testing. Failure costs (the cost of nonconformance) includes bug fixes, rework, cost of late delivery, and customer complaints.

Differences Among Quality Planning, Quality Assurance, and Quality Control

One area of confusion, especially among project managers who don't have a background in quality, is the difference between the three processes in quality management. Table 5.5 helps clarify these concepts.

TABLE 5.5 **Summary of Quality Management Processes**

	Quality Planning	**Quality Assurance**	**Quality Control**
Process Group	Planning	Executing	Monitoring and controlling
Emphasis	Planning	Implementing	Measuring and adjusting
Key Activities	Determining relevant quality standards	Applying planned activities	Monitoring results
	Determining how to apply standards	Ensuring continuous improvement	Identifying ways to eliminate unwanted results
Key Outputs	Quality management plan	Requested changes	QC measurements
	Quality improvement plan	Recommended corrective action	Validated defect repair
	Quality metrics		Recommended corrective and preventive actions
	Quality checklist		Requested changes
			Recommended defect repair
			Validated deliverables

Seven Basic Quality Tools

The seven basic quality tools are visual representations of information that help solve quality-related problems. You'll see references to these tools on the exam, so it is a good idea to be familiar with each tool and how it is used. Figure 5.2 shows an example of each of the seven basic quality tools.

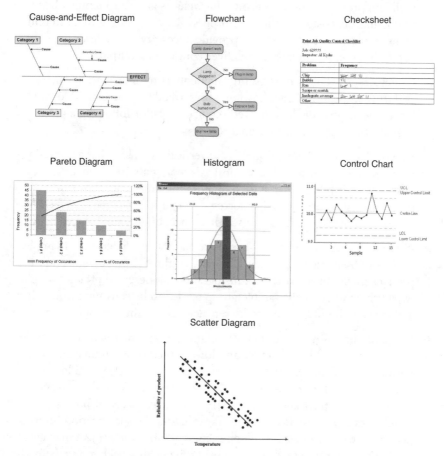

FIGURE 5.2 **Seven basic quality tools.**

The seven basic quality tools are

> ▶ **Cause-and-effect diagram**—These diagrams are also called fishbone diagrams or Ishikawa diagrams. These diagrams are useful in tracing problems back to the original cause. To create a cause-and-effect diagram, start with a problem statement on the head of the fish. Then ask why this problem occurred and place each answer on a different

bone drawn from the head. As more causes are discovered and recorded, the diagram begins to look like the bones of a fish. Eventually, you should be able to reach the root cause (or causes) of a problem.

▶ **Flowchart**—This tool is helpful in mapping the flow of a process or a group of processes from beginning to end. A flowchart contains components for each activity, decision point, branching loop, and parallel path in a process or process group. Flowcharts are very helpful when estimating the cost of quality in a process. Understanding the different paths to reach an end result can provide necessary information to determine the requirements to deliver conforming output.

▶ **Checksheet**—This tool is useful when collecting information, such as during inspections, or following a prescribed sequence of actions. Checksheets provide documented requirements for following a procedure or collecting data for further analysis.

▶ **Pareto diagram**—These diagrams are vertical bar charts that graphically depict sources of defects. The vertical axis represents 100% of all observations, while the bar at each point in the time series shows the percentage of observations that correspond to a specific type of defect. A Pareto diagram makes it easy to see the impact of different sources of defects.

▶ **Histogram**—A histogram is a bar chart that shows tendency in a sample group of observations. For example, say that the size of a manufactured product should be consistent. A histogram of all observed product weights would show whether the sample group tended to be consistent in weight and give an idea of how many discrepancies in weight were observed.

▶ **Control chart**—A control chart is simply a graph that depicts upper and lower control limits, upper and lower specification limits, and actual performance data collected from project activities. Upper and lower specification limits correspond to the requirements from the project contract. The upper and lower control limits are placed at points at which action must be taken to avoid exceeding the specification limits. If performance data exceeds the upper control limit, the project manager can implement appropriate changes to bring the quality back in line before the upper specification limit is exceeded and the project is in violation of the contract. The graph makes it easy to see when actual performance exceeds the predefined upper and lower limits.

▶ **Scatter diagram**—These diagrams are useful to see how changing one variable, X, affects another variable, Y. An example could be how increasing or decreasing the amount of ingredients affects baking time for a loaf of bread. The results can be used to arrive at an optimal balance between two variables.

Cram Quiz

Answer these questions. The answers follow the last question. If you cannot answer these questions correctly, consider reading this section again until you can.

1. Which of the following is NOT a responsibility of a project manager?

   ○ **A.** Acquiring human resources for the project team

   ○ **B.** Managing overall responsibility for quality in the organization

   ○ **C.** Managing risk on the project

   ○ **D.** Monitoring customer satisfaction on the project

2. Which subsidiary plan/component documents how an organization will achieve the quality objectives for a project?

   ○ **A.** Quality management plan

   ○ **B.** Quality baseline

   ○ **C.** Process improvement plan

   ○ **D.** Quality control checklist

3. Which quality theory outlines 14 points and calls for quality awareness at all levels of the organization?

   ○ **A.** CMM

   ○ **B.** Kaizen

   ○ **C.** TQM

   ○ **D.** Malcolm Baldrige

Cram Quiz Answers

1. Answer B is correct. Senior management is responsible for quality in the organization. The project manager is responsible for product quality on the project.

2. Answer A is correct. The quality management plan lists which quality policies apply to the project and documents how the quality objectives will be met. The quality baseline documents the quality objectives for the project. The process improvement plan documents how processes will be analyzed for improvement. A quality control checklist is used to ensure that steps of a process are completed.

3. Answer C is correct. Total quality management (TQM) uses 14 points and calls for quality awareness from everyone involved. CMM outlines five levels of process maturity. Kaizen, or continuous improvement, calls for a cycle of improvements to processes. Malcolm Baldrige is an award for quality awareness.

Human Resource Management

▶ **Plan Human Resource Management—9.1**

CramSaver

If you can correctly answer these questions before going through this section, save time by skimming the Exam Alerts in this section and then completing the Cram Quiz at the end of the section.

1. Which of the following documents provide a graphical representation of project resources, organized by type?

   ○ **A.** Organizational breakdown structure

   ○ **B.** Resource breakdown structure

   ○ **C.** Responsibility assignment matrix

   ○ **D.** RACI matrix

2. Which of the following is NOT a tool and technique of the plan human resource management process?

   ○ **A.** Organization charts and position descriptions

   ○ **B.** Networking

   ○ **C.** Ground rules

   ○ **D.** Organizational theory

Answers

1. Answer B is correct. A resource breakdown structure (RBS) provides a graphical display of resources by type. An organizational breakdown structure (OBS) graphically displays work packages. A responsibility assignment matrix (RAM) is a chart displaying resources and for which assignments they are responsible, and a RACI matrix is a specific type of RAM that shows the resources that are responsible, accountable, consulted, and informed in project activities.

2. Answer C is correct. Ground rules is a tool and technique of the develop project team process. Answers A, B, and D are incorrect because they are all valid tools and techniques of the plan human resource management process.

The project manager must fulfill the role of manager and leader of the project team. Using the same skills and techniques a line manager uses, the project manager has the following responsibilities:

▶ Determine the human resource needs of the project

▶ Negotiate with line managers for internal resources

▶ Acquire external resources through the procurement process

▶ Determine training needs

▶ Identify/plan team-building activities

▶ Determine the performance review approach for a project's human resources

▶ Determine a reward and recognition approach for motivating team members

▶ Document the team structure and each team's responsibilities

▶ Create a project organization chart

▶ Develop a staffing management plan

> **ExamAlert**
>
> PMI puts a high value on the project manager's responsibilities to the team. Make sure you are comfortable with applying PMBOK content to hypothetical situations.

Key Human Resource Principles

Human resource management is the set of processes used to organize and manage the project team, also referred to as the project staff. A subset of the project team is the project management team, composed of the project manager, project sponsor, and others responsible for project management activities, such as planning, controlling, and closing the project.

Project human resource management is composed of planning, acquiring, and developing human resources as well as managing the team. Human resource planning has a number of key deliverables, including project organization charts, the staffing management plan, and determining the roles and responsibilities of each human resource. Table 5.6 shows the inputs, tools and techniques, and outputs for the plan human resource management process.

TABLE 5.6 **Plan Human Resource Management Inputs, Tools and Techniques, and Outputs**

Inputs	Tools and Techniques	Outputs
Project management plan	Organization charts and position descriptions	Human resource management plan
Activity resource requirements	Networking	
Enterprise environmental factors	Organizational theory	
Organizational process assets	Expert judgment	
	Meetings	

It is important to understand the various methods organizations use to depict and describe human resources and their attributes. Table 5.7 summarizes the tools used in human resource planning.

TABLE 5.7 **Human Resource Planning Tools**

Name	Description	Use
Organizational breakdown structure (OBS)	Graphically displays work packages according to departments.	Identifies the work assigned to each department.
Resource breakdown structure (RBS)	Graphically displays resources by type.	Effective in tracking costs. Groups resources even if they are working on different deliverables.
Responsibility assignment matrix (RAM)	Displays resources and the assignments they are each responsible for.	Allows for easy identification of all responsibilities for a given resource.
RACI matrix	Shows the resources that are responsible, accountable, consulted, and informed in project activities.	Provides more detail than RAM.
Position description	Provides a text-based description of responsibilities.	Provides a high level of detail for a given position.

> **Note**
>
> An organizational breakdown structure (OBS) is a graphical representation of the project team, arranged according to an organization's existing structure. A resource breakdown structure (RBS) is also a graphical representation but is organized according to resource type. An RBS can contain resources other than human resources, such as equipment, and can be used to track costs.

In addition to graphical representations, resources might be documented in matrix-based documents such as a *responsibility assignment (RACI) matrix*. These documents are effective communication tools to ensure team members understand for which assignments they are responsible. Table 5.8 shows an example of a RACI matrix.

> **Note**
>
> RACI stands for responsible, accountable, consult, inform.

TABLE 5.8 **RACI Matrix**

Activity	Person		
	Bill	**Mary**	**John**
Design	Responsible	Consult	Accountable
Build	Accountable	Responsible	Consult
Test	Inform	Accountable	Consult

The Staffing Management Plan

The *staffing management plan* is used to document the type of resources needed and the timing for those resources. The plan includes how the resources will be acquired, start and end dates, training requirements, policies and procedures for the team, and the team recognition approach and budget.

Cram Quiz

Answer these questions. The answers follow the last question. If you cannot answer these questions correctly, consider reading this section again until you can.

1. Which resource planning tool provides information on resource responsibility and accountability?

    ○ **A.** OBS

    ○ **B.** RBS

    ○ **C.** RAM

    ○ **D.** RACI matrix

2. What is the primary purpose of the human resource management plan?

    ○ **A.** Identify and document roles, responsibilities, and skills necessary for project goal fulfillment

    ○ **B.** Describe how the project team will interact

    ○ **C.** Assemble the project team

    ○ **D.** Document strategies to motivate the project team

Cram Quiz Answers

1. Answer D is correct. The RACI (responsible, accountable, consult, inform) matrix provides information both on resource responsibility and accountability. The RAM only provides responsibility information. Neither the OBS nor RBS provides responsibility information.

2. Answer A is correct. Answers B, C, and D describe other processes in the executing process group.

Communications Management

▶ **Plan Communications Management—10.1**

CramSaver

If you can correctly answer these questions before going through this section, save time by skimming the Exam Alerts in this section and then completing the Cram Quiz at the end of the section.

1. Why is communication among project team members important enough to create a distinct knowledge area to address its concerns?

2. Which of the following communication methods would be most appropriate for communicating with very large general audiences?

   ○ **A.** Interactive communication

   ○ **B.** One-way communication

   ○ **C.** Push communication

   ○ **D.** Pull communication

Answers

1. Answers will vary, but the smooth operation of a project is contingent on the project team members working together to get the work of the project accomplished. The only way work in a team environment can progress is through deliberate communication among the team members. Projects are no different from any other team process. When communication breaks down, so does the progress.

2. Answer D is the best answer. Pull communication is a good choice for very large volumes of information or for very large audiences. Answer A is incorrect because interactive communication works best between two parties or a small group. Answer B is incorrect because one-way communication can represent either push or pull communication. Answer C is not the best answer because push communication works well for a group of specific recipients. The recipient group might be large, but it is a specific group and not a general audience.

Projects require the coordinated efforts of multiple team members. The success of a project is at least partially dependent on the quality of communication between team members. The communications management plan addresses the necessary elements of team communication and leaves little room for assumptions. This plan is important to set the expectations of how the project team should communicate in an effective and timely manner. It also sets the expectations of the stakeholders and makes their need for information a part of the overall project plan. Most communication issues start with a lack of clear directives as to how and when to communicate. Further, most people are reluctant to initiate unsolicited communication. The communications management plan is crucial to good project team interaction.

Identifying and Analyzing Communications Requirements

When developing the communications management plan, you should analyze the stakeholders, organization, existing documentation and policies, and any specifics that might affect the communication requirements for the project or help ensure that information is communicated in a timely and effective manner. For example, communication requirements might depend on factors such as whether the team is collocated, the number of team members, whether information to be communicated is confidential, or specific organizational policy requirements. These factors might dictate the format, frequency, distribution, retention, or other aspects of the communication. The details included in the communications management plan provide the project team guidance on how to manage communications of all different types throughout the project life cycle. Table 5.9 shows the inputs, tools and techniques, and outputs for the plan communications management process.

TABLE 5.9   **Plan Communications Management Inputs, Tools and Techniques, and Outputs**

Inputs	Tools and Techniques	Outputs
Project management plan	Communication requirements analysis	Communications management plan
Stakeholder register	Communication technology	Project documents updates
Enterprise environmental factors	Communication models	
Organizational process assets	Communication methods	
	Meetings	

ExamAlert

The plan communications management process addresses the information and communications needs of the stakeholders by determining the stakeholder information needs and defining an approach to meeting those needs.

Any time you communicate with another person, you create a communication channel with that person. When multiple people communicate, they must establish a communication channel between each two people communicating. The number of communication channels is an exponential relationship. As the number of people participating in communication increases, the level of complexity and effort required to communicate increases exponentially. See Figure 5.3 for the formula and examples for calculating communication channels.

Number of Channels = n(n-1)/2

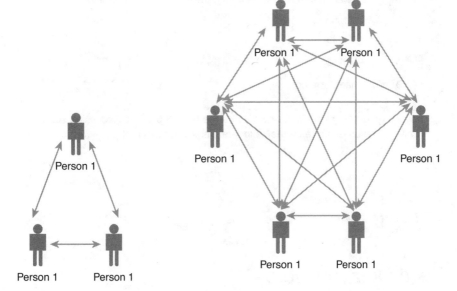

3 people, 3 channels   6 people, 15 channels

FIGURE 5.3   **Communication channels.**

On the left side of Figure 5.3, the first team has three people ($n = 3$), so the equation is

$3 * (3 - 1) / 2 = 3$ communication channels

On the right side of Figure 5.3, there are six team members ($n = 6$), so the equation is

$6 * (6 - 1) / 2 = 15$ communication channels

ExamAlert

Be able to calculate the number of communication channels, given the number of team members.

Cram Quiz

Answer these questions. The answers follow the last question. If you cannot answer these questions correctly, consider reading this section again until you can.

1. What type of communication would be best for casual, non-urgent information exchange between team members in geographically distant locations?

   ○ **A.** Telephone

   ○ **B.** Conference call

   ○ **C.** Email

   ○ **D.** Shared memo

2. Which type of communication would be the best choice for discussing schedule changes to an entire team that is located in several different physical sites?

   ○ **A.** Conference call

   ○ **B.** Email

   ○ **C.** Website

   ○ **D.** One-on-one telephone calls

Cram Quiz Answers

1. Answer C is correct. Email provides a good medium for exchanging messages among team members who are in different time zones. Telephone conversations and conference calls require much more scheduling effort, and exchanging shared memos requires additional effort.

2. Answer A is correct. In this case, a conference call provides the ability for the project manager to inform the team simultaneously and also take feedback from team members. The other options are more time-consuming and make feedback more difficult.

Risk Management

▶ **Plan Risk Management—11.1**

▶ **Identify Risks—11.2**

▶ **Perform Qualitative Risk Analysis—11.3**

▶ **Perform Quantitative Risk Analysis—11.4**

▶ **Plan Risk Responses—11.5**

CramSaver

If you can correctly answer these questions before going through this section, save time by skimming the Exam Alerts in this section and then completing the Cram Quiz at the end of the section.

1. Which risk response is most likely to involve contingency reserves?

   ○ **A.** Transfer

   ○ **B.** Mitigate

   ○ **C.** Acceptance

   ○ **D.** Share

2. Which of the following activities is NOT part of risk management planning?

   ○ **A.** Developing a risk management plan

   ○ **B.** Identifying risk categories

   ○ **C.** Updating risk register

   ○ **D.** Determining risk roles and responsibilities

3. Which of the following tools and techniques are part of the perform qualitative risk analysis process?

   ○ **A.** Data gathering and representation techniques

   ○ **B.** Probability and impact matrix

   ○ **C.** Quantitative risk analysis and modeling techniques

   ○ **D.** Contingent response strategies

4. Which of the following best describes the perform quantitative risk analysis process?

   ○ **A.** The process of determining which risks might affect your project

   ○ **B.** The process of ranking the relative severity of risks to determine which risks deserve the most attention

   ○ **C.** The process of carrying out risk response plans and evaluating risk process effectiveness

   ○ **D.** The process of assigning numerical values to risks in order to analyze the effect of the risks to the project

Answers

1. Answer C is correct. Acceptance is when no change to the project is made to accommodate a risk. Passive acceptance requires no action beyond documenting the decision. Active acceptance includes further action, such as setting aside a contingency to offset the impact of the risk. Transferring moves the risk to a third party and there most likely would be an upfront cost associated with this response. Mitigate is taking steps to reduce the probability or impact. Sharing is similar to transferring but for a positive risk.

2. Answer C is correct. Updating the risk register first happens in risk identification. All other activities occur during risk management planning.

3. Answer B is correct. A probability and impact matrix is a tool and technique for the perform qualitative risk analysis process. Answers A and C are incorrect because these are both tools and techniques for the perform quantitative (not qualitative) risk analysis process. Answer D is incorrect because contingent response strategies is a tool and technique for the plan risk response process.

4. Answer D is correct. Perform quantitative risk analysis is the process of assigning numerical values to risks in order to analyze the impact of the risks to the project. Answer A is incorrect because it describes the identify risks process. Answer B is incorrect because it describes the perform qualitative risk analysis process. Answer C is incorrect because it describes the monitor and control risks process.

PMI's risk management philosophy is based on a proactive approach to preventing negative risks and enhancing positive risks. Key points to remember about risk include

▶ Risk can be either positive or negative. Positive risks are opportunities; negative risks are threats.

▶ An RBS is used to organize risks in a hierarchical structure.

▶ Monte Carlo analysis is a technique that uses simulations and probability in determining quantitative risk analysis.

▶ Risk categories are important in classifying risk.

▶ Probability and impact are both needed to assess risks.

▶ Quantitative analysis is generally reserved for high-probability, high-impact risks.

▶ Risk management planning and risk response planning are not the same activities.

▶ Risk identification is an iterative process that is performed throughout a project, not just during planning.

▶ Decision tree analysis is a technique using probabilities and costs for structured decision making.

▶ Five of the six risk management processes are conducted during the planning process group.

▶ The risk register is an important tool for capturing and tracking risks.

ExamAlert

Risk register is a term introduced by PMI for the document detailing information on risks. The risk register includes all identified risks, the impacts of identified risks, proposed responses, responsible parties, and the current status.

Note

A risk can have either a negative or positive effect on a project.

The *risk management methodology* is a definition of how risk will be managed. It includes the approach, tools, and techniques to be used for managing risks for the project. The approach details how the steps of the risk process will be conducted. For example, the approach could specify that risk analysis will be conducted at the end of each planning meeting. The tools can include the risk register, the RBS, the probability and impact matrix, and checklists.

Risk Management Planning and Risk Response Planning

The *risk management plan* includes the risk management methodology, roles/responsibilities, budget, execution timing, and definitions for risk categories, probabilities, and impacts. It is a summation of how the project team will carry out the remainder of the risk management activities for the project. The risk management plan should not be confused with the risk response plan, which is where the project manager captures how responses to specific risks that have been identified during the risk identification process will be handled.

> **ExamAlert**
>
> The risk management plan is not the same as the risk response plan.

The risk management plan is the single output of the plan risk management process. Table 5.10 shows the inputs, tools and techniques, and outputs for the plan risk management process.

TABLE 5.10 **Plan Risk Management Inputs, Tools and Techniques, and Outputs**

Inputs	Tools and Techniques	Outputs
Project management plan	Analytical techniques	Risk management plan
Project charter	Expert judgment	
Stakeholder register	Meetings	
Enterprise environmental factors		
Organizational process assets		

Risk Breakdown Structure (RBS)

A *risk breakdown structure (RBS)* is a tool that can be used to organize risks in a hierarchical fashion. The structure is defined using the risk categories. Even if an RBS is not used, risk categories are still defined in risk management planning. Risk categories can include

▶ **Technical**—Risk associated with using new technology.

▶ **External**—Risk associated with forces or entities outside the project organization. External risks can include external suppliers, customers, weather, and market conditions.

▶ **Organizational**—Risk associated with either the organization running the project or the organization where the project will be implemented.

▶ **Project Management**—Risk associated with project management processes.

Risk Probability and Impact

Probability can be defined as the likelihood that a risk will occur. It can be expressed mathematically as a decimal value representing a percentage (.2) or as a relative scale (low, medium, high). The probability for each identified risk is developed during risk management planning.

Impact is the effect a risk has if it occurs. It can also be defined on a relative scale or mathematically. The definition for impact is developed during risk management planning.

The team documents in the project management plan detail how probabilities and impacts are measured. For example, a red/yellow/green scale might be used, where high-probability, high-impact risks are red; low-probability, low-impact risks are green; and so forth. A probability and impact matrix can also be used; for an example, refer to the *PMBOK Guide*, Fifth Edition, Figure 11-10.

ExamAlert

Both probability and impact are necessary for evaluating risks.

Risk Identification, Analysis, Response Planning, and Monitoring/Controlling

In the risk management process, completing the risk management plan is the first step. After the plan is in place, according to PMI the next steps in the risk management process are

- ▶ Identification
- ▶ Analysis (qualitative and quantitative)
- ▶ Response planning
- ▶ Monitoring/controlling (discussed in Chapter 7, "Investigate Project Monitoring and Controlling")

ExamAlert

Understand the difference between qualitative and quantitative risk analysis. Qualitative evaluation is a prioritization based on probability and impact. Quantitative evaluation uses techniques to further advance the specific probabilities and impacts of project risks. For instance, modeling techniques such as Monte Carlo determine the overall effect of risks on project objectives and are typically used for high-probability, high-impact risks.

Identify Risks

The *identify risks* process determines the risks that might affect the project and characterizes those risks.

Obviously, the ability to identify risks is key in an effective risk management process. Keep in mind that identifying risks is not just the project manager's responsibility; team members, subject matter experts, customers, stakeholders, and others are involved in this process. Table 5.11 shows the inputs, tools and techniques, and outputs for the identify risks process.

TABLE 5.11 **Identify Risks Inputs, Tools and Techniques, and Outputs**

Inputs	Tools and Techniques	Outputs
Risk management plan	Documentation reviews	Risk register
Cost management plan	Information gathering techniques	
Schedule management plan	Checklist analysis	
Quality management plan	Assumptions analysis	
Human resource management plan	Diagramming techniques	
Scope baseline	SWOT (strengths, weaknesses, opportunities, threats) analysis	
Activity cost estimates	Expert judgment	
Activity duration estimates		
Stakeholder register		
Project documents		
Procurement documents		
Enterprise environmental factors		
Organizational process assets		

The Risk Register

The *risk register* is the output of the identify risks process. The risk register contains the following information for each project risk:

▶ Risk description

▶ Date identified

▶ Category

▶ Potential responses

▶ Current status

Qualitative and Quantitative Risk Analysis

Qualitative risk analysis provides further definition to the identified risks in order to determine appropriate responses to them. The key terms are *probability* and *impact*. Probability is important because it measures how likely it is that a risk will occur. A high-probability risk deserves more attention than a low-probability risk. Likewise, impact is a measure of how the risk will affect the project if it occurs. A risk with low impact would have a different response than one with a high impact.

Qualitative risk analysis quickly prioritizes risks to conduct response planning and quantitative risk analysis, if used. Using the probability of the impact and a probability impact matrix, the project manager develops a prioritized list of risks. The output to this step is captured in the risk register. Table 5.12 shows the inputs, tools and techniques, and outputs for the perform qualitative risk analysis process.

TABLE 5.12 **Perform Qualitative Risk Analysis Inputs, Tools and Techniques, and Outputs**

Inputs	Tools and Techniques	Outputs
Risk management plan	Risk probability and impact assessment	Risk register updates
Scope baseline	Probability and impact matrix	
Risk register	Risk data quality assessment	
Enterprise environmental factors	Risk categorization	
Organizational process assets	Risk urgency assessment	
	Expert judgment	

Quantitative risk analysis assigns numerical values to risks and looks at those risks that are high on the list of prioritized risks during qualitative risk analysis. The goal of this process is to quantify possible outcomes for the project, determine probabilities of outcomes, further identify high-impacting risks, and develop realistic scope, schedule, and cost targets based on risks. Table 5.13 shows the inputs, tools and techniques, and outputs for the perform quantitative risk analysis process.

> **ExamAlert**
>
> Quantitative risk analysis is more concerned with assigning each risk a numerical value. This value can then be analyzed using various methods and presented graphically to paint a complete risk picture.

TABLE 5.13 **Perform Quantitative Risk Analysis Inputs, Tools and Techniques, and Outputs**

Inputs	Tools and Techniques	Outputs
Risk management plan	Data gathering and representation techniques	Project documents updates
Cost management plan	Quantitative risk analysis and modeling techniques	
Schedule management plan	Expert judgment	
Risk register		
Enterprise environmental factors		
Organizational process assets		

A key tool used in quantitative risk analysis is decision tree analysis. Using a decision tree diagram (see Figure 5.4), the impact of different scenarios is captured. Both probability and cost are used, resulting in an expected monetary value (EMV).

For this example, there are two vendors for a software package: Acme and WebCo. The details of the two options are presented in Table 5.14. The table shows how much two different software packages cost to purchase, along with the maintenance cost of each and the cost of a failure. The EMV is the product of the failure probability (P) and the impact of failure (I) for each risk. Note that the EMV also includes the purchase cost, which is a "risk" with a probability of 100%. The EMV helps compare the long-term value of a risk. In this case, WebCo's software will cost more if the expected risks are realized.

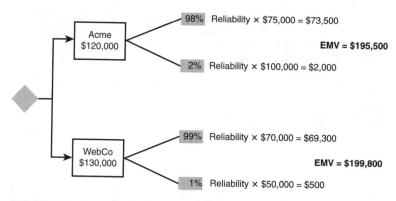

FIGURE 5.4   An example of a decision tree analysis.

TABLE 5.14   **Decision Tree Analysis Example Data**

	Acme	**WebCo**
Purchase cost	$120,000	$130,000
Maintenance	$75,000/year (98% reliability)	$70,000/year (99% reliability)
Maintenance EMV	$75,000 * 0.98 = $73,500	$70,000 * 0.99 = $69,300
Failure cost	$100,000 (2% probability)	$50,000 (1% probability)
Failure cost EMV	$100,000 * 0.02 = $2,000	$50,000 * 0.01 = $500
Total EMV	$120,000 + $73,500 + $2,000 = $195,500	$130,000 + $69,300 + $500 = $199,800

Responses to Positive and Negative Risk

After all risks are identified, options to deal with the risks must be identified. Each risk is assigned to one or more owners to carry out the planned response. The responses are documented in the risk register. Table 5.15 shows the inputs, tools and techniques, and outputs for the plan risk responses process.

TABLE 5.15   **Plan Risk Responses Inputs, Tools and Techniques, and Outputs**

Inputs	Tools and Techniques	Outputs
Risk management plan	Strategies for negative risks or threats	Project management plan updates
Risk register	Strategies for positive risks or opportunities	Project documents updates

Inputs	Tools and Techniques	Outputs
	Contingent response strategies	
	Expert judgment	

There are four responses to negative risks:

▶ Avoid

▶ Transfer

▶ Mitigate

▶ Accept

There are also four responses to positive risks:

▶ Exploit

▶ Share

▶ Enhance

▶ Accept

They are summarized in Table 5.16.

TABLE 5.16 **Summary of Risk Responses**

Response	Description	Risk Type
Avoid	Eliminating the threat by changing the project management plan.	Negative
Transfer	Shifting the risk to a third party.	Negative
Mitigate	Reducing either the probability or impact of the risk.	Negative
Exploit	Taking steps to make the opportunity happen.	Positive
Share	Using a third party to help capture the opportunity.	Positive
Enhance	Increasing the probability or positive impact of the risk.	Positive
Accept	Taking no steps in the project because of the risk. Contingency reserves might be established.	Positive and Negative

Risk Monitoring and Controlling

The risk evaluation process is not just performed once during the planning process. Throughout the project, risks must be continually monitored, with additional analysis and risk response development as new risks are identified. *Risk monitoring and controlling* focuses both on identification and analysis of new risks, as well as tracking previously identified risks and risk triggers.

> **Note**
>
> *Risk triggers*, also sometimes referred to as *risk symptoms* or *warning signs*, are indications that risks have occurred or are about to occur. They are identified during risk identification and monitored throughout the project.

Risks should be reevaluated when the following events occur:

▶ A risk trigger is identified.

▶ A change request is approved.

▶ Key project milestones are reached.

▶ Project phases end.

▶ Deviations are detected in variance and trend analysis.

▶ Corrective or preventive actions are implemented.

Cram Quiz

Answer these questions. The answers follow the last question. If you cannot answer these questions correctly, consider reading this section again until you can.

1. Which input is NOT used for the identify risks process?

   ○ **A.** Project charter

   ○ **B.** Scope baseline

   ○ **C.** Cost management plan

   ○ **D.** Academic studies

2. In evaluating project risk, a decision tree analysis is most helpful in which of the following scenarios?

○ **A.** Describing a potential risk and the implications for each available choice and outcome associated with the risk

○ **B.** Describing a potential risk and the most likely choice and outcome associated with the risk

○ **C.** Describing a potential risk and the least likely choice and outcome associated with the risk

○ **D.** None of the above

3. The identification of risks associated with a project

○ **A.** Occurs only at the beginning of a project, when the risk management plan is developed

○ **B.** Is an ongoing process, regularly scheduled throughout the life cycle of a project

○ **C.** Occurs as needed throughout the life cycle of a project

○ **D.** Both B and C

4. Which of the following is the only valid tool and technique for the plan risk management process?

○ **A.** Reserve analysis

○ **B.** Planning meetings and analysis

○ **C.** Checklist analysis

○ **D.** Contingent response strategies

5. Which input is NOT used for the qualitative risk analysis process?

○ **A.** Cost management plan

○ **B.** Risk register

○ **C.** Risk management plan

○ **D.** Scope baseline

6. Which tool and technique is NOT used for the plan risk responses process?

○ **A.** Strategies for positive risks or opportunities

○ **B.** Contingent response strategies

○ **C.** Risk audits

○ **D.** Expert judgment

Cram Quiz Answers

1. Answer A is correct. The project charter is not used. The scope baseline and cost management plan are used. Academic studies are part of enterprise environmental factors that also include commercial databases, benchmarking, or other industry studies.

2. Answer A is the correct response. A decision tree diagram can be used to consider potential risks and all the implications associated with the risk. You can include every conceivable choice and outcome. Every option is considered. Answer B is incorrect because choice and outcome are limited to the most probable scenario. Answer C is incorrect because choice and outcome are limited to the least probable scenario. Answer D is incorrect.

3. Answer D is the best response. Risk analysis is not limited to the beginning of a project's life cycle, when the risk management plan is developed. The risk management plan should include a tool for risk assessment as a continuous process throughout the project. Risk reassessment should be a scheduled component of the project but should also have the flexibility to occur as needed at greater or lesser intervals, based on the level of risk.

4. Answer B is correct. Planning meetings and analysis is the only tool and technique defined for the plan risk management process. All the other answers refer to tools and techniques from other processes.

5. Answer A is correct. The cost management plan is an input for the perform quantitative risk analysis process. All the other answers are valid inputs for the perform qualitative risk analysis process.

6. Answer C is correct. Risk audits are a tool and technique for the monitor and control risks process. All other answers are valid tools and techniques for the plan risk response process.

Procurement Management

▶ **Plan Procurement Management—12.1**

CramSaver

If you can correctly answer these questions before going through this section, save time by skimming the Exam Alerts in this section and then completing the Cram Quiz at the end of the section.

1. Which contract type would be best for the seller if the scope of work is not well defined?

   ○ **A.** Fixed price

   ○ **B.** Purchase order

   ○ **C.** Time and material

   ○ **D.** Cost plus incentive fee

2. Which of the following is NOT a tool and technique for the plan procurement management process?

   ○ **A.** Make-or-buy analysis

   ○ **B.** Expert judgment

   ○ **C.** Market research

   ○ **D.** Bidder conferences

Answers

1. Answer D is correct. Cost plus incentive fee is always the lowest risk for the buyer. Fixed price and purchase order are the best choices when the item is well defined. Time and materials balances the risk between buyer and seller.

2. Answer D is correct. Bidder conferences is a tool and technique for the conduct procurements process. All other answers list valid tools and techniques for the plan procurement management process.

Procurement management involves the relationship between the buyer and the seller when products, services, or other results are being purchased by the project team in order to complete the project. Consider these key PMI principles for procurement management:

▶ The contract statement of work (SOW) is a key document that defines the work in order to allow buyers the ability to evaluate and bid on the work.

▶ There are three primary contract types:

- ▶ Fixed price

- ▶ Time and material

- ▶ Cost reimbursement

▶ The risk to both the buyer and seller depends on the type of contract chosen.

▶ The contract is a formal, written document, and any changes are submitted in writing.

Table 5.17 shows the inputs, tools and techniques, and outputs for the plan procurement management process.

TABLE 5.17 **Plan Procurement Management Inputs, Tools and Techniques, and Outputs**

Inputs	Tools and Techniques	Outputs
Project management plan	Make-or-buy analysis	Procurement management plan
Requirements documentation	Expert judgment	Procurement statement of work
Risk register	Market research	Procurement documents
Activity resource requirements	Meetings	Source selection criteria
Project schedule		Make-or-buy decisions
Activity cost estimates		Change requests
Stakeholder register		Project documents updates
Enterprise environmental factors		
Organizational process assets		

The Make-or-Buy Decision

The first step in procurement is resolving the make-or-buy decision. This decision is made during the plan procurement management process. An analysis is done to determine whether the product or service can be produced by the project team or whether it should be purchased. This analysis might also include buying versus renting/leasing a product. Many factors may be considered when performing this make-or-buy analysis, such as the capabilities and availability of the project team, the direct and indirect costs, and the type of contract.

The Contract Statement of Work

In addition to making the make-or-buy decision during the plan procurement management process, it is during this step that the contract statement of work (SOW) is developed and the type of contract to be used is determined. The SOW is a document that defines the work to be performed. A contract SOW describes work performed under contract. The contract SOW is developed from the scope statement and WBS and should be sufficiently detailed to allow the potential sellers to determine their ability to perform the work. A project can have multiple SOWs.

One of the project manager's responsibilities is to determine how to select the best vendors and the methods used to determine costs for the project. The evaluation criteria used can include any of the following:

▶ Seller's overall understanding of the need

▶ Price

▶ Overall life cycle cost

▶ History of the seller with the company

▶ Seller capabilities and approach, including technical, managerial, and financial

▶ Seller's production capacity, business size, and interest in the product/ service

▶ Seller's desire to assert intellectual property or proprietary rights on the product or service

▶ References

Contract Types

A number of contract types are used in the procurement processes. To be prepared for the exam, understand the benefit of each type, as summarized in Table 5.18.

TABLE 5.18 **Contract Types**

Name	Description	Pro/Con
Firm fixed price (FFP) (or lump sum)	The work is completed for a predetermined price.	Benefits the buyer. Seller at risk if item isn't clearly defined. Seller must manage changes closely.
Fixed price incentive fee (FPIF)	Similar to fixed price, but an incentive is offered for early completion.	More administrative effort for buyer and seller.
Fixed price with economic price adjustment (FP-EPA)	Similar to fixed price but with an agreed-upon final adjustment due to changing economic conditions.	Used for very long-term performance when costs can increase or decrease over time. To protect the buyer and seller, the EPA clause must relate to a well-known financial index.
Purchase order	A form of fixed price, usually for off-the-shelf items.	Optimal for both parties when the item is a commodity (such as computers).
Cost reimbursement, includes CPFF, CPIF, and CPAF (see following exam alert)	The seller is reimbursed for costs, plus an additional fee.	Benefits the seller because the seller's cost is covered. Risk to buyer if costs are higher than anticipated; the budget is affected.
Time and material (T&M)	Hybrid arrangement between fixed price and cost reimbursement where elements of both are used; a fixed unit rate can be set for certain elements of work, while other components are completely reimbursable. For example, a programmer might be acquired at $125 per hour without defining how long he will be used.	Seller benefits if amount of work can be extended, which affects the buyer's budget.

ExamAlert

PMI identifies three types of common cost-reimbursement contracts that only vary in how the fee is calculated: cost plus fixed fee (CPFF), cost plus incentive fee (CPIF), and cost plus award fee (CPAF). Be familiar with all three variations of cost-reimbursement contracts.

Figure 5.5 illustrates the risks to buyer and seller for the contract types.

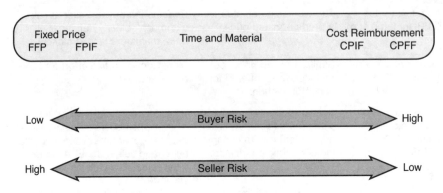

FIGURE 5.5   **The buyer and seller risk for contract types.**

The Procurement Management Plan

The procurement management plan is developed to describe how procurement activities will be carried out. The plan can include content that provides guidance for

▶ Type of contracts to be used

▶ Risks and risk management issues

▶ Criteria for independent estimates

▶ Standard procurement documents and procedures

▶ Coordinating procurement with other projects and multiple vendors

▶ Project assumptions or constraints that affect procurements

▶ Handling procurement schedules

▶ Addressing make-or-buy decisions

▶ Identifying and managing performance requirements

▶ Identifying prequalified sellers

▶ Procurement metrics used to evaluate sellers and manage contracts

> **Note**
>
> The steps of the procurement process are necessary only if the decision is made to buy outside resources.

Cram Quiz

Answer these questions. The answers follow the last question. If you cannot answer these questions correctly, consider reading this section again until you can.

1. The responsibility for tailoring a contract for goods and services to the needs of the project lies with whom?

   ○ **A.** The project manager

   ○ **B.** The project management team

   ○ **C.** The attorneys

   ○ **D.** The contract manager

2. What is the name for the decision about whether a product or service can be produced by the project management team or can be purchased?

   ○ **A.** Buyer assessment

   ○ **B.** Expert judgment

   ○ **C.** Make-or-buy analysis

   ○ **D.** Procurement evaluation

Cram Quiz Answers

1. Answer B is the best response. The responsibility for tailoring a contract for goods and services to the needs of the project lies with the project management team. The project management team can include the project manager, attorneys, and/or contract manager, but the responsibility does not rest solely with one individual.

2. Answer C is the best response. The decision about whether a product or service can be produced by the project management team or can be purchased is called *make-or-buy analysis*.

Stakeholder Management

▶ **Plan Stakeholder Management—13.2**

CramSaver

If you can correctly answer these questions before going through this section, save time by skimming the Exam Alerts in this section and then completing the Cram Quiz at the end of the section.

1. Which of the following reasons best summarizes why stakeholders are so important to projects?

   ○ **A.** Stakeholders authorize projects.

   ○ **B.** Stakeholders fund projects.

   ○ **C.** Stakeholders provide resources for projects.

   ○ **D.** Stakeholders can resist or support projects.

2. Which of the following is NOT a tool and technique for the plan stakeholder management process?

   ○ **A.** Meetings

   ○ **B.** Expert judgment

   ○ **C.** Analytical techniques

   ○ **D.** Stakeholder analysis

Answers

1. Answer D is correct. Each stakeholder can potentially resist or support each project. Depending on the stakeholder's power or influence, this support or resistance can have a noticeable impact on a project. Answers A and B are incorrect because the project sponsor authorizes and funds a project. Although the project sponsor is a stakeholder, these answers are not true in a general sense. Answer C is incorrect because not all stakeholders provide resources for the project.

2. Answer D is correct. Stakeholder analysis is a tool and technique for the identify stakeholders process. All other answers list valid tools and techniques for the plan stakeholder management process.

Stakeholder management is one aspect of project management that is often overlooked, or at least minimized. Many project managers with experience leading small projects may not fully appreciate the importance of stakeholders to the success of a project. Larger projects tend to have more stakeholders and more divergent requirements that must be satisfied. Effective stakeholder management can mean the difference between project success and failure. The plan stakeholder management process involves developing the management strategies to keep stakeholders engaged throughout the project life cycle. The identify stakeholders process results in a list of all stakeholders, along with their level of interest, power, and influence (the stakeholder register). Use this information to plan how to interact with stakeholders and ensure that they are part of the project when their interests and needs dictate involvement.

Table 5.19 shows the inputs, tools and techniques, and outputs for the plan stakeholder management process.

TABLE 5.19 **Plan Stakeholder Management Inputs, Tools and Techniques, and Outputs**

Inputs	Tools and Techniques	Outputs
Project management plan	Expert judgment	Stakeholder management plan
Stakeholder register	Meetings	Project documents updates
Enterprise environmental factors	Analytical techniques	
Organizational process assets		

Analytical Techniques

Successful stakeholder management planning involves ensuring that each stakeholder is engaged at an appropriate level at each stage in the project. This first means that the project manager must determine what the appropriate level of engagement is for each stakeholder. There are various techniques to classify stakeholders and their engagement level. Most techniques result in classifying current and desired stakeholder engagement. Stakeholders generally are engaged at one of the following levels:

▶ **Unaware**—No awareness of the project and possible impacts

▶ **Resistant**—Aware of the project and resistant to any change

▶ **Neutral**—Aware of the project but not actively supporting or resisting any changes

▶ **Supportive**—Aware of the project and actively supportive of changes

▶ **Leading**—Aware of the project and actively engaged to ensure project success

Relationships with stakeholders are crucial for a project manager. It is often difficult to establish a relationship with all stakeholders, especially on larger projects. A good project manager understands which stakeholders can have the most impact (both positive and negative) on a project's success and focuses on these stakeholders. The project manager must understand who the most important stakeholders are at each point in the project and ensure that they are engaged to promote the project's success.

The Stakeholder Management Plan

The stakeholder management plan is a part of the project management plan. The plan identifies strategies to keep the necessary stakeholders engaged at appropriate points in the project life cycle. While it is desirable to have all stakeholders engaged throughout a project, the stakeholder management plan focuses on the stakeholders who have the biggest impact. The plan can include

▶ Desired and current key stakeholder engagement levels

▶ Impact of change to key stakeholders

▶ Relationships between stakeholders and overlap of influence or interest

▶ Requirements to maintain communication with key stakeholders

▶ Information content and format requirements for stakeholder distribution

▶ The process for updating the stakeholder management plan throughout the project life cycle

Cram Quiz

Answer these questions. The answers follow the last question. If you cannot answer these questions correctly, consider reading this section again until you can.

1. Which type of stakeholder should be managed most closely throughout the project life cycle?

    ○ **A.** Low interest, high power

    ○ **B.** Low interest, low power

    ○ **C.** High interest, high power

    ○ **D.** High interest, low power

2. Why must the stakeholder management plan include provisions to change the plan?

    ○ **A.** The initial plan may be insufficient as more stakeholders are identified.

    ○ **B.** Stakeholders may gain or lose interest in the project as work progresses.

    ○ **C.** Stakeholders may change positions and responsibilities.

    ○ **D.** Project work beyond the defined scope may impact different stakeholders.

Cram Quiz Answers

1. Answer C is the best response. Stakeholders with high interest in the project and who possess high power to impact the project must be managed most closely to ensure that they are engaged and satisfied. All other combinations of interest and power have less impact and do not need to be managed as closely.

2. Answer B is the best response. As project work progresses, different stakeholders may become more or less interested in the project due to awareness or changing operational focus. Many factors may change how interested any stakeholder may be at any point in the project life cycle. Answer A is incorrect because the identify stakeholders process should produce a complete list of stakeholders. Answer C can be true in some cases but generally happens less frequently than Answer B and therefore is not the best answer. Answer D is incorrect because work beyond the project scope is not allowed.

What Next?

If you want more practice on this chapter's exam topics before you move on, remember that you can access all of the Cram Quiz questions on the CD. You can also create a custom exam by topic with the practice exam software. Note any topic you struggle with and go to that topic's material in this chapter.

CHAPTER 6

Understand Project Execution

In the executing process group, the work of the project takes place. The activities of the executing process group overlap with the monitoring and controlling process group (as well as the other process groups, to some extent). The specific activities that PMI identifies as part of executing are

▶ Direct and manage project work

▶ Perform quality assurance

▶ Acquire the project team

▶ Develop the project team

▶ Manage the project team

▶ Manage communications

▶ Conduct procurements

▶ Manage stakeholder engagement

ExamAlert

The executing progress group questions comprise 30% of the PMP exam. That's the largest number of questions from any process group. PMI puts a lot of emphasis on this process group, so you should, too.

Integration Management

▶ **Direct and Manage Project Work—4.3**

CramSaver

If you can correctly answer these questions before going through this section, save time by skimming the Exam Alerts in this section and then completing the Cram Quiz at the end of the section.

1. Which project document is best suited for tracking costs of resources?

- ○ **A.** Resource breakdown structure
- ○ **B.** Organizational breakdown structure
- ○ **C.** Work breakdown structure
- ○ **D.** Risk breakdown structure

2. Which of the following is the best description of the direct and manage project work process?

- ○ **A.** Performing the work defined by the project management plan to create the project's deliverables
- ○ **B.** Developing a document that formally authorizes a project or phase and documenting the initial stakeholders' expectations
- ○ **C.** Documenting the tasks necessary to create all subsidiary plans
- ○ **D.** Reviewing all change requests and approving and managing all changes to project components

Answers

1. Answer A is correct. The resource breakdown structure organizes all resources in a hierarchical structure, allowing for cost tracking. An organizational breakdown structure is used to document the project organization (human resources). A work breakdown structure shows deliverables but is not a detail of cost. A risk breakdown structure is used for risk analysis.

2. Answer A is correct. The direct and manage project work process is the process of performing the work defined by the project management plan to create the project's deliverables. Answer B is incorrect because it describes the develop project charter process. Answer C is incorrect because it describes the develop project management plan process. Answer D is incorrect because it describes the perform integrated change control process.

PMI includes the *direct and manage project work process* within the project integration management knowledge area and defines the process as "executing the work defined in the project management plan to achieve the project's objectives." Table 6.1 shows the inputs, tools and techniques, and outputs for the direct and manage project work process.

TABLE 6.1 **Direct and Manage Project Work Inputs, Tools and Techniques, and Outputs**

Inputs	Tools and Techniques	Outputs
Project management plan	Expert judgment	Deliverables
Approved change requests	Project management information system	Work performance data
Enterprise environmental factors	Meetings	Change requests
Organizational process assets		Project management plan updates
		Project documents updates

The PMBOK includes a list of activities that are included in the direct and manage project work process. The purpose of these activities is to produce the deliverables that are defined within the project's scope. The work also includes completed approved changes, corrective action, preventive action, and defect repair. Finally, work performance data is produced. This data is used to monitor and control activities against the project plan baseline.

One key output of this activity is the set of deliverables. They might be tangible deliverables such as a road or computer software or intangible deliverables such as training.

The project management information system (PMIS) includes the scheduling tools, tools for reporting, document repositories, and any other systems used in project execution. The PMIS also includes the techniques used for gathering, integrating, and disseminating process outputs. The PMIS can be either manual, automated, or a combination.

As a result of monitoring/controlling activities, additional work might be required in execution. For example, a quality control activity might indicate that a deliverable does not meet the quality standards, which would cause rework. A summary of the controlling activities, potential impacts, and resulting work is provided in Table 6.2.

> **Note**
>
> Understand the difference between corrective action and preventive action. *Preventive action* is anything done to prevent or avoid a specific situation. *Corrective action* is "after the fact" activities that fix an issue after it has occurred.

TABLE 6.2 **Impact of Monitoring/Controlling Activities on Project Execution**

Monitoring/Controlling Process	Potential Output	Resulting Work in Execution
Monitor/control project work	Corrective action to bring actual results in line with planned activities	Implementation of corrective action
Perform integrated change control	Change request	Implementation of approved change request
Validate scope	Change request	Implementation of approved change request
Control scope, schedule, and cost	Change request	Implementation of approved change request
Control quality	Identification of deliverables not meeting quality standards	Rework to bring deliverable up to quality standards, preventive action to eliminate cause of problem
Control communications	Forecast indicating that project is behind schedule	Corrective action to bring performance in line with plans
Control risks	Planned risk emerges	Application of risk response, risk reassessment
Control procurements	Seller's deliverables	Payment to seller completed
Control stakeholder engagement	Change request	Implementation of approved change request

> **ExamAlert**
>
> Ensure that you have a clear understanding of the activities and the interfaces that are part of the direct and manage project work process and the monitoring and controlling project work process.

Cram Quiz

Answer these questions. The answers follow the last question. If you cannot answer these questions correctly, consider reading this section again until you can.

1. Which activity is NOT performed as part of the direct and manage project work process?

   ○ **A.** Staff, train, and manage the project team.

   ○ **B.** Create and verify deliverables.

   ○ **C.** Manage risks and implement risk responses.

   ○ **D.** Monitor implementation of approved changes.

2. You're part of a project team constructing a manufacturing plant. You begin using process engineering to define the assumptions and constraints of the manufacturing process to be performed at the plant. This information is then used to design the major manufacturing units within the plant, which in turn serves as the starting point for designing the detailed plant layout and all other associated facilities. Next, design drawings are completed for fabrication and construction requirements. Changes and modifications occur during actual construction, requiring change control management and "as-built" documents. Finally, user acceptance testing and turnover of the completed manufacturing plant results in more adjustments and corrections. This is an example of

   ○ **A.** Analogous estimating

   ○ **B.** Assumptions analysis

   ○ **C.** Fast tracking

   ○ **D.** Progressive elaboration

3. What does crashing a project schedule imply?

   ○ **A.** Project cost and project schedule trade-offs occur to achieve the maximum schedule compression for the least cost to the project without compromising the intended scope of the project.

   ○ **B.** Project cost and project schedule overruns may result in a project coming in over budget and over time but within the original defined project scope.

   ○ **C.** It involves throwing more resources at the project to meet the planned project end date and planned project scope.

   ○ **D.** This is another term for fast tracking a project.

Cram Quiz Answers

1. Answer D is correct. During the direct and manage project work process, approved changes are implemented, but monitoring of those changes is part of the monitor and control project work process. All other activities are performed as part of direct and manage project work process.

2. Answer D is the correct response. Progressive elaboration is a technique for continuous improvement in your planning efforts. More details are added to your planning documents as the information becomes available, and each successive iteration of your planning process results in a better plan.

3. Answer A is the correct response. *Crashing* is a schedule compression technique whereby the project cost and project schedule are optimized to obtain the highest degree of schedule compression for the least cost to the project. Crashing does not always result in a viable project solution and can increase the overall cost of a project. Answer B is incorrect because crashing is not a term used for a project that is over time and over budget. Answer C is incorrect because crashing does not necessarily allow you to meet the planned project end date. Answer D is incorrect because fast tracking is another schedule compression tool used to perform multiple phases of project development in parallel.

Quality Management

▶ **Perform Quality Assurance—8.2**

CramSaver

If you can correctly answer these questions before going through this section, save time by skimming the Exam Alerts in this section and then completing the Cram Quiz at the end of the section.

1. What is the name for the technique to identify the underlying cause of a problem and take steps to prevent further occurrence?

   ○ **A.** Continuous improvement

   ○ **B.** Root cause analysis

   ○ **C.** Quality audits

   ○ **D.** Ishikawa analysis

2. Which of the following is NOT a valid input to the perform quality assurance process?

   ○ **A.** Quality metrics

   ○ **B.** Quality checklists

   ○ **C.** Process improvement plan

   ○ **D.** Quality control measurements

Answers

1. Answer B is correct. Root cause analysis looks at the underlying causes of an issue and applies corrective action to prevent further occurrence.

2. Answer B is correct. Quality checklists are an input to the perform quality control process. All the other answers are valid inputs to the perform quality assurance process.

Quality assurance is the process of auditing quality requirements and the results from quality control measurements that are used to ensure that the project employs all processes needed to meet requirements. It differs from quality control, which is monitoring specific project results to ensure they meet quality standards.

ExamAlert

Understand the difference between quality assurance and quality control.

Table 6.3 shows the inputs, tools and techniques, and outputs for the perform quality assurance process.

TABLE 6.3   **Perform Quality Assurance Inputs, Tools and Techniques, and Outputs**

Inputs	Tools and Techniques	Outputs
Quality management plan	Quality management and control tools	Change requests
Process improvement plan	Quality audits	Project management plan updates
Quality metrics	Process analysis	Project documents updates
Quality control measurements		Organizational process assets updates
Project documents		

PMI stresses the importance of continuous improvement, which is an iterative process for improving quality. Continuous improvement is an ongoing cycle of process analysis that leads to process improvements, at which point further process analysis is undertaken. Process analysis is an in-depth look at what processes are being executed, how they are executed and by whom, and related processes.

> **Note**
>
> The benefits of continuous improvement include reduced waste and reduction in non–value-added processes, leading to increased efficiency and effectiveness.

Quality metrics and quality control measurements are important inputs to perform quality assurance. Quality control measurements are the results of quality control activities. Quality metrics are the attributes that should be measured during quality control and the defined variances that are allowed. Taken together, metrics and measurements show whether production is within allowable variances. It is important to understand that measurements without metrics have very little meaning. For example, a temperature measurement of 73 degrees Fahrenheit doesn't mean anything by itself. However, if a specific metric states that the sample temperature must be between 65 and 71 degrees Fahrenheit, it is easy to determine that the measured temperature falls outside the valid range.

ExamAlert

Memorize and understand all the inputs to quality assurance.

Note

The tools used in quality planning and quality control can also be used in quality assurance. Refer to Chapters 5, "Explore More Elements of Project Planning," and 7, "Investigate Project Monitoring and Controlling," for more details.

Along with the tools used in quality planning and quality control, two other tools in quality assurance are quality audits and process analysis. *Quality audits* are independent reviews to verify compliance with quality standards. For example, a review team looks at control charts to determine whether the processes were being controlled properly and whether proper actions were taken when processes fell outside control limits. *Process analysis* supports continuous improvement, as explained in the previous section.

Note

Root cause analysis is a technique to examine a problem, determine the underlying cause of the problem, and implement corrective action to prevent further occurrence.

The application of quality assurance might result in changes to the project, which take the form of change requests or recommended corrective action. Updates are made to the project management plan, other project documents, and organizational process assets.

Cram Quiz

Answer these questions. The answers follow the last question. If you cannot answer these questions correctly, consider reading this section again until you can.

1. What is the name for comparing planned project practices or actual project best practices from other comparable projects to your project in an effort to improve the quality of your project and establish performance measurement baselines?

   ○ **A.** Benchmarking

   ○ **B.** Continuous improvement

   ○ **C.** Metric creation

   ○ **D.** Quality assurance (QA)

2. A structured, independent review to determine whether project activities adhere to your project management plan and other project documentation, including all project policies, procedures, and standards, is called a(n)

○ **A.** Assurance review

○ **B.** Organizational process assessment

○ **C.** Process analysis

○ **D.** Quality audit

3. Which of the following is NOT one of the seven basic quality tools?

○ **A.** Cause-and-effect diagram

○ **B.** Statistical sampling

○ **C.** Histogram

○ **D.** Scatter diagram

Cram Quiz Answers

1. Answer A is the best response. *Benchmarking* is the practice of comparing your project to other planned project practices or actual project best practices in an effort to improve your project and establish performance measurement benchmarks. Answer B is incorrect because continuous improvement is a Plan–Do–Check–Act cycle for improving quality in the product developed by a project. Answer C is incorrect because metrics are specific defined tools for describing and measuring key values for quality control. Answer D is incorrect because quality assurance (QA) is the application of planned, systematic activities to achieve specific quality objectives. QA is the overarching process in which continuous process improvement is practiced. Benchmarking is one task within the process, and using metrics is a way to assess quality initiatives.

2. Answer D is the correct response. A quality audit is a structured, independent review that provides an assessment of whether a project's activities meet organizational and project policies, processes, and procedures.

3. Answer B is the correct response. Statistical sampling is a quality control technique, but it is not one of the seven basic quality tools. The seven basic quality tools are cause-and-effect diagrams, control charts, flowcharts, histograms, Pareto diagrams, checksheets, and scatter diagrams. Answers A, C, and D are incorrect because these items are part of the seven basic quality tools.

Human Resource Management

▶ **Acquire Project Team—9.2**

▶ **Develop Project Team—9.3**

▶ **Manage Project Team—9.4**

CramSaver

If you can correctly answer these questions before going through this section, save time by skimming the Exam Alerts in this section and then completing the Cram Quiz at the end of the section.

1. Which document is best suited for tracking the assignment of all resources to specific tasks?

   ○ **A.** Staffing management plan

   ○ **B.** Organizational breakdown structure

   ○ **C.** Position description

   ○ **D.** RACI matrix

2. Which of the following is NOT a tool and technique for the develop project team process?

   ○ **A.** Conflict management

   ○ **B.** Ground rules

   ○ **C.** Colocation

   ○ **D.** Training

3. As part of the team acquisition process, the project manager hires a new employee and assigns her to the project team. According to Maslow's hierarchy of needs, what need level is she most likely at?

   ○ **A.** Self-actualization

   ○ **B.** Safety and security

   ○ **C.** Social need

   ○ **D.** Physical need

Answers

1. Answer D is correct. The RACI matrix lists responsibilities of all resources. The staffing management plan only lists types of resources and timing. The organizational breakdown structure lists resources according to the organization to which they belong. A position description only lists responsibilities for a specific position.

2. Answer A is correct. Conflict management is a tool and technique for the manage project team process. All the other answers are valid tools and techniques for the develop project team process.

3. Answer C is correct. Because she is new to the company, she is most likely looking for acceptance and friendship. She needs to achieve this and self-esteem before being able to move to self-actualization. Because the new employee recently secured employment, you can assume that her basic safety and security and physical needs are currently being met.

The project cannot be completed without people. Using the procedures defined during planning, the project manager acquires the necessary resources. Note, however, that the project manager might not have direct control over what resources are assigned to the project. When the project manager has the ability to influence or direct staff assignments, the following should be considered:

▶ **Availability**—Does the person's schedule allow him or her to support the project?

▶ **Ability**—Does the person have the proper skill set?

▶ **Experience**—Will the project require an individual with significant experience?

▶ **Interest**—Will the person want to work on the project, which is an important factor in motivation?

▶ **Cost**—How much will the person cost? This can be in terms of hiring a contractor. If the resource is internal, other factors might be considered, including the effect on another project that the individual supports.

Table 6.4 shows the inputs, tools and techniques, and outputs for the acquire project team process.

TABLE 6.4 **Acquire Project Team Inputs, Tools and Techniques, and Outputs**

Inputs	Tools and Techniques	Outputs
Human resource management plan	Pre-assignment	Project staff assignments
Enterprise environmental factors	Negotiation	Resource calendars
Organizational process assets	Acquisition	Project management plan updates
	Virtual teams	
	Multi-criteria decision analysis	

A number of tools can be used in acquiring human resources; they are summarized in Table 6.5.

TABLE 6.5 **Summary of Human Resource Acquisition Tools**

Tool	Description
Pre-assignment	Assignments made prior to beginning of execution. They might be named in the proposal, contract, or charter, or they might be assigned because of a specific skill.
Negotiation	The project manager/team negotiates with functional managers or other managers for the resources they want. Organizational politics might be a factor in obtaining the desired resources.
Acquisition	Outside resources, such as consultants or contractors, are brought in through the acquisition process.
Virtual teams	A team might not be located in the same place and might rely on electronic tools (email, conference calls, and so forth) for communication. With decreasing communications costs and improved reliability, virtual teams have become more prevalent. This can also include offshoring, where some of the project work is done in a different country.
Multi-criteria decision analysis	When evaluating potential team members, it is often helpful to prioritize them based on attributes that will impact the project. Some common attributes include availability, cost, experience, ability, knowledge and skills, and even attitude. The project manager can determine which attributes are most beneficial to the project team and rank potential team members accordingly. This type of analysis can make the process of deciding between multiple resources clearer.

> **Note**
>
> The use of virtual teams requires additional work during the communication planning process to ensure that all the communication needs of the virtual team are met.

> **ExamAlert**
>
> Know your tools and techniques! You need to know how to apply the concepts discussed here to answer exam questions about the project team.

Develop Project Team

Team development has two facets: increasing the competency of the team and improving interaction among team members. Although team development should occur throughout the project, it is especially important early in the project life cycle.

> **ExamAlert**
>
> Teamwork is a critical factor for project success, and developing effective project teams is one of the primary responsibilities of the project manager.

Table 6.6 shows the inputs, tools and techniques, and outputs for the develop project team process.

TABLE 6.6 Develop Project Team Inputs, Tools and Techniques, and Outputs

Inputs	Tools and Techniques	Outputs
Human resource management plan	Interpersonal skills	Team performance assessments
Project staff assignments	Training	Enterprise environmental factors updates
Resource calendars	Team-building activities	
	Ground rules	
	Colocation	
	Recognition and rewards	
	Personnel assessment tools	

PMI lists a number of tools for team development, including general management skills, training, team-building activities, ground rules, colocation, recognition and rewards, and personnel assessment tools:

▶ **Interpersonal skills**—These skills, sometimes referred to as soft skills, include empathy, creativity, influence, and group facilitation skills.

▶ **Training**—Training is used to increase competency. It might be formal or informal and can include classroom training, computer-based training, and coaching/mentoring.

▶ **Team-building activities**—This is any activity used to improve team cohesiveness. Team building can encompass anything from a short activity at the beginning of a meeting to an offsite event. Even team participation in a project activity such as risk identification can serve to build team cohesiveness. Most teams progress through five stages of development:

    ▶ **Forming**—This is the phase in which the team meets and first learns about the project and their roles. Team members are still independent and not yet team oriented.

    ▶ **Storming**—The team begins to consider the project work and make decisions. Collaboration is important in this phase.

    ▶ **Norming**—Team members begin to adjust to one another, work together more closely, and build trust.

    ▶ **Performing**—The team is well formed and works together well.

    ▶ **Adjourning**—The team completes project work and migrates to post-project work.

▶ **Ground rules**—These rules dictate the expected behavior of the team. Having the team develop ground rules can serve as a team-building activity.

▶ **Colocation**—This is the opposite of virtual teams. PMI uses the term *war room* to describe a room where the team activities take place. Critical projects might use colocation to improve communication among team members.

▶ **Recognition and rewards**—These are used to motivate the team and reinforce positive behavior. The approach should be developed during planning and take into account the culture of team members, the type of behavior to be rewarded, and the budget.

▶ **Personnel assessment tools**—Tools that provide insight into potential team members' strengths and weaknesses help the project manager acquire the right resources for the project. These tools can include surveys to determine attitude, assessments for aptitude or performance, interviews, and focus groups. The use of these tools can foster more confidence among team members and increase overall team commitment.

Power is an important concept in the team environment. Although the project manager is in charge, he or she might not have legitimate power over all team members. Other team members must also defer to someone with power to accomplish their tasks. A summary of the types of power is in Table 6.7.

TABLE 6.7 **Summary of Types of Power**

Type of Power	Description
Legitimate	Power based on position or title, such as senior executives.
Referent	Power transferred from someone with legitimate power. A project charter approved by a vice president assigning the project manager gives the project manager referent power.
Expert	Power based on knowledge. A team leader might have expert power because of her knowledge of a programming language.
Reward	Power based on the ability to give or hold back rewards. A project manager who can award performance bonuses has this type of power.
Coercive	Power based on force or intimidation.

> **Note**
>
> Referent power is important for project managers. Often their authority does not equal their responsibilities on the project. This is especially true in a matrix environment, where project managers don't have direct authority over team members. A project manager should be able to integrate and apply specific types of power as situations demand.

Manage Project Team

Once the project team members have been assembled and developed, they are ready for action. As the team begins the actual work of the project, the focus shifts to the day-to-day management of the team. PMI addresses the task of managing the project team in the manage project team process. Table 6.8 shows the inputs, tools and techniques, and outputs for the manage project team process.

TABLE 6.8 **Manage Project Team Inputs, Tools and Techniques, and Outputs**

Inputs	Tools and Techniques	Outputs
Human resource management plan	Observation and conversation	Change requests
Project staff assignments	Project performance appraisals	Project management plan updates
Team performance assessments	Conflict management	Project documents updates
Issue log	Interpersonal skills	Enterprise environmental factor updates
Work performance reports		Organizational process assets updates
Organizational process assets		

As mentioned previously, recognition and rewards are used to motivate the team. Motivation also occurs in managing the project team in the areas of interpersonal skills and conflict management. Knowledge of motivation theories is often tested in the PMP exam. A summary of the leading theories is presented in Table 6.9.

TABLE 6.9 **Summary of Motivation Theories**

Theory	Developer	Description
Hierarchy of needs	Abraham Maslow	People have a hierarchy of needs, described as a pyramid. When one level is satisfied, they move on to the higher-level needs. The base of the pyramid is physical needs (food, shelter), and then the higher levels are safety and security, social needs (love, friendship), esteem, and finally self-actualization. On a project team, a worker would very likely be motivated by esteem, which can be self-esteem for mastery of a task or the esteem that comes from recognition by others for accomplishments.
Motivation-hygiene theory (or factor theory)	Fredrick Herzberg	There are motivators and hygiene factors. Hygiene factors (pay, adequate supplies) prevent dissatisfaction but otherwise don't motivate. Motivation comes from factors such as learning new skills or being promoted. A project manager must ensure that hygiene factors are present and create motivators as part of the assignment.

Theory	Developer	Description
Expectancy theory	Victor Vroom	People are motivated by the expectation of being rewarded for their work. In addition, if a team is told it is high performing, it will act that way, with the corollary for low performance also being true.
Achievement theory	David McClelland	The three motivators for people are power, affiliation, and achievement. A person might not have one of these factors and therefore might not be motivated in his job.
X and Y theories	McGregor	Theory X states that people are lazy and need autocratic leadership. Theory Y states that people are generally hard workers and do not require constant supervision.
Theory Z	William Ouchi	Theory Z is not related to McGregor's work. It states that people are not only self-motivated to do their work but also have a desire to want to help make the company succeed.
Contingency theory	Fred Fiedler	The most effective leadership style is contingent on the situation. It is influenced by the leader's relationship with the team, the task to be completed, and the positional power of the leader.
Situational leadership	Ken Blanchard	Individuals move through four stages of development, and leaders need to apply the correct leadership style. The progression of leadership styles is directing, coaching, supporting, and delegating.

ExamAlert

Understand how a project manager uses the theories of motivation to influence team members.

Note

Expectancy theory says that motivation is a factor of valence (the value of the reward), expectancy (belief in the ability to complete a task), and instrumentality (belief that you will receive the reward if you complete the task).

Team Formation

The theories presented in Table 6.9 focus primarily on development of individuals. PMI also discusses how the team forms as a cohesive unit. A leading theory in team development was developed by Bruce Tuckman. His theory states that teams go through stages: forming, storming, norming, and performing. He later added a fifth stage, adjourning. His model is summarized in Table 6.10.

TABLE 6.10 **Tuckman's Model of Team Formation**

Stage	Description
Forming	Initial stage, when team is first brought together. Team goals and individual roles are unclear. High dependence on the project manager for direction.
Storming	Team members attempt to establish themselves within the team. Cliques might form. Still some uncertainty in goals.
Norming	Roles are accepted. Consensus exists. There might be social interactions outside the project.
Performing	Very clear focus. Little direction is needed from the project manager.
Adjourning	Break-up of the team after completion of the project. Feelings of insecurity might exist.

Blanchard's situational leadership model, briefly described in Table 6.9, can also apply to teams. The four leadership styles can be used in Tuckman's five stages of team development. Figure 6.1 compares these two theories.

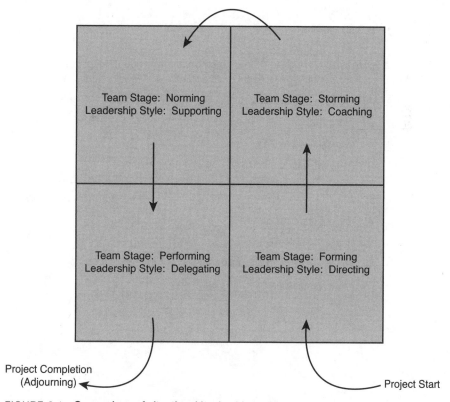

FIGURE 6.1   Comparison of situational leadership and team formation.

Cram Quiz

Answer these questions. The answers follow the last question. If you cannot answer these questions correctly, consider reading this section again until you can.

1. A project manager has budgeted money to provide cash awards to team members who exceed expectations. A project team member who is motivated by the chance to earn a cash reward can most accurately be explained by which theory?

   ○ **A.** Hierarchy of needs

   ○ **B.** Theory X

   ○ **C.** Achievement theory

   ○ **D.** Expectancy theory

2. A project is a month into the executing phase. There are some cliques forming among the team members. Which leadership style is most appropriate?

   ○ **A.** Directing

   ○ **B.** Delegating

   ○ **C.** Coaching

   ○ **D.** Supporting

3. A project team is composed of team members in two countries plus a contractor team in a third country. What tool would optimize communication?

   ○ **A.** Project schedule tool

   ○ **B.** War room

   ○ **C.** Manual filing system

   ○ **D.** Extranet-based electronic document repository

4. Which of the following is NOT an output of the acquire project team process?

   ○ **A.** Project staff assignments

   ○ **B.** Resource calendars

   ○ **C.** Team performance assessments

   ○ **D.** Project management plan updates

Cram Quiz Answers

1. Answer D is correct. The person is working hard because he expects to be rewarded. The other theories do not talk about rewards as motivators.

2. Answer C is correct. The formation of cliques occurs during the storming stage of team development. During this stage, the correct situational leadership style is coaching.

3. Answer D is correct. An electronic document repository allows all team members, regardless of location, access to the documents. Manual filing and war rooms are optimal for a project team in one location. A project scheduling tool might allow team members on a shared network to share data but would not be helpful for a third-party team.

4. Answer C is correct. Team performance assessments is an output of the develop project team process. All other answers are valid outputs of the acquire project team process.

Communications Management

▶ **Manage Communications—10.2**

CramSaver

If you can correctly answer these questions before going through this section, save time by skimming the Exam Alerts in this section and then completing the Cram Quiz at the end of the section.

1. Project communication includes which of the following tasks?

○ **A.** Determining and limiting who may communicate with whom and who receives what information

○ **B.** Combining the type and format of information needed with an analysis of the value of the information for communication

○ **C.** Understanding how communication affects the project as a whole

○ **D.** All of the above

2. Which of the following is NOT an input to the manage communications process?

○ **A.** Communications management plan

○ **B.** Work performance reports

○ **C.** Organizational process assets

○ **D.** Issue log

Answers

1. Answer D is the best response. Project communication includes all these tasks: determining and limiting who may communicate with whom and who receives what information, combining the type and format of information needed with an analysis of the value of the information for communication, and understanding how communication affects the project as a whole.

2. Answer D is the best response. The issue log is an input to the control communications process, not the manage communications process. All other answers are valid inputs to the manage communications process.

Communicating with the project team, and with any other stakeholders, is one of the project manager's most important tasks. In fact, a project manager spends the majority of his time communicating. Some say as much as 90% of a project manager's time is spent communicating. Exchanging information is the only way a project manager can know how a project is progressing. The manage communications process keeps stakeholders informed. This includes communication outlined in the communications management plan as well as responses to ad hoc requests. Communication must be both timely and accurate. Table 6.11 shows the inputs, tools and techniques, and outputs for the manage communications process.

TABLE 6.11 **Manage Communications Inputs, Tools and Techniques, and Outputs**

Inputs	Tools and Techniques	Outputs
Communications management plan	Communication technology	Project communications
Work performance reports	Communication models	Project management plan updates
Enterprise environmental factors	Communication methods	Project documents updates
Organizational process assets	Information management systems	Organizations process assets updates
	Performance reporting	

Communication management is an elemental topic due to both its importance to the smooth operation of the project team and its complexity.

Tools and Techniques for Managing Communications

Notice that in Table 6.11 the tools and techniques for the manage communications process include communication technology, communication models, communication methods, information management systems, and performance reporting. Each of these tools and techniques helps project teams communicate effectively and without wasted or missed messages.

Communication Technology

Communication technology refers to the mechanisms used to provide information and receive feedback among team members. The specific type of technology selected for any particular message depends on the urgency of the message, the availability of the desired transmission mechanism, the ability for the sender and receiver to access the technology, and the sensitivity of the message. Technology mechanisms can range from impromptu meetings, to email, to written memos. Each team member should consider technology needs and applicability when communicating with other team members.

Communication Models

Communication models consist of different ways to communicate with different parties. The components of various models include encoding, transmitting, and decoding the message, as well as any acknowledgement and potential feedback. Different models serve different purposes. For instance, a project manager would likely use a broadcast model (one sender sending to many recipients) for general, non-sensitive communication. On the other hand, a project manager would use a more direct model with requested receipt acknowledgement when sending legal agreements to a specific party. The chosen model should support the purpose and sensitivity requirements of each communication session.

Communication Methods

Communication methods are a part of general management skills. *Communication* comprises a sender, a receiver, and the communication channel. The sender is responsible for making the message clear and accurate. The receiver is responsible for understanding the message. Communication can include the following:

▶ Written and oral

▶ Listening and speaking

▶ Internal and external

▶ Formal and informal

▶ Vertical and horizontal

Issues can result if communications are not managed effectively on a project. For example, because email cannot easily convey emotions, an email could be sent with a comment meant to be sarcastic, but the receiver doesn't understand that and is upset based on the text of the email. The project manager should plan communications to avoid these types of issues, including the best method for delivering messages based on the audience and content.

If there are unique needs for information gathering and retrieval systems, they should be identified during planning. For example, a project that involves subcontractors might need a document repository that exists outside the company's computer network. This would allow anyone with permission to access documents through a common web browser, even from remote locations.

Information Management Systems and Performance Reporting

Today's project managers rely on electronic communication more than ever before. Whereas project managers from several decades ago relied on hard-copy communication, today email, instant messaging, document collaboration, and social media are more common choices to communicate with team members working on projects. Regardless of the medium chosen, it is more and more likely that an information management system be a part of project communication. Information management systems empower team members to use electronic means to share content and exchange messages. They also ease the burden of any team member to find pertinent content and search historical information.

As a project moves toward its goals, the only way a project manager can assess the project's progress is by measuring team members' performance. The process of collecting and distributing information that describes the performance of a project is called *performance reporting*. Performance reporting isn't just reports to the project manager. It also includes the distribution of performance information to the project team and stakeholders. There are several different types of performance reports, including

- ▶ Status reports
- ▶ Progress measurements
- ▶ Forecasts

These reports, along with other project information, can be distributed several ways. Common distribution methods include

- ▶ Hard-copy documents
- ▶ Electronic communication, including email, telephone, and videoconferencing
- ▶ Project management/document management software, including online collaboration tools

Performance report formats and content vary depending on the target audience. Performance reports intended for upper-level management will contain summary information. Reports intended for other team members will likely contain more detailed information. Regardless of the audience, the purpose of performance reports is to convey the progress a project team has made toward the project goals.

Cram Quiz

Answer these questions. The answers follow the last question. If you cannot answer these questions correctly, consider reading this section again until you can.

1. How many communication channels exist for a team of 20 members?

   ○ **A.** 20

   ○ **B.** 80

   ○ **C.** 190

   ○ **D.** 230

2. Communication technology factors that can affect a project include

   ○ **A.** The urgency of the need for information

   ○ **B.** The expected staffing on the project and the individuals' competencies

   ○ **C.** The length of the project

   ○ **D.** All of the above

Cram Quiz Answers

1. Answer C is correct. Using the formula $(n) * (n - 1) / 2$, the calculation is $20 * (20 - 1) / 2$.

2. Answer D is the best response. Communication technology factors include the urgency of the need for information, the expected staffing for the project, the staff members' individual skill sets, and the length of the project.

Procurement Management

▶ **Conduct Procurements—12.2**

CramSaver

If you can correctly answer these questions before going through this section, save time by skimming the Exam Alerts in this section and then completing the Cram Quiz at the end of the section.

1. Which of the following techniques would you NOT use to conduct procurements?

   ○ **A.** Bidder conference

   ○ **B.** Make-or-buy analysis

   ○ **C.** Independent estimates

   ○ **D.** Analytical techniques

2. Which of the following is the best description for the conduct procurements process?

   ○ **A.** Completing each procurement

   ○ **B.** Documenting project purchasing decisions, specifying the approach, and identifying potential sellers

   ○ **C.** Managing procurement relationships, monitoring contract performance, and making changes and corrections as needed

   ○ **D.** Obtaining seller responses, selecting a seller, and awarding a contract

Answers

1. Answer B is the correct answer. Answers A, C, and D all represent tools and techniques for the conduct procurements process. The make-or-buy analysis is a tool and technique for the plan procurement management process.

2. Answer D is the correct answer. Answer A is incorrect because it describes the close procurements process. Answer B is incorrect because it describes the plan procurement management process. Answer C is incorrect because it describes the conduct procurements process.

Procurement

During planning, the procurement approach is mapped out. PMI has consolidated several steps from older PMBOK editions into a single, unified process to address procurement execution issues: *the conduct procurements process.*

Conduct Procurements

Using the procurement management plan and other procurement documents, such as the invitation for bid, statement of work, or request for quotation, developed during planning, the project team seeks out potential sellers for the items being procured. The request might be made via a bidder conference, advertising, or through the use of a qualified seller list. The most important outputs from this process are the selected sellers list, agreements, and resource calendars. Table 6.12 shows the inputs, tools and techniques, and outputs for the conduct procurements process.

TABLE 6.12 **Conduct Procurements Inputs, Tools and Techniques, and Outputs**

Inputs	Tools and Techniques	Outputs
Procurement management plan	Bidder conferences	Selected sellers
Procurement documents	Proposal evaluation techniques	Agreements
Source selection criteria	Independent estimates	Resource calendars
Seller proposals	Expert judgment	Change requests
Project documents	Advertising	Project management plan updates
Make-or-buy decisions	Analytical techniques	Project documents updates
Procurement statement of work	Procurement negotiations	
Organizational process assets		

ExamAlert

The bidder conference is also known as the contractor conference, vendor conference, or pre-bid conference. Understand that these terms are interchangeable.

With proposals in hand, the project team must select the seller or sellers that are best able to deliver the product or service. In addition to the proposals, evaluation criteria were identified during planning that are used to evaluate the proposals.

PMI lists other inputs with which you should be familiar, including the procurement management plan, procurement policies, the procurement document package, proposals, the qualified seller list, and the project management plan.

Conduct Procurements Tools

A number of tools are used during seller selection, as summarized in Table 6.13.

TABLE 6.13 **Conduct Procurements Tools**

Tool	Description
Bidder conference	Meeting for prospective buyers and sellers prior to submitting a bid or proposal. Such meetings help ensure that all parties have a clear understanding of the procurement requirements.
Proposal evaluation techniques	These techniques can incorporate the other tools, such as a weighting system or expert judgment, as well as the process that will be used to evaluate proposals. Often scorecards are used as part of the process. The technique includes the overall process for comparing results of screening processes, weighting results from multiple contributors, or applying expert judgment to make the final decision.
Independent estimates	Independent estimates are prepared by outside organizations or the procurement department as a check against the proposal pricing. These estimates can be compared to proposals to determine whether the proposals are within reason.
Expert judgment	A review team with expertise in the items being contracted uses expert judgment to evaluate the proposals.
Analytical techniques	Systems can be used to quantify the importance of all the evaluation criteria. Some criteria might be more important than others and therefore be weighted more. For example, if reliability is more important than cost, a seller with better reliability would score higher than one with better cost.
Procurement negotiation	Procurement negotiations are used to provide clarification on proposals. This can become a process on its own in large procurement situations. Negotiations cover technical details, financing, pricing, payment schedules, responsibilities of both parties, change and conflict resolution processes, and rights to intellectual or proprietary property. The result of contract negotiation is the signed contract. These negotiations might be led by someone other than the project manager.

The proposal evaluation technique should be able to take into account both objective and subjective criteria. The technique incorporates the weighting system for the evaluation criteria. The proposal evaluation is conducted by multiple reviewers. An example of a proposal evaluation scorecard is shown in Table 6.14. In this example, Vendor 2 had the higher score and would be selected as the seller.

TABLE 6.14 **Sample of Proposal Evaluation Scorecard**

Criteria	Vendor 1			Vendor 2		
	Raw Score	Weight	Weighted Score	Raw Score	Weight	Weighted Score
Price	4	.7	2.8	5	.7	3.5
Delivery schedule	3	.5	1.5	4	.5	2.0
Technical knowledge	3	.5	1.5	2	.5	1.0
Experience	1	.3	0.3	3	.3	0.9
Total			6.2			7.4

ExamAlert

Understand the concept of using a source selection weighting system for the exam.

The weighting system is developed based on the criteria that the organization has determined is important for the project. In Table 6.15, price received the highest weight, while experience received the lowest weight. Using that scorecard, a vendor with a lower price receives a higher weighted score than a vendor with significant experience. The raw scores are determined by the individuals or team reviewing the proposals.

The weighting system can be used to either select a final seller or to prioritize the list of sellers for contract negotiations. If a satisfactory contract cannot be arranged with the seller receiving the top score, contract negotiations could begin with the next seller.

Cram Quiz

Answer these questions. The answers follow the last question. If you cannot answer these questions correctly, consider reading this section again until you can.

1. Which of the following is NOT a benefit of a bidder conference?

   ○ **A.** All prospective vendors hear questions and answers from all parties

   ○ **B.** Featured vendors receive preferential access

   ○ **C.** Procurement requirements are communicated to all prospective vendors

   ○ **D.** Questions can be collected before the conference to allow for complete answers

2. Which technique for selecting a seller is useful when there are several differences between the sellers and no clear "best choice"?

   ○ **A.** Weighting system

   ○ **B.** Expert judgment

   ○ **C.** Seller rating system

   ○ **D.** Screening system

Cram Quiz Answers

1. Answer B is correct. The main goal of a bidder conference is to eliminate any preferential treatment for any prospective vendor. Answers A, C, and D are all features and benefits of bidder conferences.

2. Answer A is the best answer. While Answers B, C, and D could be viable choices, only a weighting system allows for easy comparison of sellers when multiple variables are involved.

Stakeholder Management

▶ **Manage Stakeholder Engagement—13.3**

CramSaver

If you can correctly answer these questions before going through this section, save time by skimming the Exam Alerts in this section and then completing the Cram Quiz at the end of the section.

1. Which of the following best describes the manage stakeholder engagement process?

   ○ **A.** Adjusting strategies to engage stakeholders

   ○ **B.** Developing strategies to engage stakeholders throughout the project

   ○ **C.** Keeping track of overall project stakeholder relationships

   ○ **D.** Communicating and working with stakeholders to address their needs and issues

2. Which of the following is NOT an input to the manage stakeholder engagement process?

   ○ **A.** Stakeholder management plan

   ○ **B.** Change log

   ○ **C.** Communications management plan

   ○ **D.** Work performance reports

Answers

1. Answer D is the best response. Manage stakeholder engagement includes activities related to communicating and working with stakeholders in an effort to meet their requirements and expectations, as well as address any issues that arise throughout the project.

2. Answer D is the best response. The manage stakeholder engagement process focuses on communicating with stakeholders and addressing their needs and issues. Answer D refers to work performance reports, which are inputs to or outputs from various processes, but not the manage stakeholder engagement process.

Stakeholders

A good project manager must do more than just send out timely status updates. In addition to keeping the team informed and ensuring that all stakeholders have the necessary information, the project manager must also manage the impact of the disseminated information on project stakeholders. It is important that the stakeholders remain committed to the project. One of the project manager's jobs is to recognize any shift in stakeholder commitment and react in an effective manner. The manage stakeholder expectations process addresses this concern. Table 6.15 shows the inputs, tools and techniques, and outputs for the manage stakeholder engagement process.

TABLE 6.15 **Manage Stakeholder Engagement Inputs, Tools and Techniques, and Outputs**

Inputs	Tools and Techniques	Outputs
Stakeholder management plan	Communication methods	Issue log
Communications management plan	Interpersonal skills	Change requests
Change log	Management skills	Project management plan updates
Organizational process assets		Project documents updates
		Organizational process assets updates

Notice that the tools and techniques exclusively address the issues of interacting with other people. That's what managing stakeholders is all about. It is the job of the project manager to ensure that all the stakeholders continue to contribute in a material manner to the success of the project.

Cram Quiz

Answer these questions. The answers follow the last question. If you cannot answer these questions correctly, consider reading this section again until you can.

1. What is the key benefit of the manage stakeholder engagement process?

  ○ **A.** It maintains an updated roster of engaged stakeholders.

  ○ **B.** It provides an opportunity to align stakeholders with closely related team members.

  ○ **C.** It enables the project manager to strengthen support and decrease resistance from stakeholders.

  ○ **D.** It gives the project manager the authority to persuade stakeholders to support project activities.

2. Which output of the manage stakeholder engagement process may result in alterations to the project product?

  ○ **A.** Project documents updates

  ○ **B.** Project management plan updates

  ○ **C.** Issue log

  ○ **D.** Change requests

Cram Quiz Answers

1. Answer C is correct. The manage stakeholder engagement process gives project managers the ability to engage stakeholders in more positive ways and reduce resistance to project activities.

2. Answer D is the correct answer. The only approved method of altering the project product is through the change management process. This process starts with submitted change requests.

What Next?

If you want more practice on this chapter's exam topics before you move on, remember that you can access all of the Cram Quiz questions on the CD. You can also create a custom exam by topic with the practice exam software. Note any topic you struggle with and go to that topic's material in this chapter.

CHAPTER 7

Investigate Project Monitoring and Controlling

Monitoring and controlling refers to all the activities and processes necessary to successfully manage a project and its associated risks. For the PMP exam, monitoring and controlling relates to 11 out of the 47 project management processes defined in the PMBOK.

In essence, *monitoring and controlling* is all the effective activities that a project manager performs to keep project performance and resource utilization at optimal levels. The magnitude and frequency of these activities are dictated by the size and organizational impact of a project. No matter the size of a project, there are three core elements that support effective monitoring and controlling:

▶ Effective definition of the project baseline and milestones

▶ Effective tracking of project activities and resource utilization

▶ Effective risk definition for proposed corrective or preventive actions

The following sections address the various processes associated with monitoring and controlling and how these processes ensure that a project stays on track.

ExamAlert

The monitoring and controlling process group questions comprise 25% of the PMP exam. Although that's not as many questions as a couple other process groups, it still demands a respectable amount of attention.

Integration and Scope Management

▶ **Monitor and Control Project Work—4.4**

▶ **Perform Integrated Change Control—4.5**

▶ **Validate Scope—5.5**

▶ **Control Scope—5.6**

CramSaver

If you can correctly answer these questions before going through this section, save time by skimming the Exam Alerts in this section and then completing the Cram Quiz at the end of the section.

1. What is a corrective action?

   ○ **A.** An action to correct something in a project

   ○ **B.** An action that fixes the requisition process

   ○ **C.** An action that brings future project events into alignment with the project plan

   ○ **D.** Both B and C

2. Which type of diagram is most helpful in determining the root cause of project plan variances?

   ○ **A.** Control chart

   ○ **B.** Ishikawa diagram

   ○ **C.** Responsibility assignment matrix

   ○ **D.** Histogram

3. Which of the following is a tool and technique for the perform integrated change control process?

   ○ **A.** Facilitated workshops

   ○ **B.** Questionnaires and surveys

   ○ **C.** Meetings

   ○ **D.** Prototypes

4. Which of the following is NOT an output of the control scope process?

   ○ **A.** Accepted deliverables

   ○ **B.** Work performance information

   ○ **C.** Change requests

   ○ **D.** Project management plan updates

Answers

1. Answer C is correct. Remember that for the PMP exam, you are looking for the best possible answer. As per the *PMBOK Guide*, Fifth Edition, the best possible answer is C. Answer A is accurate, but it is not the best possible answer. Answer B is the result of a corrective action, but it is not the definition of what a corrective action is.

2. Answer B is correct. An Ishikawa diagram, also called a cause-and-effect diagram, is used to determine the root cause of an outcome.

3. Answer C is correct. Meetings are a tool and technique for the perform integrated change control process. All other answers are tools and techniques for the collect requirements process.

4. Answer A is correct. Accepted deliverables is an output of the validate scope process. All other answers are tools and techniques for the control scope process.

The monitoring and controlling process group addresses 9 of the 10 PMI knowledge areas, permeating nearly all aspects of a project. The activities in this process group help to prescribe a measured and controlled project execution environment.

Note

Why is monitoring and controlling important? In general, all project failures and cancellations can be traced back to lack of effective controls in one or more of these areas: scope, cost, quality, and risk management.

Figure 7.1 shows how the process groups of the project management methodology are related. You can see that all of them must be monitored and controlled for effective project completion. Note, however, that Figure 7.1 only shows a single closing iteration. Remember that closing can occur at every phase in a multi-phase project. It doesn't happen only once in all cases.

Monitoring and Controlling

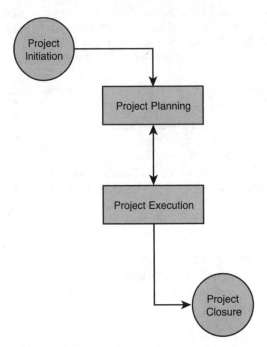

FIGURE 7.1   **The project monitoring and controlling process group framework.**

Factors That Cause Project Change

To effectively monitor and control a project, a project manager must prepare organizational processes that work like sentinels on the fence. These sentinels help the project manager identify events (people, cultural, or strategic) that might force a change to the project or the environment where the project is executing. In other words, your project will be influenced by elements outside its normal execution and identified risks. These processes can include elements such as

▶ Execution trend analysis

▶ Risk trigger management

▶ Forecast reports (like weather forecasts)

▶ Work package progress status and variances reports

▶ Lessons learned from similar projects

▶ Best practices

▶ Corporate strategy committee resolutions

These are some examples of project control processes and their elements:

▶ You could use earned value analysis to determine how your project is performing against the planned activities, schedule, and cost.

▶ You can prescribe corrective or preventive actions after performing trend analysis in work packages variances.

▶ You can identify a potential project change request after evaluating defect and frequency control charts.

▶ When executing enterprise projects, you can arrange a monthly meeting with the company CEO to discuss progress and new corporate initiatives.

Note

Monitoring and controlling is an iterative group of processes. Milestones tend to have a compilation of work packages and deliverables under them. If you monitor and control activities only at their completion, you might not learn of problems until late in the project. Like the autopilot in an airplane, the main function of project control is to make frequent minor course corrections instead of waiting until you are far off the planned course.

Monitor and Control Project Work

The monitor and control project work process is the first process in the monitoring and controlling process group. This process formally specifies what the project manager requires as inputs to properly monitor and control the project execution activities. As with all other PMI processes, the monitor and control project work process also defines the tools and techniques that are used and the expected outputs of the process. Table 7.1 shows the inputs, tools and techniques, and outputs for the monitor and control project work process.

TABLE 7.1 **Monitor and Control Project Work Inputs, Tools and Techniques, and Outputs**

Inputs	Tools and Techniques	Outputs
Project management plan	Expert judgment	Change requests
Schedule forecasts	Analytical techniques	Work performance reports
Cost forecasts	Project management information system	Project management plan updates
Validated changes	Meetings	Project documents updates

Inputs	Tools and Techniques	Outputs
Work performance information		
Enterprise environmental factors		
Organizational process assets		

As you can see, this process is a high-level process that requires expert judgment on the part of the project manager to assess whether the project is within the constraints of the plan. Any deviations require intervention or requests for changes to the plan.

Perform Integrated Change Control

When an opportunity for change is identified, the project manager must make time to acknowledge the request for change, evaluate its associated risks, and consider its potential not just to the timeline but also to scope, cost, staff, quality, make-or-buy decisions, and communication. The perform integrated change control process helps identify whether a requested change is gold plating or whether it has a direct effect on the project deliverables and its return on investment.

ExamAlert

What is gold plating? *Gold plating* is a change to a project or a work package within a project that has not gone through an adequate change control management process. Such requests often initiate from informal requests. Ensure that all change requests are routed through the formal procedures.

Table 7.2 shows the inputs, tools and techniques, and outputs for the perform integrated change control process.

TABLE 7.2 **Perform Integrated Change Control Work Inputs, Tools and Techniques, and Outputs**

Inputs	Tools and Techniques	Outputs
Project management plan	Expert judgment	Approved change requests
Work performance reports	Meetings	Change log
Change requests	Change control tools	Project management plan updates
Enterprise environmental factors		Project documents updates
Organizational process assets		

After you determine that a proposed change has merit and supports the project objectives, the change request is submitted to the change control board for final determinations. For the most part, the interaction with the change control board is defined in the planning stage and can remain in place until the completion of the project. In the event that the organization has a project management office, the members of the change control board can change to accommodate strategic impact or affected areas in the project organization.

> **Note**
>
> What is a change control board? A *change control board* is an enterprise decision-making body tasked with approving the changes to projects or their impact in strategic initiatives.

In addition, you should monitor any trends in requested changes that could indicate inadequate requirements definition in the planning stage of your project.

The Project Feedback Loop

Earlier chapters discussed the five distinct PMI process groups: initiating, planning, executing, monitoring and controlling, and closing. But what of the external changes that occur during the execution of a project? This is where iterative information gathering and dissemination processes serve as information feedback loops.

One of the challenges of the traditional linear methodology approaches is that they do not clearly provide methods to incorporate organizational changes midstream and do not verify their range to target impacts. In other words, a project without feedback loops makes the assumption that nothing outside the project will change throughout the life of the project; the requirements will not change or are frozen.

> **Note**
>
> A project with frozen structure and processes is likely to encounter problems or even fail because it does not take into account any discoveries or organizational changes that might occur during its execution.

Remember that enterprise changes can have a direct effect on the viability of a project. Some examples of events that you might want to be made aware of in advance are

▶ A hostile takeover

▶ A divestment of a business unit

▶ Personnel or resource availability reduction

▶ A corporate relocation

Validating and Controlling Project Scope

The scope management knowledge area defines two processes in the monitoring and controlling process group. The first process, *validate scope*, is the formal process of accepting project deliverables. It provides a mechanism to verify that deliverables meet or exceed project requirements. The second process, *control scope*, is the process of managing the project's status and any changes to the scope baseline. Let's look at each of the processes individually.

The validate scope process provides a project manager with a formal process to classify deliverables as acceptable or unacceptable. Table 7.3 shows the inputs, tools and techniques, and outputs for the validate scope process.

TABLE 7.3 **Validate Scope Inputs, Tools and Techniques, and Outputs**

Inputs	Tools and Techniques	Outputs
Project management plan	Inspection	Accepted deliverables
Requirements documentation	Group decision-making techniques	Change requests
Requirements traceability matrix		Work performance information
Verified deliverables		Project documents updates
Work performance data		

One output of the validate scope process is the collection of change requests. These requests are individually addressed through the perform integrated change control process and might result in approved change requests.

ExamAlert

Pay attention to how the outputs of processes are used as inputs to other processes. As you just saw with change control, processes in the executing process group and the monitoring and controlling process group are intermingled. In other words, processes are not just ordered by their PMI section number. The actual flow is important. Know how PMI process outputs and inputs match up.

The next process in the monitoring and controlling process group is the control scope process. This process monitors and controls all changes to the scope baseline to ensure that the changes are being handled in a structured manner. Table 7.4 shows the inputs, tools and techniques, and outputs for the control scope process.

TABLE 7.4 **Control Scope Inputs, Tools and Techniques, and Outputs**

Inputs	Tools and Techniques	Outputs
Project management plan	Variance analysis	Work performance information
Requirements documentation		Change requests
Requirements traceability matrix		Project management plan updates
Work performance data		Project documents updates
Organizational process assets		Organizational process assets updates

A primary component of the project management plan is the scope baseline. The *scope baseline* defines the project scope and its associated deliverables, and it documents the acceptance parameters of the final product. This baseline helps in clarifying any details that might have been left in a to-be-determined (TBD) mode during the project initiation phase or items that require further clarification with the project sponsor or its stakeholders. The project process indicators in this process are

▶ The work breakdown structure (WBS)

▶ Work package progress reports

The idea behind effectively defining the WBS is to create the roadmap that defines all the activities that will be executed to accomplish the project goal.

The WBS is an element that changes with the passage of time and resource utilization. Why? As you perform the tasks outlined in your baseline, the recorded changes accommodate any differences between the planned theory and the actual execution.

An effective WBS assists the stakeholders in understanding the activities and events that help in delivering the project promise, as well as outlining internal and external resource use. The entire project execution team looks at the WBS to inquire about present, past, and future deliverables and their effectiveness.

Due to the nature and importance of the WBS, its creation should not be taken lightly. It must be considered as the one element that all project participants might want to have considered when formulating an opinion.

Cram Quiz

Answer these questions. The answers follow the last question. If you cannot answer these questions correctly, consider reading this section again until you can.

1. The change control system is a subsystem of what?

   ○ **A.** Configuration management

   ○ **B.** Project management

   ○ **C.** Risk management

   ○ **D.** Scope management

2. Approved change requests can cause a change to which of the following project elements?

   ○ **A.** Scope

   ○ **B.** Quality

   ○ **C.** Schedule

   ○ **D.** All of the above

3. Which of the following best describes the monitor and control project work process?

    ○ **A.** Tracking, reviewing, and regulating the progress made toward fulfilling project objectives

    ○ **B.** Performing the work defined in the project management plan

    ○ **C.** Reviewing change requests, approving change requests, and managing changes to the project

    ○ **D.** Monitoring the status of the project and product scope, as well as changes to the scope baseline

4. Which of the following is NOT a valid output of the validate scope process?

    ○ **A.** Accepted deliverables

    ○ **B.** Project management plan updates

    ○ **C.** Change requests

    ○ **D.** Project document updates

Cram Quiz Answers

1. Answer A is the correct response. The change control system is a subsystem of the configuration management system and, according to the PMBOK, is defined as "a collection of formal documented procedures that define how project deliverables and documentation will be controlled, changed, and approved."

2. Answer D is the best response. Approved change requests can cause a change to project scope, project quality, and project schedule.

3. Answer A is the best response. The monitor and control project work process tracks, reviews, and regulates the progress made toward fulfilling the project objectives. Answer B is incorrect because it describes the direct and manage project work process. Answer C is incorrect because it describes the perform integrated change control process. Answer D is incorrect because it describes the control scope process.

4. Answer B is correct. Project management plan updates is an output of the control scope process. All other answers are valid outputs of the validate scope process.

Time, Cost, and Quality Management

▶ **Control Schedule—6.7**

▶ **Control Costs—7.4**

▶ **Control Quality—8.3**

CramSaver

If you can correctly answer these questions before going through this section, save time by skimming the Exam Alerts in this section and then completing the Cram Quiz at the end of the section.

1. What can you tell about a project with a CPI of 1.6?

   ○ **A.** A critical path index of 1.6 means the project is falling behind.

   ○ **B.** A central performance index of 1.6 means the project is running ahead of schedule.

   ○ **C.** A control performance index of 1.6 means the project is using fewer resources than anticipated.

   ○ **D.** A cost performance index of 1.6 means the project is consuming fewer resources than anticipated.

2. What does an SPI of 1.6 mean?

   ○ **A.** Each resource assigned to the project costs 1.6 units.

   ○ **B.** A scope performance index of 1.6 suggests that the project is running ahead of the schedule.

   ○ **C.** A schedule performance index of 1.6 suggests that the project is running ahead of the schedule.

   ○ **D.** None of the above

3. Which of the following is NOT an output of the control quality process?

   ○ **A.** Quality metrics

   ○ **B.** Validated changes

   ○ **C.** Validated deliverables

   ○ **D.** Change requests

Answers

1. Answer D is correct. A cost performance index of 1 or greater suggests that the project is delivering more with less money.

2. Answer C is correct. A schedule performance index of 1 or greater suggests that the project is ahead of schedule.

3. Answer A is correct. Quality metrics is an output of the plan quality process. All other answers are valid outputs of the control quality process.

After a project enters the executing phase, work is performed to produce the project's deliverables. All work should be performed according to the project schedule, budget, and quality standards. But is it? Is the project schedule accurate, and is the work being performed at the planned time? Is the project costing more than planned? Is the quality of the deliverables sufficient? These questions must be answered to keep the project on track. The processes in the time, cost, and quality management knowledge areas ensure that the project stays on schedule and on budget and that the project produces deliverables of the necessary quality.

Manage the Project Schedule and Budget

Two processes monitor and control how project work is progressing with respect to the project schedule and budget. The first process, control schedule, ensures that project work is being carried out according to the planned schedule. Table 7.5 shows the inputs, tools and techniques, and outputs for the control schedule process.

TABLE 7.5 **Control Schedule Inputs, Tools and Techniques, and Outputs**

Inputs	Tools and Techniques	Outputs
Project management plan	Performance reviews	Work performance information
Project schedule	Project management software	Schedule forecasts
Work performance data	Resource optimization techniques	Change requests
Project calendars	Modeling techniques	Project management plan updates
Schedule data	Leads and lags	Project documents updates
Organizational process assets	Schedule compression	Organizational process assets updates
	Scheduling tool	

The control schedule process identifies any departures from the project schedule. What happens if work is falling behind? Your recourse is to implement corrective or preventive actions or a change request to align the project execution with its expected results and timelines.

ExamAlert

A *corrective* or *preventive action* is an action that is implemented to bring future project events and tasks into alignment with the project plan and its baseline.

Some options available at this time could be to

▶ Update the project baseline to reflect the current situation, using the documented change process.

▶ Level resources. When possible, reassign over-allocated resources to avoid schedule conflicts.

▶ Crash the schedule. Add people (internal/external) or resources to the tasks that have fallen behind and have a direct effect on the critical path; the downside is that this might cause unscheduled expenses.

▶ Fast track. Rearrange your activities to perform activities in parallel.

▶ Outsource the project or the affected part.

▶ Reduce the scope of the project.

The second process, control costs, ensures that the work is occurring within the project budget and identifies any variances early in the process. Table 7.6 shows the inputs, tools and techniques, and outputs for the control costs process.

TABLE 7.6 **Control Costs Inputs, Tools and Techniques, and Outputs**

Inputs	Tools and Techniques	Outputs
Project management plan	Earned value management	Work performance information
Project funding requirements	Forecasting	Cost forecasts
Work performance data	To-complete performance index (TCPI)	Change requests
Organizational process assets	Performance reviews	Project management plan updates
	Project management software	Project documents updates
	Reserve analysis	Organizational process assets updates

The control costs process identifies any areas that are costing more than planned. As a project moves toward completion, the value of the project's deliverables changes. The "value" of a project at any point in time is known as its earned value. One method of comparing the earned value of a project to the budget is earned value analysis.

> **Note**
>
> What is earned value analysis? *Earned value analysis* in its simplest form is the value of the work performed to date against the project baseline expectations. The steps to calculating earned value (and other project-related values) are covered in the "Identifying Variance with Earned Value Management" section, later in this chapter.

Remember that the whole idea behind a corrective or preventive action is to help preserve the healthy execution of your project and maximize its resource utilization.

The following are some of the items used to measure and keep control of the schedule and cost variances:

Item	Description
Planned value or budgeted cost of work scheduled (BCWS)	The budgeted cost of the work according to the schedule.
Budgeted at completion	The project baseline cost.
Earned value	The value of the work performed to date against the project schedule. Use the formula % completed * budgeted at completion
Actual cost or actual cost of work performed (ACWP)	The cost of the work performed to date.
Scheduled variance	The earned value less the planned value.
Cost variance	The earned value less the actual cost.
Cost performance index	The result from dividing the earned value by the actual cost. A result less than one suggests that the project is at budget risk.
Scheduled performance index	The result of dividing the earned value by the planned value. A result less than one suggests that the project is at schedule risk.
Estimate at completion	The result of dividing the budget at completion into the cost performance index.
Estimated to completion	The result of subtracting the estimate at completion from the actual cost.
Variance at completion	The result of subtracting the estimate at completion from the budget at completion.

Identifying Variance with Earned Value Management

Earned value analysis is a tool used to help in identifying how well a team is performing and where the project might end up in comparison to the project plan. It was initially conceived by the U.S. Department of Defense (DoD) as a tool to standardize the way contractors report on the progress of their assigned projects.

The three key variables involved in the project earned value analysis are

▶ Budgeted cost for work scheduled (BCWS)

▶ Budgeted cost for work performed (BCWP)

▶ Actual cost for work performed (ACWP)

ExamAlert

BCWS is also referred to as planned value. The total BCWS or planned value for a project can be called the *budget at completion* (*BAC*).

ACWP is also referred to as *actual cost* (*AC*).

BCWP is also referred to as *earned value* (*EV*).

To successfully report on earned value management, your project must have a well-defined WBS and an effective task planned versus actual performance reporting system.

A basic utilization example is as follows:

The budgeted cost for work scheduled (BCWS) is the planned value of the work according to the project budget. The BCWS of a project with 12 milestones and 144 work packages is $200,000, and the cost for every 3 milestones has been estimated to be $50,000.

The actual cost for work performed (ACWP) is how much you really have incurred in the project. In this example, you are at milestone 6, and the project has used $80,000; therefore, your ACWP is $80,000.

The budgeted cost for work performed (BCWP) is the value of how much work has been completed. So while your ACWP is $80,000, your BCWP is $100,000.

Armed with this information, you can determine derivative calculations such as the schedule performance index (SPI) and the cost performance index (CPI). In this example, it would be

SPI	=	EV / PV (BCWP / BCWS)
	=	(100,000 / 200,000
	=	.5 (Your project is behind schedule.)
CPI	=	EV / AC (BCWP / ACWP)
	=	(100,000 / 80,000)
	=	1.25 (Your project is using less money than expected.)

Control Quality

In the project context, quality is not only defined as delivering the right thing at the right time and at the right cost but also delivering to customer expectations. Therefore, you, the project manager, have to ensure that the required metrics, tolerances, reports, and checklists are in place to ensure that a quality-prone execution and delivery sandbox is in place. The control quality process enables a project manager to assess the level of quality of a project's deliverables and take any required action. Table 7.7 shows the inputs, tools and techniques, and outputs for the control quality process.

TABLE 7.7 **Control Quality Inputs, Tools and Techniques, and Outputs**

Inputs	Tools and Techniques	Outputs
Project management plan	Seven basic quality tools	Quality control measurements
Quality metrics	Statistical sampling	Validated changes
Quality checklists	Inspection	Verified deliverables
Work performance data	Approved change requests review	Work performance information
Approved change requests		Change requests
Deliverables		Project management plan updates
Project documents		Project documents updates
Organizational process assets		Organizational process assets updates

ExamAlert

Some of the tools available to a project manager in controlling quality are

▶ The Ishikawa (also called the fishbone or cause-and-effect) diagram

▶ Control charts, such as the ones available using Three Sigma or Six Sigma:

    ▶ Six Sigma—99.99% defect free, or about 0.002 defective parts per million

    ▶ Three Sigma—99.73% defect free, or about 2,700 defective parts per million

▶ Pareto charts (the 80/20 rule)

▶ Statistical sampling, such as that used in the standard audit processes

Diagrams and Charts Used to Measure Quality Control

The three diagrams that follow are typically used to help monitor quality control:

▶ **Ishikawa diagram**—This diagram type can be easily identified because it resembles fishbones. It is used to determine the root cause of a defect (see Figure 7.2).

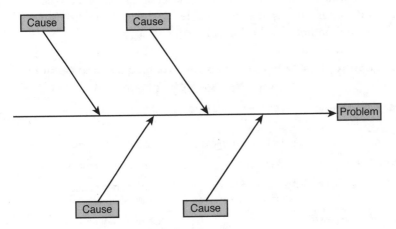

FIGURE 7.2 **Cause-and-effect diagram.**

Remember that a product or task defect is a symptom, but not the cause, of the problem. A fishbone diagram is effective in graphically displaying what might be causing a problem at the end of the production line.

▶ **Control chart**—A control chart is a statistical tool used to identify process points that are outside the normal flow of a process. They help to graphically display process execution boundaries, trending, and overall performance over time (see Figure 7.3).

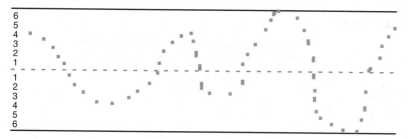

FIGURE 7.3 **Trending and performance control chart.**

▶ **Pareto chart**—Vilfredo Pareto postulated that the distribution of income and wealth follows a regular logarithmic pattern where 20% of the population controls 80% of the wealth. Subsequently in 1937, Dr. Joseph M. Juran adapted Pareto's economic observations to business applications, which he called the "vital few and trivial many." Translated to project terms, 80% of the problems are caused by 20% of the activities. This is called the *80/20 rule*, and a Pareto chart reflects this rule (see Figure 7.4).

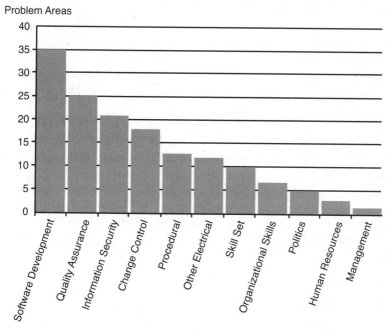

FIGURE 7.4 **Pareto chart displaying an error trend in a software development project.**

Cram Quiz

Answer these questions. The answers follow the last question. If you cannot answer these questions correctly, consider reading this section again until you can.

1. The activity that is most concerned with the current status of the project schedule is

   ○ **A.** Project time management

   ○ **B.** Project risk management

   ○ **C.** Monitoring and controlling

   ○ **D.** Control schedule

   ○ **E.** Both C and D

2. The Ishikawa diagram, control chart, Pareto chart, and statistical sampling are examples of tools used in

   ○ **A.** The assure quality process

   ○ **B.** The control quality process

   ○ **C.** Six Sigma

   ○ **D.** None of the above

3. The most commonly used performance measure for evaluating whether work is being completed as planned at any given point in a project is which of the following?

   ○ **A.** Cost variance (CV)

   ○ **B.** Schedule variance (SV)

   ○ **C.** Both A and B

   ○ **D.** Neither A nor B

4. You're managing a project using the earned value technique (EVT) for cost management. The project planned value (PV) is $200,000. The project earned value (EV) is $100,000. The actual value (AV) is $150,000. What is the cost variance (CV) for the project?

   ○ **A.** 100,000

   ○ **B.** –100,000

   ○ **C.** 50,000

   ○ **D.** –50,000

Cram Quiz Answers

1. Answer D is correct. One of the control schedule deliverables is to determine the current status of the project schedule.

2. Answer B is correct. The Ishikawa diagram, control chart, Pareto chart, and statistical sampling are examples of basic tools of the control quality process.

3. Answer C is the best response. The most commonly used performance measures for evaluating whether work is being completed as planned at any given time in a project are cost variance (CV) and schedule variance (SV). Answers A and B are both individually correct, but Answer C is the best answer. Answer D is incorrect.

4. Answer D is the correct response. Cost variance (CV) is calculated by subtracting the actual cost (AC) from the earned value (EV): CV = EV − AV. In the example given, the AC is $150,000, and the EV is $100,000. Therefore, $100,000 − $150,000 = −$50,000. Answer A is incorrect. Answer B is the schedule variance (SV), not the CV, so it is incorrect. Answer C is incorrect.

Communications, Risk, Procurement, and Stakeholder Management

▶ **Control Communications—10.3**

▶ **Control Risks—11.6**

▶ **Control Procurements—12.3**

▶ **Control Stakeholder Engagement—13.4**

CramSaver

If you can correctly answer these questions before going through this section, save time by skimming the Exam Alerts in this section and then completing the Cram Quiz at the end of the section.

1. What is the communication channel delta if the stakeholders are increased from 4 to 11?

   ○ **A.** 6

   ○ **B.** 49

   ○ **C.** 55

   ○ **D.** 109

2. In general, performance reporting takes into account information from the following areas EXCEPT

   ○ **A.** Scope

   ○ **B.** Schedule

   ○ **C.** Execution

   ○ **D.** Cost

   ○ **E.** Quality

3. Which of the following is NOT a tool and technique of the control risks process?

   ○ **A.** Risk audits

   ○ **B.** Variance and trend analysis

   ○ **C.** Contingent response strategies

   ○ **D.** Reserve analysis

4. Which of the following best describes the control procurements process?

  ○ **A.** Obtaining seller responses, selecting a seller, and awarding a contract

  ○ **B.** Managing procurement relationships, monitoring contract performance, and making necessary changes

  ○ **C.** Reviewing change requests, approving change requests, and managing changes to the project

  ○ **D.** Documenting purchasing decisions, specifying the approach, and selecting potential sellers

Answers

1. Answer B is correct. The communication channels calculation is $(n * (n - 1)) / 2$. In this case, the initial number of communication channels is 6, and the second is 55. Therefore, $55 - 6 = 49$.

2. Answer C is correct. Project performance reporting takes into account trending and exceptions in the project scope, schedule, cost, and quality.

3. Answer C is correct. Contingent response strategies is a tool and technique of the plan risk responses process. All other answers are valid tools and techniques of the control risks process.

4. Answer B is the best response. The control procurements process manages procurement relationships, monitors contract performance, and makes necessary changes. Answer A is incorrect because it describes the conduct procurements process. Answer C is incorrect because it describes the perform integrated change control process. Answer D is incorrect because it describes the plan procurement management process.

The remaining processes in the monitoring and controlling process group provide a project manager with tools and direction for assessing project communication, risk, procurement, and stakeholders. These processes complete the description of how the project manager ensures that the project is operating as intended.

Communicating How a Project Is Performing

Communicating with the project team and the outside world is one of the project manager's primary jobs. As a communicator, a project manager must understand the mechanics involved in sending a message. This process involves an initiator, encoding of the message, sending of the message, and a receiver who decodes the message, acknowledges the message, and confirms receipt of the message. It is important to maintain open communication with the stakeholders to provide timely and informative updates on the project's progress. The control communications process addresses issues with communicating with the stakeholders. Table 7.8 shows the inputs, tools and techniques, and outputs for the control communications process.

TABLE 7.8 **Control Communications Inputs, Tools and Techniques, and Outputs**

Inputs	Tools and Techniques	Outputs
Project management plan	Information management systems	Work performance information
Project communications	Expert judgment	Change requests
Issue log	Meetings	Project management plan updates
Work performance data		Project documents updates
Organizational process assets		Organizational process assets updates

In the normal exchange of information with the stakeholders, the project manager will use methods and techniques that help with formal and informal communication. Formal methods include items such as contracts, status reports, public speeches, and performance appraisals. Informal methods are those such as "the scuttlebutt," email, and telephone conversations.

ExamAlert

One way to determine how complex communication will be in a project is to determine its communication channels by using the formula $(n * (n - 1)) / 2$, where n represents the number of participants in a project. For example, a project with 10 participants will require 45 communication channels: $(10 * 9) / 2 = 90 / 2 = 45$.

With this in mind, it is important to adjust a message and its delivery method based on the audience and the level of impact the project might have on the individuals with whom the project manager is communicating. For example, consider a board member versus the person doing the work. For the worker, getting information about revenue projections and return on investment might be of little or no consequence in her daily duties. However, providing figures on how many additional widgets can be made in an hour would definitely have an impact on her duties and equipment maintenance cycles.

In addition, the project manager must be aware that when delivering a message, nonverbal communication and physical appearance have a direct effect on the message delivered. For example, the project manager delivers a message to a construction team. It's important to ensure that language and colloquialisms used are appropriate to the group. Bear in mind, though, that the same approach might not work when giving a project update to the company senior team. It is important to ensure that the message and intentions are clearly understood by the audience who is the target of the message.

Examples of common tools used to communicate are a budget, a contract, a teleconference, and a chart.

Control Risks

The control risks process enables a project manager to keep track of how risk responses are performing against the plan, as well as the place where new risks to the project are managed.

> **Note**
>
> There could be cases in which risk might be identified as having a material impact on the enterprise but not on the project. For these risk types, the project must allow for an alternative communication path that forwards alerts to the people in enterprise risk management functions. In addition, the project manager must remember that risks can have negative and positive effects. For example, consider a project for a bridge that interconnects two roads with a max traffic flow of 10,000 cars and 300 tons. A weather event forces a traffic change from other roads, which doubles the capacity requirements for the bridge for at least 18 months after project completion. Although this wrinkle does not directly affect the project's deliverable, it is important to consider the new information. In this case, the added traffic could affect the life span and performance of the deliverable after delivery.

Table 7.9 shows the inputs, tools and techniques, and outputs for the control risks process.

TABLE 7.9 Control Risks Inputs, Tools and Techniques, and Outputs

Inputs	Tools and Techniques	Outputs
Project management plan	Risk assessment	Work performance information
Risk register	Risk audits	Change requests
Work performance data	Variance and trend analysis	Project management plan updates

Inputs	Tools and Techniques	Outputs
Work performance reports	Technical performance measurement	Project documents updates
	Reserve analysis	Organizational process assets updates
	Meetings	

Remember that to determine how much of an effect a risk will have, you multiply its probability by its material impact. As the probability of risk materialization increases, the risk register should make resource (money, equipment, people, and time) allocations ahead of time, thus increasing reserves. It is also important that the risk management plan include the processes that would replenish these reserves before they become depleted.

The purpose of project risk control is to

▶ Identify the events that can have a direct effect on the project deliverables

▶ Assign qualitative and quantitative weight—the probability and consequences of events that might impact the project deliverables

▶ Produce alternate paths of execution for events that are out of your control or cannot be mitigated

▶ Implement a continuous process for identifying, qualifying, quantifying, and responding to new risks

ExamAlert

The utility theory, or utility function, assigns subjective value to a management decision in risk mitigation strategies in uncertain conditions.

The risk register accounts for positive and negative risks. A positive risk is a risk that a project takes because its potential benefits are greater than those of the traditional approach. A negative risk is one that could negatively influence the cost of the project or its schedule.

One of the techniques to evaluate risk control and monitoring effectiveness is to compare actual risk resolution practices to those that were planned at the time the risk was identified. Any deviations (negative or positive) would be cause to implement a corrective action in the risk management plan.

> **Note**
>
> Risk triggers are events that cause the threat of a risk to become a reality. For example, say that you have identified the fact that you have only one water pump station available and the replacement takes six weeks to arrive. In the middle of your irrigation and recycling process tests, you discover that water pressure tends to fluctuate beyond pump tolerance levels. If you do not find a way to solve this problem, your risk will become a reality.

Remember that for each identified risk, it is important to provide a response plan. It is not much help if a risk becomes a reality and there is no alternate execution path or emergency procurement plan.

> **Note**
>
> Business risks and pure risks are different because a pure risk takes into account impacts on loss of financial profits, and a business risk concentrates on events that might cause a company to lose position with its investors or to have financial difficulty.

In addition, the risk reserves must be evaluated to determine the best way to replenish them. Some examples of events that could have negative impacts in your risk mitigation and control strategies are

▶ Resource shortage

▶ Scope creep

▶ Contractual issues

▶ Lack of key resources availability

Control Procurements

The *control procurements* process is the blueprint for managing the procurements process and making any changes necessary. It is the process of comparing vendor or service performance to the contractual service-level agreements (SLAs). Due to its implications and its potential effect across several sections of a project or enterprise, all team members must be aware of the legal ramifications of any change in the contractual relationship. In addition, project-vendor disbursements tend to tie the SLAs, or performance agreements, and deliverables to direct cash expenditures.

> **Note**
>
> At all costs, you must avoid any undocumented or unapproved cash disbursements or changes that might go against your project deliverables.

Table 7.10 shows the inputs, tools and techniques, and outputs for the control procurements process.

TABLE 7.10 Control Procurements Inputs, Tools and Techniques, and Outputs

Inputs	Tools and Techniques	Outputs
Project management plan	Contract change control system	Work performance information
Procurement documents	Procurement performance reviews	Change requests
Agreements	Inspections and audits	Project management plan updates
Approved change requests	Performance reporting	Project document updates
Work performance reports	Payment systems	Organizational process asset updates
Work performance data	Claims administration	
	Records management system	

In general, the project procurements administrator is from the procurement management office and/or legal department and has the authority to issue change requests or early terminations.

Remember that all communications pertaining to procurement administration must follow formal channels and be logged in your project log.

Your procurement administration process should include mechanisms that allow for contract renegotiation, management response, and payment terms definitions.

Control Stakeholder Engagement

The *control stakeholder engagement* process is one of the new processes introduced in the *PMBOK Guide*, Fifth Edition. This process focuses on monitoring the relationships between stakeholders and the project. In addition to simply monitoring stakeholder relationships, the process also provides for adjusting plans and strategies necessary to keep stakeholders effectively engaged throughout a project's life cycle.

Table 7.11 shows the inputs, tools and techniques, and outputs for the control stakeholder engagement process.

TABLE 7.11 **Control Stakeholder Engagement Inputs, Tools and Techniques, and Outputs**

Inputs	Tools and Techniques	Outputs
Project management plan	Information management systems	Work performance information
Issue log	Expert judgment	Change requests
Work performance data	Meetings	Project management plan updates
Project documents		Project documents updates
		Organizational process assets updates

Although you may see references to stakeholders in the project communications management knowledge area, pay particular attention to the processes in the project stakeholder management knowledge area. Any activities specifically related to interacting with stakeholders are addressed by processes in this knowledge area.

Cram Quiz

Answer these questions. The answers follow the last question. If you cannot answer these questions correctly, consider reading this section again until you can.

1. Before risk mitigation can occur, what two processes must be accomplished?

   ○ **A.** Acceptance and delivery requirements

   ○ **B.** Identification and trigger recognition

   ○ **C.** Phasing and interactions

   ○ **D.** Quantitative analysis and qualitative

   ○ **E.** None of the above

2. Which of the following is NOT an output of the control risks process?

   ○ **A.** Change requests

   ○ **B.** Work performance information

   ○ **C.** Risk-related contract decisions

   ○ **D.** Project document updates

3. Which of the following processes utilizes inspections as a tool or technique?

   ○ **A.** Perform integrated change control

   ○ **B.** Control schedule

   ○ **C.** Control risks

   ○ **D.** Control procurements

4. Which of the following is NOT a tool and technique of the manage communications process?

   ○ **A.** Variance analysis

   ○ **B.** Interpersonal skills

   ○ **C.** Forecasting methods

   ○ **D.** Communication methods

Cram Quiz Answers

1. Answer B is correct. Before risks can be mitigated, you need to know how probable is it that they will occur and what their triggering events are.

2. Answer C is correct. Risk-related contract decisions is not an output of the control risks process. Change requests, work performance information, and project document updates are all outputs of the control risks process.

3. Answer D is correct. Of the processes listed, only control procurements utilizes inspections and audits as a tool or technique. None of the other processes utilize inspections. Of all the 47 processes, validate scope and control quality also utilize inspection.

4. Answer B is correct. Interpersonal skills is a tool and technique of the manage stakeholder engagement process. All the other answers are valid tools and techniques of the manage communications process.

What Next?

If you want more practice on this chapter's exam topics before you move on, remember that you can access all of the Cram Quiz questions on the CD. You can also create a custom exam by topic with the practice exam software. Note any topic you struggle with and go to that topic's material in this chapter.

CHAPTER 8

Explain Project Closing

This chapter covers the following PMP exam topics:

▶ Close Project or Phase—4.6

▶ Close Procurements—12.4

(For more information on the official PMP exam topics, see "About the PMP Exam" in the Introduction.)

The closing process group accounts for 8% of the PMP exam. *Closing* is where you formally end a project phase or the entire project, release all the resources that were assigned to the project, and build reference material for future projects. In addition, this is the process group where all plans are compared to actual performance data. The road to this point is about keeping focus, control, and processes optimization. Project closing ensures that the other side of the bell curve of execution looks the same way as when you started the process. Simply put, this is where the project manager wraps up the project and ties up all the loose ends.

The Closing Process Group

▶ **Close Project or Phase—4.6**

▶ **Close Procurements—12.4**

CramSaver

If you can correctly answer these questions before going through this section, save time by skimming the Exam Alerts in this section and then completing the Cram Quiz at the end of the section.

1. Part of the project closure process is to gain formal acceptance. From whom do you need to gain this formal acceptance?

   ○ **A.** The quality director

   ○ **B.** The head of the project management office

   ○ **C.** The project sponsor

   ○ **D.** The customer

   ○ **E.** Both C and D

2. Which one of these is NOT an input to the close project or phase process?

   ○ **A.** Project management plan

   ○ **B.** Expert judgment

   ○ **C.** Accepted deliverables

   ○ **D.** Organizational process assets

3. Which of the following is NOT a tool and technique of the close procurements process?

   ○ **A.** Procurement audits

   ○ **B.** Procurement negotiations

   ○ **C.** Procurement performance reviews

   ○ **D.** Records management system

Answers

1. **Answer E is correct.** Formal acceptance is the formal confirmation from the sponsor or the customer that the product or service delivered by the project meets the project deliverables. Remember that in the PMI realm, all of a project's products and services must comply with the project objectives and deliverables and must be accepted by the project client and the project sponsor.

2. **Answer B is correct.** The inputs for the close project or phase process are the project management plan, accepted deliverables, and organizational process assets. Answer B pertains to the tools and techniques of the close project or phase process, which include expert judgment.

3. **Answer C is correct.** Procurement performance reviews is a tool and technique of the control procurements process. Answers A, B, and D are all valid tools and techniques of the close procurements process.

Look at it from this perspective: If you would have known everything that you know today about your project(s) when you started, would you have done things the same way? Would you have used the same resources?

Of course, probably by now you are thinking, "What a joke. We are not born experts. How am I supposed to know when to do what and how to avoid execution problems?" This is where trusted consultants and an experienced project manager come into play; they help in identifying what pitfalls to avoid.

One of the key recurring messages of the PMI methodology is to leverage expert resources and to use the project archives; executing the proper closing process ensures that the groundwork for your own internal expert resource and knowledge base is built, combining the knowledge and experience of your people, culture, and enterprise.

This process takes into account the needs for documentation and the understanding of the associated risks, the risks analysis techniques, and the decision-making process.

Figure 8.1 depicts the general close project process flow.

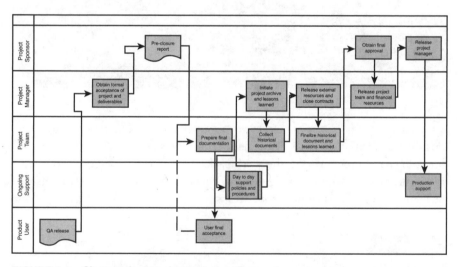

FIGURE 8.1 **Close project or phase process flow.**

> **ExamAlert**
>
> What is a project deliverable? A *project deliverable* is a specific, quantifiable product or service that is attained after the completion of a project phase or a project.

Table 8.1 shows the inputs, tools and techniques, and outputs for the close project or phase process.

TABLE 8.1 **Close Project or Phase Inputs, Tools and Techniques, and Outputs**

Inputs	Tools and Techniques	Outputs
Project management plan	Expert judgment	Final product, service, or result transition
Accepted deliverables	Analytical techniques	Organizational process assets updates
Organizational process assets	Meetings	

The key input elements for the close project or phase process are

▶ Project management plan

▶ Accepted deliverables

ExamAlert

For PMP exam purposes, you must remember that the close project or phase process and close procurements process are both processes of the closing process group and that the close procurements process happens *before* the close project or phase process.

Why have these been designated as key input elements? The intent is to take this time to verify that all of the project deliverables are met. Use the work breakdown structure (WBS), the work packages, and the packages' resource assignments as a roadmap to identify any remaining critical work elements to be completed and ensure the proper transitions.

Note

A *work package* is the lowest descriptive level of work in a WBS.

If there are any unfinished tasks, you need to make arrangements to prepare their termination plan and measure their combined risk materiality against the long-term viability of the project, services, and deliverables.

For example, one of the contracts calls for the return of all graphite composite containers to the lease company within 30 days of project completion. Your job as project manager is to issue all the proper closeout work orders and see that these containers are returned to the provider on time. Does this task have anything to do with the long-term functionality of your project? Probably not. However, if it is not addressed by the deadline, it has the potential of affecting your company at a potentially high annual cost.

This process must be repeated throughout the entire work package dictionary to ensure that deliverables are in line with the project and the performance metrics that you assigned to the service provider.

One of the most important realizations in the project management process should be that the project does not stop when the end is in sight or the product or services are delivered. If anything, this is where you need to concentrate and make sure that all tasks and their peripheral activities are completed. Examples of some of these activities are

▶ Client or user final acceptance

▶ Updates to all pertaining historical records

▶ Transitions to ongoing support

▶ Release of all project resources

▶ Final signoff and release from the project sponsor

Close Procurements

At project build-up, you might have been faced with the need to have extra capacity by bringing in external resources. The close procurements process is the place where you accept delivery of the product and close the corresponding procurement agreements.

> **Note**
>
> One thing to remember is that this process also applies to any company internal contract or agreements that might have been arranged in order to leverage internal business expertise or processes.

For example, say that you work for a multinational company that decides to leverage its internal expertise in building bridges over long water bodies by combining the resources from the steel and cement business units with its engineering unit. In addition to coordinating the building of the bridge, you are now faced with the challenge of having to orchestrate all the intercompany contracts, expenses, and revenue-generating models in order to ensure the proper level of synergies.

This isn't any different from using external resources; however, you need to pay close attention to the human factor. The *human factor* refers to any cultural and personal differences between your culture and the inbound resources.

Another example for contract management might include a combination of internal, external, and outsourced relationships. These relationships might call for a different set of closing instructions that depend on the type of relationship. For example, relationships that exist within a single organization are different from outsourced relationships. Likewise, closing procedures are apt to be different.

Table 8.2 shows the inputs, tools and techniques, and outputs for the close procurements process.

TABLE 8.2 Close Procurements Inputs, Tools and Techniques, and Outputs

Inputs	Tools and Techniques	Outputs
Project management plan	Procurement audits	Closed procurements
Procurement documents	Procurement negotiations	Organizational process asset updates
	Records management system	

As per the PMI methodology, the formal outputs of the close procurements process are

- ▶ Closed procurements
- ▶ Organizational process assets (updates)

Of course, this also means that you are part of contract negotiation and interpretation, thus requiring a special dose of leadership and management techniques in an environment with multiple moving parts.

For closing procurements, you need to be well aware of your vendor's or provider's

- ▶ Performance metrics
- ▶ Assigned work packages

▶ Deliverables

▶ Schedule performance

▶ Quality control metrics

▶ If applicable, inspection reports pertaining to regulatory requirements

In addition, you need to address items such as

▶ Consideration to perform product or service verification which ensures that all work was completed in accordance with the service-level agreements (SLAs) and the deliverables specified in the contract

▶ Review of contract terms and conditions in the event that the product is not delivered to specifications

▶ Enabling of early terminations clauses and remediation due to the vendor's inability to deliver the product, agreed budget being exceeded, or failure to assign the required resources

Note

When it comes to contracts, you must be aware that in the PMI world, there are several types of contracts: *cost reimbursable*, *fixed price* or *lump sum*, *time and material*, and *unit price*.

ExamAlert

Early contract terminations can result from a mutual agreement or may be due to a failure to fulfill the contract deliverables. Early termination can occur at any time during a project.

What does it mean to be faced with an early termination? It all goes back to your contract, the execution clauses that were stipulated at the beginning of the business relationship, and the parameters for contract termination and vendor replacement plan.

The *vendor replacement plan* refers to the implementation of an alternate path for future project fulfillment needs. If you don't have an alternate path, a good place to start is to consider second and third runners-up in your original selection process.

A way to effectively measure how well a contract might have served your project is to take into account the following:

▶ Activities to be performed in a project or a project phase

▶ Supporting schedules for time, deliverables, and cost

▶ Issue log and issue management plan

▶ Project delivery metrics

▶ Invoice and payment register

> **ExamAlert**
>
> A *procurement audit* provide a structured review of the processes and practices involved in resource planning and acquisition. These audits can also be used to identify and evaluate deviations in regard to materiality and risk analysis of future procurement activities.

After all contractual agreement clauses are satisfied and you have delivered the provider execution report card, a company representative executes the stipulated documents to signify that the contract was completed and executed according to agreed specifications.

Closing a Project or Phase Criteria

Everyone hopes for successful project completion, but the cold hard reality is that on occasion, some projects are presented with challenges from their inception up to their ultimate demise. Some of the outside reasons that can trigger an early termination could be linked to elements such as

▶ **Market conditions**—The company or client may be forced to discontinue a project simply because the initiative is no longer in line with the long-term market share or presence objectives.

▶ **Customer requirements**—Your client may decide to implement changes that are well beyond the capabilities of the current initiative, making it cost-prohibitive to tackle the project at this time.

▶ **Insufficient resources**—You may not have the people, money, facilities, supplies, and so on to complete a project.

▶ **Technical problems**—In the project management arena, technical problems go beyond computers. Technical problems could include things such as variances in the density of the material used in a building or the inability to devise a way to hold the insulation in a space shuttle's main fuel tank.

▶ **Enterprise culture**—A project and its product or services may contradict the culture of the company. For example, say that a company is known for its face-to-face customer service practices and, after implementing a test of self-service point-of-sale checkout lines, discovers that implementing this initiative has a direct impact on customer perception.

▶ **Bankruptcy**—If your client or company will not gain a cash position or additional market share by implementing your project, the project may be cancelled.

Even in these instances, you must ensure a successful transition by leading your project toward project closing criteria elements, which include

▶ The formal acceptance of the project results or product by your customer

▶ Documentation and forms resulting from organizational requirements

▶ Project performance metrics and reports

▶ Budget expenditures

▶ Cost–benefit metrics and verifications

▶ Lessons learned

Think of the project closing criteria as those elements that give reasonable assurance that your project took into account the initial deliverables, the client, and sponsor approval.

In addition, this process works closely with the communication management and procurement management plans to formalize the ending of your project.

Some of the key participants in this process are

▶ **Project sponsor**—This person gives final validation that the project's services and products are in line with the original objectives and deliverables of the project before the official handoff to the client and the operational support team takes place.

▶ **Project manager**—This person keeps coordinating the execution of the communication, procurement, human resources, cost management, and quality plans until the project is officially closed. The project manager then turns over all the archives.

▶ **Team members**—These people assist the project manager in performing the aforementioned tasks, plus assist in transitioning the new product or service to operational support.

▶ **Quality assurance team**—These people ensure that all work adheres to agreed project quality expectations and deliverables.

ExamAlert

Formal acceptance is a binding process between a customer and a seller (provider) of a product or service that the product or service has been accepted. Its form and contents are predicated on the service agreement or negotiated in the contract.

Note

Why is formal acceptance important? If during the execution and control processes the project acceptance criteria changed but the documentation did not, this could be the place where you update all your records to represent the final product. It is important that project acceptance and procurement closing be documented and signed by the project sponsor.

The key item to remember when preparing for closing a project or phase is that the actual project criteria plan and requirement definition began the day that the project charter and the project scope were defined and agreed upon by the client, sponsor, and the rest of the project team.

You need to make sure that there is an effective transition between what was agreed upon at the beginning of a project and what was delivered and accepted by the client.

Lessons Learned

Contrary to popular practice, lessons learned should be part of all phases of a project and recorded as they occur. Do not confuse this with the postmortem connotation used by some project managers. If you follow that approach, you might miss the opportunity to write down important elements that might prove essential in future projects.

Why make lessons learned important throughout the project? An out-of-context example would be not writing down the license plate and color of a car involved in a hit and run; the more time that passes, the less clarity you have about the details.

The main intent of the lessons learned is to help build an information store that allows anyone in your company to look back in time and understand the decisions made and the circumstances that surrounded the decision-making process.

Some of the triggering events for lessons learned records are

▶ Significant course corrections are implemented.

▶ Corrective or preventive actions are taken.

▶ Scope changing events occur.

▶ Root cause analysis occurs for variances between planned and actual project events.

You must make every effort to be extremely honest and include items that performed well and those that did not. You must highlight individuals involved in the process and the risk factors considered at the time of making the decision. Some of the elements of this report might be

▶ Executive summary

▶ Project phase

▶ Related work package

▶ Event description

▶ Event duration

▶ Action taken

▶ Decision makers

▶ Results

▶ Areas of improvement

▶ Time stamp

> **Note**
>
> Do not make the mistake of confusing a project execution satisfaction survey with a lessons learned document; these two documents have different functions.

In addition to recording lessons learned, you must make every effort to collect any evidence and include it as part of the project archive.

> **ExamAlert**
>
> Ideally, lessons learned are included as part of the enterprise risk repository to assist with the risk identification, best practices, and mitigation strategies in future projects.

Ending a Procurement or a Project

Ending a procurement is not the same as ending a project. There might be cases where they coincide, but that is not to be expected as the normal behavior. You could have a case where a contract for a service ends but the project continues with another provider or project phase.

In contract execution, there are two actors: the buyer of goods and services and the seller of those goods and services. During the life of a project, contracts might end for one of the following reasons:

▶ **Successful completion**—Successful completion occurs when goods and services have been delivered in accordance with the contract specifications. At this point, no further action is required, with the exception of formal acceptance of the product or services and final payment.

▶ **Collective agreement**—This occurs when both parties agree to end the contract. A collective agreement or mutual consent termination allows you to present and negotiate contract closing terms, such as a no-cost settlement, payment of all fees and charges accrued prior to the effectiveness of the cancellation, and payment at a reduced cost by settlement.

For the most part, the parameters of what is available as recourse are specified in the contract by a paragraph that reads something like "This agreement may be terminated by either party at the renewal/anniversary date by giving the other party notice at least 15 days prior to the renewal/anniversary date of the Term. This Agreement may also be suspended or terminated by...."

You must issue your collective agreement notice for cancellation of services with something such as, "Pursuant to the termination section of the professional services agreement between client and provider, this contract is hereby terminated effective on *dd-mm-yy*. You are directed to cease all work upon presentment of this notice and start the close procurement process" (which you need to have defined by now).

▶ **When there is a breach**—In a breach of contract, one of the parties is not complying with the terms and specifications of the contract. A breach of contract or contract default situation requires immediate and special attention from legal counsel. Remember that the actions to take are as varied as the different clauses stipulated in the contract.

In addition, because good providers are difficult to find, executing a breach of contract procedure should be viewed as a last resort. Of course, it all depends on your long-term objectives with the relationship and the provider's willingness to solve the problem that caused the breach. For example, if a default occurs at the SLA level, your contract might allow you to consider mitigating factors and make adjustments to the SLA. Or you might be able to outsource, supplement, or augment the function in question at the provider's expense in order to deliver according to the SLA.

Another key element to consider is a cure or remediation period. Basically, this is a cooling-off period that allows the provider a specified amount of time to remediate the problem before taking any actions.

For contracts where the deliverables, products, and services go according to plan, the next step is to ensure that

▶ All issues have been resolved.

▶ All contract deliverables have been delivered and accepted by the client and the sponsor.

▶ The project manager gives final approval.

▶ All assets have been accounted for.

▶ Final payment has been issued.

Project contracts rarely go beyond the actual life of the project; project phases might end several times throughout the project, but there is only *one* project closing.

Some of the reasons a project might conclude are

▶ The company loses interest in the project and its deliverables.

▶ The company, project, or group is replaced or displaced.

▶ The project comes to a normal end after all the products and services are delivered.

▶ The project becomes its own organization, living beyond the end date as an organizational process.

▶ The project is replaced by another initiative.

ExamAlert

For test purposes, you need to be familiar with project conclusion states such as *extinction*, *inclusion*, *integration*, *starvation*, *addition*, *collapse*, *absorption*, and *deterioration*.

Another element to consider when processing a project closing is what to do with the team that was assigned to your project. A project might end, or terminate, in one of several states:

▶ **Integration mode**—A project that ends in integration mode has its resources assigned to other areas and integrated into the normal operations of the business. Most often they are reintegrated to the department or group from which they came.

One challenge to this project ending mode is that the responsibilities of the position could have been reassigned or replaced by new processes. This gives the returning team member the special opportunity to flex her muscles and take on new and more demanding responsibilities.

▶ **Extinction or collapsed mode**—A project that ends in extinction or collapsed mode is a project that ends before meeting its stated objectives. Simply stated, in this situation, people do not have a place to which to return.

▶ **Inclusion, absorption, or addition mode**—A project that ends in inclusion, absorption, or addition mode is a project that has been accepted and has transitioned to be part of the organization. With this type of project ending, your team members keep performing their assigned project functions as their new day-to-day responsibilities, maintaining the project performance in accordance to specifications.

▶ **Starvation or deterioration mode**—A project that ends in starvation or deterioration mode is a project for which all resources have been cut. Just an empty shell remains.

Note

From the PMBOK perspective, closing a contract is part of the project procurement management knowledge area, and closing a project is part of the project integration management knowledge area.

Final Review Meetings

When you have received final approval from the client and the sponsor, compiled the final set of reports, released all your team members, and delivered the project products and services, your next task is to meet with the project sponsor for the final review meeting. In this meeting, the project manager gets final release, receives project performance reports, and is able to return to the bench to wait for the next assignment.

The bench could be going back to your regular job or actually sitting in your company's project management office to oversee the final archiving steps and get a new assignment.

Cram Quiz

Answer these questions. The answers follow the last question. If you cannot answer these questions correctly, consider reading this section again until you can.

1. The primary output of the close project or phase process is

   ○ **A.** Formalize and distribute all information pertaining to the project closing

   ○ **B.** Lessons learned

   ○ **C.** Release all personnel assigned to the project

   ○ **D.** Get customer and sponsor approval

   ○ **E.** Both B and D

2. Which one of these is NOT an output of the close procurements process?

   ○ **A.** Closed procurements

   ○ **B.** Contract file

   ○ **C.** Lessons learned documentation

   ○ **D.** Organizational process assets updates

   ○ **E.** Both B and C

3. Lessons learned are

   ○ **A.** Best collected at the end of a project

   ○ **B.** Collected for the historical knowledge base

   ○ **C.** Necessary only at the end of a project

   ○ **D.** A store of historical information

   ○ **E.** Used to collect information about good and bad outcomes through-out a project

Cram Quiz Answers

1. Answer A is correct. The primary output of the project closing process is to formalize and distribute all the information pertaining to the closing of the project. This coordinated message is distributed by administrative closure, contract closure procedure, final product, service, or result, and organizational process assets (updates).

2. Answer E is correct. The only two outputs of the close procurements process are closed procurements and organizational process asset updates.

3. Answer E is correct. Lessons learned are used to collect information pertaining to good and bad outcomes throughout project execution. If you look at the output sections of the PMI methodology, lessons learned are part of virtually all the execution processes.

What Next?

If you want more practice on this chapter's exam topics before you move on, remember that you can access all of the Cram Quiz questions on the CD. You can also create a custom exam by topic with the practice exam software. Note any topic you struggle with and go to that topic's material in this chapter.

PMP Practice Exam

Test-Taking Tips

When you sit for the PMP certification examination, there will be 200 multiple-choice questions, and you will have up to four hours to complete the examination. This breaks down to 50 questions per hour and gives you a little more than 1 minute per question. The practice exam included in this book is also 200 questions and simulates the questions you will see on the real exam. Not all questions require equal time. Don't agonize over every question. Read the question and each possible answer in its entirety prior to selecting an answer. Select the best answer to each question based on the response that seems to adhere to the PMBOK and PMI.

More than one answer might seem plausible and correct. Select the best answer from those provided rather than aiming for the "correct" answer. In some cases, multiple choices among the available answers might seem equally valid, so it is important to rule out obviously incorrect choices to narrow your options.

If more than one answer seems logical, look for an answer that includes both responses. Sometimes the exam presents choices such as "Both X and Y," "Neither X nor Y," "All of the above," and "None of the above." Just because a question has a choice that includes multiple answers does not mean it is the correct answer. Some of the choices can be tricky in this regard.

Many of the available choices include terminology, concepts, and processes endorsed by the PMBOK and PMI. Just because you recognize a term does not mean that it is the correct answer. The exam uses terms in similar contexts to ensure that you thoroughly understand and can apply the material. Be sure to read each question carefully to avoid any confusion about terminology or process names.

In your response to every test question, you should strive to select the best answer, based on how you believe PMI and the PMBOK would respond to the question and not necessarily from your own project management experience. The best answer as determined by PMI is provided as one of the four possible responses.

Be suspicious of answers offering definitive responses such as *never* and *always*. Some answers might tout non-PMI methods and reflect common project management misconceptions. Some answers might offer information that is correct but that is not pertinent to the question at hand and is simply included to confuse you. Similarly, some questions might contain factually correct information that has no bearing on the possible answers. If you do not have a firm grasp of the material and immediately know the best answer, you can waste valuable test time trying to figure out a way to use and apply irrelevant information. This is particularly tricky when mathematical calculations are requested in response to an examination question. Remember that the purpose of this exam is to measure your ability to understand and apply the PMI methodology, not your past experiences as a project manager. Whenever there is a discrepancy between your experience and the PMBOK, go with the PMBOK answer.

It is important to apply the same test conditions to taking this practice exam as you expect to experience on the day of the actual test. Be aware of your time to avoid having to rush at the end to complete the examination. You should leave adequate time to review any responses you are unsure of and/or to return to unanswered questions. If you are spending more than 1 minute on a question, it is better to skip over the question and mark it for review later than to agonize over the question and lose the opportunity to answer other questions to which you know the answers.

During the actual computerized exam, you can mark questions for later review and/or make multiple passes through the exam. Mark every question you are unsure of even if you have selected an answer. This approach saves you time when you review your responses because you do not need to review any unmarked questions. If on a second review you determine an answer, unmark the question. Continue this process of going through all the marked questions until they all have answers or you are nearing the end of the allotted time period.

Save the last 20 minutes or so of the test to finalize any unmarked answers and ensure that you have provided an answer to each question. For the practice test, if you adhere to the suggested 1-minute-per-question rule of thumb, you have 10 minutes to review your answers and respond to any marked questions. On the actual exam day, try to make a best guess by ruling out definitely wrong answers, as described earlier. Select an answer for each question even if you have to guess. Ruling out obviously wrong answers as discussed earlier is extremely valuable because it increases your chances of guessing from the remaining answers that are plausible. For example, if you can rule out two of four answers as obviously wrong, then you have a 50% chance of guessing the correct answer. There is no penalty for incorrect answers, so make sure to answer all questions if at all possible.

Exam Topics

The PMP certification examination tests for knowledge in the five project management process groups. In addition, questions that relate to the area of professional responsibility are included within each process group. The project management process groups are

▶ Initiating

▶ Planning

▶ Executing

▶ Monitoring and Controlling

▶ Closing

Exam Questions

1. You are a project manager working for a large utility company. You have managed many successful projects and have decided to pursue the PMP certification. After studying the processes in the monitoring and controlling process group, you find that the PMI processes differ a lot from the processes you currently use in your own organization. The processes your organization uses work very well, and you are confused about the PMI approach. To answer questions on the PMP exam, you should

   ○ **A.** Use your experience with managing projects, along with the information in the PMBOK.

   ○ **B.** Use your experience as a project manager to find the best answers.

   ○ **C.** Use the PMBOK as the primary resource and use your experience as a project manager to apply the PMBOK knowledge.

   ○ **D.** Use the PMBOK information only. No other information is relevant.

2. To study for the PMP exam, you decide to join a study group. At the first meeting, another student offers to share some "actual, live questions" from the PMP exam. What should you do?

   ○ **A.** Study with the real questions

   ○ **B.** Report the study group to PMI

   ○ **C.** Leave the study group

   ○ **D.** Find out where the student got the questions and report the source to PMI

3. While building your project team, you decide to include a business analyst with extensive experience in implementing, using, and managing tasks with the new chosen accounting software. This individual has managed and participated in other projects that are similar and knows how to work well with users, technical personnel, and management to get the software up and running. Your choice to include this individual is due to the fact he possesses expertise in which PMI knowledge area?

   ○ **A.** General management knowledge and skills

   ○ **B.** Interpersonal skills

   ○ **C.** Application area specific knowledge and standards

   ○ **D.** Software implementation

4. Which quality management tool would be used to determine potential causes of a production problem?

   ○ **A.** Control chart

   ○ **B.** Fishbone diagram

   ○ **C.** Scatter diagram

   ○ **D.** Histogram

5. Smoothing out resource requirements from period to period is called

○ **A.** Allocation

○ **B.** Partitioning

○ **C.** Leveling

○ **D.** Quantification

6. At what point in a project do you have the highest probability that it will fail?

○ **A.** The beginning of the project

○ **B.** After the initial project plan is published but before work actually begins

○ **C.** After the halfway point of the project is reached

○ **D.** Just before the end of the project

7. You have just completed the collect requirements and define scope processes. What should you do next?

○ **A.** Validate scope

○ **B.** Define activities

○ **C.** Create WBS

○ **D.** Control scope

8. You have just been assigned as the project manager for a new project. You have collected the necessary input information and delivered the project charter to the stakeholders. What should you do next?

○ **A.** Develop the project scope statement

○ **B.** Get the project charter signed

○ **C.** Start the initial project planning process

○ **D.** Ask the stakeholders for resources

9. Which of the following activities is NOT concerned with identifying areas in which changes are required?

○ **A.** Perform integrated change control

○ **B.** Manage communications

○ **C.** Control schedule

○ **D.** Control quality

10. Which of the following is the same as a lump-sum contract?

- ○ **A.** Fixed-price contract

- ○ **B.** Price-fixing contract

- ○ **C.** Purchase order

- ○ **D.** All of the above

11. Which function audits quality requirements and the results from quality control measurements?

- ○ **A.** Quality control

- ○ **B.** Quality planning

- ○ **C.** Quality assurance

- ○ **D.** Quality improvement

12. A member of the project team is sabotaging the project because of a basic disagreement with functional processes. As the project manager, what should you do?

- ○ **A.** Fire the project team member

- ○ **B.** Present the problem to the appropriate management

- ○ **C.** Present the problem to the appropriate management with the suggestion that the team member be removed from the project

- ○ **D.** Present the problem to the appropriate management with a demand to fire the team member

13. Which factor has the greatest effect on the way a project manager sends and receives information?

- ○ **A.** How others relate to the project manager

- ○ **B.** The project manager's level in the organization

- ○ **C.** The size of the project

- ○ **D.** The project manager's salary and age

14. How do you calculate the expected value of an outcome?

- ○ **A.** Divide the value of each outcome by its probability and then sum the results

- ○ **B.** Divide the value of the desired outcome by the value of all possible outcomes

- ○ **C.** Multiply the value of each outcome by its probability and then sum the results

- ○ **D.** Use linear regression to assess the expected value of the outcome

15. You are managing a road paving project and are assessing risks to your project. You find that weather forecasters estimate that there is a 25% chance that the upcoming week will be drier than normal. This would allow your team to work more hours and save $80,000 in downtime. However, there is also a 10% chance that fuel prices will rise substantially over the next week, costing your team $45,000. What is the expected monetary value, based on these two project risks?

    ○ **A.** $24,500

    ○ **B.** $15,500

    ○ **C.** –$15,500

    ○ **D.** –$24,500

16. A lessons learned session should be held at what point in a project?

    ○ **A.** At the project conclusion

    ○ **B.** When something goes wrong

    ○ **C.** At key milestones

    ○ **D.** All of the above

17. Who is ultimately responsible for project quality control?

    ○ **A.** The project quality officer

    ○ **B.** The company quality group

    ○ **C.** The plant manager

    ○ **D.** The project manager

18. Which of the following activities is NOT part of the acquisition process?

    ○ **A.** Source selection

    ○ **B.** Invitation to bid

    ○ **C.** Contract award

    ○ **D.** Notice to proceed

19. While in the executing phase of a project, a functional manager informs you that he will not have sufficient resources available next month to support your project and two other projects. How should you handle this situation?

    ○ **A.** Ask the functional manager to make the decision about which project to support

    ○ **B.** Ask the functional manager to work with his management to prioritize the work

    ○ **C.** Ask your sponsor to meet with the functional manager

    ○ **D.** Ask the functional manager to set up a meeting with you and the other project managers to work out the problem yourselves

20. You are the project manager for a building project and have just received notice that a vendor is completing a large portion of the project. You have heard a rumor that the vendor is losing many of its workers due to labor issues. With the rumored information, what should you do?

○ **A.** Suspend work with the vendor until the labor issues are resolved

○ **B.** Contact the vendor to talk about the rumor

○ **C.** Pursue another vendor to replace the current vendor

○ **D.** Negotiate with the labor union to secure the workers on your project

21. Which of the following types of communication is least desirable to explain to a team member why his or her performance is substandard?

○ **A.** Project office memo

○ **B.** Counseling session

○ **C.** Project team meeting

○ **D.** Formal letter

22. The ultimate way to ensure successful quality control is by

○ **A.** Outsourcing the quality function

○ **B.** Making the quality department report to facilities

○ **C.** Making quality a priority at the organizational level

○ **D.** Playing a movie about quality in the auditorium

23. One of your project deliverables is to perform a post-implementation review of the water treatment plant you just delivered. You have been asked to do what?

○ **A.** Present all the lessons learned

○ **B.** Meet with the project sponsor to discuss what could have been improved in your project

○ **C.** Investigate and report on the plan performance and maintenance requirements

○ **D.** Meet with your project team and discuss plant support options

24. The delay between the start/finish of one activity and the start/finish of another activity is referred to as

○ **A.** Slack

○ **B.** Free float

○ **C.** Lag

○ **D.** Total float

25. Which style of leadership is a project manager demonstrating by allowing the team to make the majority of the decisions?

- ○ **A.** Laissez-faire
- ○ **B.** Boss centered
- ○ **C.** Subordinate centered
- ○ **D.** Autocratic

26. Which of the following activities is NOT an element of procurement management?

- ○ **A.** Purchasing
- ○ **B.** Expenditure
- ○ **C.** Marketing
- ○ **D.** Inspection

27. You are the project manager for a project and have received overall cost estimates from three vendors. One of the estimates is significantly higher than similar project work in the past. In this scenario, you should do which of the following?

- ○ **A.** Ask the other vendors about the higher estimate from the third vendor
- ○ **B.** Use the cost estimates from the historical information
- ○ **C.** Discuss the issue with the vendor that submitted the high cost before reviewing the issue with the other vendors
- ○ **D.** Ask the vendor that supplied the high estimate for information on how the estimate was prepared

28. What should a project manager do to determine whether a team member correctly understands a message?

- ○ **A.** Reduce the filtering
- ○ **B.** Eliminate barriers
- ○ **C.** Obtain feedback
- ○ **D.** Use more than one medium

29. The critical path

- ○ **A.** Has the greatest degree of risk
- ○ **B.** Will elongate the project if the activities on this path take longer than anticipated
- ○ **C.** Must be completed before all other paths
- ○ **D.** All of the above

30. You are the project manager of a project that just went into integration mode. This means that your project

- ○ **A.** Is still running but missing resources
- ○ **B.** Will be closed due to lack of resources
- ○ **C.** Is having resources assigned to other areas of the business
- ○ **D.** Has been accepted by the sponsor and the client

31. The project charter includes

- ○ **A.** Measurable project objectives
- ○ **B.** A summary milestone schedule
- ○ **C.** Project approval requirements
- ○ **D.** All of the above

32. You are the project manager of a project that just went into extinction. This means that your project

- ○ **A.** Is still running but missing resources
- ○ **B.** Will be closed due to lack of resources
- ○ **C.** Has had resources assigned to other areas of the business
- ○ **D.** Has ended before its stated objective

33. Your customer authorizes and funds a scope change that results in a major change to the schedule. The baseline schedule

- ○ **A.** Now becomes the new schedule, including the changes, and the original baseline is disregarded
- ○ **B.** Is still the original baseline but is annotated to reflect that a change has taken place
- ○ **C.** Is amended to reflect the scope change, but the original baseline is still maintained for post-project review
- ○ **D.** Is meaningless because every schedule update changes the baseline

34. The customer of your project has requested that you inflate your cost estimates by 25%. He tells you that his management always reduces the cost of the estimates, so this is the only way to get the budget needed to complete the project. Which of the following is the best response to this situation?

- ○ **A.** Do as the customer asked to ensure that the project requirements can be met by adding the increase as a contingency reserve.
- ○ **B.** Do as the customer asked to ensure that the project requirements can be met by adding the increase across each task.

○ **C.** Do as the customer asked by creating an estimate for the customer's management and another for the actual project implementation.

○ **D.** Complete an accurate estimate of the project. In addition, create a risk assessment on why the project budget would be inadequate.

35. How do you calculate the earned value (EV) for a task that has just been completed?

○ **A.** Multiply the actual hours worked on the project by the budgeted labor rate.

○ **B.** Multiply the budgeted hours to complete the task by the budgeted labor rate.

○ **C.** Divide the actual hours required to complete the task by the budgeted labor rate.

○ **D.** It cannot be determined.

36. You are the project manager of a project that just went into inclusion mode. This means that your project

○ **A.** Is still running but missing is resources

○ **B.** Will be closed due to lack of resources

○ **C.** Has become part of the business processes

○ **D.** Has been accepted by the sponsor and the client

37. A project is

○ **A.** An organized group of activities arranged to fulfill single and multiple objectives

○ **B.** Related activities coordinated to accomplish a generic goal

○ **C.** Beginning-to-end activities that are to be accomplished in a specific time frame and utilizes various resources

○ **D.** An undertaking with a specific time frame and well-defined objectives that utilizes various types of resources within constraints

38. What is the impact to a project if an activity is crashed by two weeks?

○ **A.** The project's schedule will be reduced by two weeks.

○ **B.** The available slack on the noncritical paths will increase.

○ **C.** A new critical path might appear after the crash.

○ **D.** All of the above.

39. Quality assurance

   ○ **A.** Is the prevention of product defects

   ○ **B.** Is an auditing function that provides feedback about the quality of output being produced

   ○ **C.** Is the technical process that results in control charts that specify acceptability limits for conforming output

   ○ **D.** Both A and B

40. During which phase in the project life cycle are most of the project expenses generally incurred?

   ○ **A.** Initiating phase

   ○ **B.** Planning phase

   ○ **C.** Executing phase

   ○ **D.** Closing phase

41. Administrative closure refers to the tasks involved in

   ○ **A.** Validating the project products and services

   ○ **B.** Collecting user acceptance of the project product or service

   ○ **C.** Closing all activities pertaining to a specific project or phase

   ○ **D.** None of the above

42. Product validation pertains to

   ○ **A.** All the activities that ensure that the products and services delivered are in line with quality requirements

   ○ **B.** All the activities that ensure that the products and services delivered are in line with project deliverables and sponsor and client satisfaction

   ○ **C.** All activities that verify tangible assets

   ○ **D.** Both A and C

43. The main goal of having lessons learned is to

   ○ **A.** Keep the names of the team for posterity

   ○ **B.** Close all open contracts

   ○ **C.** Record variances and the mental state behind corrective and preventive actions taken

   ○ **D.** Record all the qualitative reasoning behind corrective and preventive actions taken in the project

44. The difference between the earned value (EV) and planned value (PV) is referred to as the

- ○ **A.** Schedule variance
- ○ **B.** Cost variance
- ○ **C.** Estimate at completion
- ○ **D.** Actual cost of the work performed

45. Which of the following is most likely to become a source of conflict among members of a project team?

- ○ **A.** Performance trade-offs
- ○ **B.** Ambiguity of roles
- ○ **C.** Administrative procedures
- ○ **D.** Determination of earned value

46. You have been assigned as the project manager for a project that takes place in a country that is not where you are from. The project leader from the other country presents a team of workers that are all from his family. What should you do?

- ○ **A.** Reject the team leader's recommendations and build your own project team.
- ○ **B.** Review the resume and qualifications of the proposed project team before approving the team.
- ○ **C.** Determine whether the country's traditions include hiring from the immediate family before hiring from outside the family.
- ○ **D.** Replace the project leader with an impartial project leader.

47. When can conflict be beneficial?

- ○ **A.** When a diversion is needed
- ○ **B.** When conflict situations are in their early stages and emotional involvement is low
- ○ **C.** When conflict situations are in their late stages and emotional involvement is high
- ○ **D.** When conflict might cause a loss of status or position power

48. What is the main reason for making sure all procurements are closed at the end of a project?

- ○ **A.** Materials must be returned.
- ○ **B.** Contractors need to return all excess materials.
- ○ **C.** Contracts are legally binding.
- ○ **D.** You would like to avoid any penalties.

49. Work performance data is

- ○ **A.** Considered a necessity for entering a contract
- ○ **B.** Required as part of the vendor performance evaluation
- ○ **C.** Needed only for contracts in distress
- ○ **D.** An output from the direct and manage project work process

50. Your project team is working with a vendor to correct some programming errors found during user acceptance testing. The decision is made to work through lunch and order take-out. When the food is delivered, the vendor says the bill has been taken care of. What do you do?

- ○ **A.** You accept and thank the vendor for your lunch.
- ○ **B.** You accept and tell him you will pay for lunch for everyone tomorrow.
- ○ **C.** You keep working and pretend you did not hear what the vendor said.
- ○ **D.** You decline and pay for your own meal.

51. What does a statement of work (SOW) identify?

- ○ **A.** The business need for the project
- ○ **B.** The project or product requirements
- ○ **C.** The strategic plan
- ○ **D.** All of the above

52. As a project manager, you direct the performance of all planned project activities and manage the technical and organizational resources available to and interacting with your project. Your work is performed in conjunction with whom?

- ○ **A.** The external project sponsor
- ○ **B.** The project management team
- ○ **C.** Both A and B
- ○ **D.** Neither A nor B

53. The earned value technique (EVT) measures project performance from project initiation through which of the following phases?

- ○ **A.** Planning
- ○ **B.** Executing
- ○ **C.** Monitoring and controlling
- ○ **D.** Closing

54. Which of the following is a deliverable-oriented hierarchical decomposition of the work to be performed by a project team?

- ○ **A.** Organizational breakdown structure (OBS)
- ○ **B.** Milestone schedule
- ○ **C.** Work breakdown structure (WBS)
- ○ **D.** Master schedule

55. In communications, which of the following is described as "assimilating through the mind or senses (as in new ideas)"?

- ○ **A.** Understanding
- ○ **B.** Communicating
- ○ **C.** Receiving
- ○ **D.** Decoding

56. Which of the following is the best long-lasting approach to settling project conflict?

- ○ **A.** Problem solving
- ○ **B.** Compromise
- ○ **C.** Withdrawal
- ○ **D.** Smoothing

57. Your project is ahead of schedule. Management decides to incorporate additional quality testing into the project to improve the quality and acceptability of the project deliverable. What activity does this action exhibit?

- ○ **A.** Scope creep
- ○ **B.** Change control
- ○ **C.** Quality assurance
- ○ **D.** Integrated change control

58. _____ is the subdivision of project deliverables into smaller, more manageable components. The final product categorizes project deliverables at the work package level.

- ○ **A.** Baselining
- ○ **B.** Critical path mapping
- ○ **C.** Decomposition
- ○ **D.** Resource leveling

59. You are the project manager for a research organization and have just been alerted that new legislation will affect your project and change your project scope. What should you do?

- ○ **A.** Create a documented change request
- ○ **B.** Proceed as planned, assuming that the project will be grandfathered beyond the new change in the law
- ○ **C.** Consult with the project sponsor and stakeholders
- ○ **D.** Stop all project work until the issue is resolved

60. Applying sound project management techniques guarantees that

- ○ **A.** Budget will be met.
- ○ **B.** Schedule will be met.
- ○ **C.** The project will be a success.
- ○ **D.** None of the above.

61. One component of the scope baseline for a project is

- ○ **A.** The preliminary project scope
- ○ **B.** The approved preliminary project scope
- ○ **C.** The project scope statement
- ○ **D.** The approved project scope statement

62. A project is a(n) _____ endeavor undertaken to create a unique product, service, or result.

- ○ **A.** Permanent
- ○ **B.** Temporary
- ○ **C.** Ongoing
- ○ **D.** None of the above

63. Which of the following can best assist a project manager during project execution?

- ○ **A.** Stakeholder analysis
- ○ **B.** Change control board
- ○ **C.** A PMIS
- ○ **D.** Verification of scope

64. With respect to integrated change control, what must the project manager ensure is present?

○ **A.** Supporting detail for the change

○ **B.** Approval of the change from the project team

○ **C.** Approval of the change from an SME

○ **D.** Risk assessment for each proposed change

65. You are the project manager for a project to design and implement a new accounting application. Management has requested that you document any changes or enhancements to the technical attributes of the project deliverable. Which one of the following would satisfy management's request?

○ **A.** Configuration management

○ **B.** Integrated change control

○ **C.** Scope control

○ **D.** Change management plan

66. The risk of project failure is highest during which phase of a project?

○ **A.** Initiating

○ **B.** Planning

○ **C.** Executing

○ **D.** Controlling

67. The cost of changes to project scope generally do which of the following over the life cycle of a project?

○ **A.** Increase

○ **B.** Decrease

○ **C.** Stabilize

○ **D.** None of the above

68. Project cost and project staffing resources follow a typical pattern during the life cycle of a project. Which of the following is common?

○ **A.** Cost and staffing levels are high at the beginning of the project, stabilize during the middle phases of the project, and drop rapidly toward project closing.

○ **B.** Cost and staffing levels are high at the beginning of the project, are high during the middle phases of the project, and drop rapidly toward project closing.

    ○ **C.** Cost and staffing levels are low at the beginning of the project, peak during the middle phases of the project, and drop rapidly toward project closing.

    ○ **D.** Cost and staffing levels are low at the beginning of the project, rise during the middle phases of the project, and peak toward project closing.

69. An organization comprising a full-time project manager with moderate project authority and a full-time project management administrative staff is an example of what type of structure?

    ○ **A.** Functional

    ○ **B.** Weak matrix

    ○ **C.** Strong matrix

    ○ **D.** Projectized

70. One type of progressive elaboration occurs when the work to be performed in the near term is planned in detail while work scheduled for further out is defined at only a high level in the work breakdown structure (WBS). As a task draws nearer, the amount of detail for the task is further defined. Which of the following terms defines this type of progressive elaboration?

    ○ **A.** Activity sequencing

    ○ **B.** Precedence diagramming method (PDM)

    ○ **C.** Activity-on-node (AON)

    ○ **D.** Rolling wave planning

71. What is the most common precedence relationship used in the precedence diagramming method (PDM)?

    ○ **A.** Finish-to-start

    ○ **B.** Finish-to-finish

    ○ **C.** Start-to-finish

    ○ **D.** Start-to-start

72. As the project manager for a project with an international team, you are about to enter negotiations with foreign vendors. Where do you find what business practices are allowed and discouraged?

    ○ **A.** The project charter

    ○ **B.** The project plan

    ○ **C.** Organizational process assets

    ○ **D.** The PMP Code of Ethics and Professional Conduct

73. Which of the following is NOT a type of dependency available in activity sequencing?

- A. Discretionary dependencies
- B. External dependencies
- C. Chronological dependencies
- D. Mandatory dependencies

74. When a scheduled activity cannot be estimated with an adequate degree of certainty, the work within the activity can be decomposed. The resource requirements for each lower, more detailed work package can be estimated and aggregated to form a basis for estimating the overarching scheduled activity. What is this type of estimating called?

- A. Bottom-up estimating
- B. Decomposed estimating
- C. Should-cost estimating
- D. Three-point estimating

75. You have been assigned two concurrent projects. Because of the nature of the projects, you have a conflict of interest. You should

- A. Do the best you can and tell no one
- B. Ask to be removed from one of the projects
- C. Ask to be removed from both of the projects
- D. Inform your sponsor and ask for her advice

76. Cost control of a project entails determining and evaluating which of the following factors?

- A. The cause of a cost variance
- B. The magnitude of a cost variance
- C. Both A and B
- D. Neither A nor B

77. Which of the following activities is NOT included in configuration management?

- A. Controlling changes to the project deliverables
- B. Scope verification
- C. Automatic change request approvals
- D. Identification of the attributes of the project deliverables

78. You are the project manager for a performance analysis project for a client's database application. Your client provides you with a test database to use for your analysis. The IT director for your organization disagrees with the database provided by the client and tells you to use a different database with different data that should give better results. This is a violation of the SOW. What should you do?

- ○ **A.** Use the client's database
- ○ **B.** Use the replacement database without telling the customer
- ○ **C.** Use the replacement database and discuss the reasons with the customer
- ○ **D.** Ask your sponsor for clarification, assuming that the IT director is not your sponsor

79. Which set of tools is part of the project plan execution?

- ○ **A.** PMIS, WBS, EVM
- ○ **B.** General management skills, status review meetings, EVM
- ○ **C.** General management skills, status review meetings, work authorization systems
- ○ **D.** General management skills, status review meetings, EVM

80. Planned value (PV) is

- ○ **A.** The budgeted cost for work scheduled to be completed on an activity up to a specific time
- ○ **B.** The budgeted cost for the work actually completed on the schedule activity during a specific time period
- ○ **C.** The total cost for work on the schedule activity during a specific time period
- ○ **D.** None of the above

81. A cost performance index (CPI) value less than 1.0 indicates that a project has which of the following?

- ○ **A.** An overrun of the cost estimates
- ○ **B.** An underrun of the cost estimates
- ○ **C.** Neither a cost overrun nor a cost underrun
- ○ **D.** None of the above

82. Which of the following requires a concise definition of the end users' needs?

- ○ **A.** Work breakdown structure
- ○ **B.** Budget estimate
- ○ **C.** Functional requirements
- ○ **D.** Risk register

83. You are managing a project using the earned value technique (EVT) for cost management. The project planned value (PV) is $200,000. The project earned value (EV) is $100,000. The actual value (AV) is $150,000. What is the schedule variance (SV) for the project?

- ○ **A.** 100,000
- ○ **B.** −100,000
- ○ **C.** 50,000
- ○ **D.** −50,000

84. EVM is used during which process group(s)?

- ○ **A.** Controlling
- ○ **B.** Executing
- ○ **C.** Closing
- ○ **D.** Entire project

85. To maintain the customer's schedule, substantial overtime will be required during a traditional holiday season. Many team members have requested vacation during this time. You should

- ○ **A.** Let the schedule slip and inform the customer
- ○ **B.** First give the team members the choice of working overtime
- ○ **C.** Make the team members cancel their vacation plans and work overtime
- ○ **D.** Acquire temporary employees for the overtime

86. Which of the following is a business philosophy to find methods to continuously improve products, services, and business practices?

- ○ **A.** TQM
- ○ **B.** ASQ
- ○ **C.** QA
- ○ **D.** QC

87. You're managing a project using the earned value technique (EVT) for cost management. The project planned value (PV) is $200,000. The project earned value (EV) is $100,000. The actual value (AV) is $150,000. Calculate the cost performance index (CPI) for the project. What is the cost-efficiency of the project?

   ○ **A.** Over budget

   ○ **B.** Under budget

   ○ **C.** On budget

   ○ **D.** Unable to determine from the information given

88. You're managing a project using the earned value technique (EVT) for cost management. The project planned value (PV) is $200,000. The project earned value (EV) is $100,000. The actual value (AV) is $150,000. What is the schedule performance index (SPI) for the project?

   ○ **A.** 0.5

   ○ **B.** 1.5

   ○ **C.** 1.75

   ○ **D.** 2

89. Monitoring project activities and results to evaluate whether the findings comply with applicable quality standards as well as identifying mitigation strategies are _____ activities.

   ○ **A.** Quality assessment

   ○ **B.** Quality assurance

   ○ **C.** Quality control

   ○ **D.** Quality improvement

90. You are the project manager for a project requiring that quality maps to federal guidelines. During a quality audit, you discover that a portion of the project work is faulty and must be done again. The requirement to redo the work is an example of which of the following?

   ○ **A.** Cost of quality

   ○ **B.** Cost of adherence

   ○ **C.** Cost of nonconformance

   ○ **D.** Cost of doing business

91. Which of the following techniques is the best for most project management situations?

- ○ **A.** Confronting
- ○ **B.** Compromising
- ○ **C.** Forcing
- ○ **D.** Avoidance

92. Ishikawa diagrams are also known as

- ○ **A.** Cause-and-effect diagrams
- ○ **B.** Scatter diagrams
- ○ **C.** Fishbone diagrams
- ○ **D.** Both A and C

93. A Pareto diagram is a type of

- ○ **A.** Cause-and-effect diagram
- ○ **B.** Control chart
- ○ **C.** Histogram
- ○ **D.** Scatter diagram

94. Project communication planning includes which of the following tasks?

- ○ **A.** Determining and limiting who will communicate with whom and who will receive what information
- ○ **B.** Combining the type and format of information needed with an analysis of the value of the information for communication
- ○ **C.** Understanding how communication affects a project as a whole
- ○ **D.** All of the above

95. The complete review of a seller's technical performance, cost performance, and delivery schedule is referred to as

- ○ **A.** Project or phase evaluation
- ○ **B.** Contract evaluation
- ○ **C.** Postmortem
- ○ **D.** Seller performance evaluation

96. The procurement closing of a project dictates that

- ○ **A.** All project monies have been spent
- ○ **B.** No budget category amounts have been exceeded

○ **C.** No other work from this client will be considered

○ **D.** No further charges can be made against the project

97. Which of the following is an example of coercive power?

○ **A.** A project manager has lunch with the project team on the same day each week.

○ **B.** A project manager openly punishes any team member who is late with an activity.

○ **C.** A project manager has worked with the technology on the project for several years.

○ **D.** A project manager is friends with all the project team members.

98. While managing a project, you find that the project customer and a team member are in conflict over the level of quality needed on a sample. You decide to split the difference between what the two stakeholders want. This is an example of which of the following?

○ **A.** A win–win solution

○ **B.** A win–lose solution

○ **C.** A lose–lose solution

○ **D.** A leave–lose solution

99. You are the project manager for a project with a very tight schedule. Because the project is running late, you feel that you do not have time to consider all the possible solutions due to a disagreement between two team members. You quickly decide to side with the team member who has the greater seniority. This is an example of which of the following?

○ **A.** Problem solving

○ **B.** Compromising

○ **C.** Forcing

○ **D.** Withdrawal

100. The most important decision for the sponsors to make during the close project or phase process is

○ **A.** Allocating budget allocations for the next phase

○ **B.** Authorizing scope changes for the next phase

○ **C.** Authorizing budget increases for the next phase based on scope changes

○ **D.** Cancelling the project

101. Historical records collected during closing are useful to do what for future projects?

- ○ **A.** Predict trends and highlight issues
- ○ **B.** Analyze successes and shortfalls
- ○ **C.** Analyze strengths and document results
- ○ **D.** Justify results and set standards

102. In small organizations, project managers and functional managers are

- ○ **A.** Never the same person
- ○ **B.** Generally the same person
- ○ **C.** Sometimes the same person
- ○ **D.** Always subordinate to the project initiator

103. Which of the following is an accurate statement?

- ○ **A.** Qualitative risk analysis occurs prior to quantitative risk analysis.
- ○ **B.** Quantitative risk analysis occurs prior to qualitative risk analysis.
- ○ **C.** Qualitative risk analysis is performed on risks that have been prioritized during quantitative risk analysis.
- ○ **D.** Both B and C.

104. The project charter

- ○ **A.** Is a good thing to have to enter restricted areas
- ○ **B.** Tells the newspapers when the project will end
- ○ **C.** Authorizes equipment acquisition
- ○ **D.** Provides a high-level definition of the effort and its stakeholders

105. Scorecard modeling, cost–benefit analysis, payback periods, and internal rate of return are examples of

- ○ **A.** Project selection methods
- ○ **B.** Enterprise benefits measurement methods used in selecting a project
- ○ **C.** Ways to ensure stakeholder commitment
- ○ **D.** Integral parts of the statement of work

106. What is the primary purpose of project control?

- ○ **A.** To plan ahead for uncertainties
- ○ **B.** To generate status reports
- ○ **C.** To keep the project on track
- ○ **D.** To develop the project road map

107. An activity was estimated to require one month for completion, with 800 hours of labor and a burdened cost of $47,000. The activity was completed in 800 hours but at a higher burdened cost of $58,000. What is the most likely reason for the increase?

- ○ **A.** Higher-salaried employees were assigned to the activity than planned
- ○ **B.** Overtime was required
- ○ **C.** The overhead rate increased
- ○ **D.** Any of the above

108. Project scope

- ○ **A.** Defines all the equipment that will be used in a project
- ○ **B.** Is a document that identifies stakeholder responsibilities
- ○ **C.** Is part of the project charter
- ○ **D.** Defines at a high level the project execution framework and its deliverables

109. Which one of the following will result in the most productive results when negotiating?

- ○ **A.** Yielding
- ○ **B.** Forcing
- ○ **C.** Collaborating
- ○ **D.** Compromising

110. Which of the following is an output of the control communications process?

- ○ **A.** Trend analysis
- ○ **B.** EVM
- ○ **C.** Variance analysis
- ○ **D.** Change requests

111. Project success can be achieved only if

- ○ **A.** The project manager is an expert in managing resources.
- ○ **B.** The project manager is part of the executive management team.
- ○ **C.** There is a clear link between the project deliverables and the business strategy.
- ○ **D.** The project sponsor leads the initiatives.

112. Reaching an agreement of concessions is accomplished in the _____ stage of negotiations.

   ○ **A.** Protocol

   ○ **B.** Posturing

   ○ **C.** Bargaining

   ○ **D.** Closure

113. The two processes in the closing process group are called

   ○ **A.** Close procurements and validate scope

   ○ **B.** Validate scope and close project or phase

   ○ **C.** Close project or phase and close procurements

   ○ **D.** Control communications and close procurements

114. The project management plan is

   ○ **A.** The steps needed to complete a project task

   ○ **B.** Prepared at the beginning and fixed throughout the execution of a project

   ○ **C.** Not needed until resources have been assigned

   ○ **D.** An outline that identifies all the steps and processes that will be used after a project is initiated

115. In what process group does source selection happen?

   ○ **A.** Initiating

   ○ **B.** Planning

   ○ **C.** Executing

   ○ **D.** Closing

116. Which of the following is NOT an input to the control procurements process?

   ○ **A.** Work performance reports

   ○ **B.** Source selection criteria

   ○ **C.** Approved change requests

   ○ **D.** Agreements

117. What is the primary function of a project manager?

   ○ **A.** Systems design

   ○ **B.** Client interfacing

   ○ **C.** Quality assurance

   ○ **D.** Integration

118. What does fast tracking mean?

- ○ **A.** Speeding up a project by performing some activities in parallel
- ○ **B.** Swapping one activity for another
- ○ **C.** Reducing the number of activities, if possible
- ○ **D.** Both B and C

119. The work breakdown structure is

- ○ **A.** A list of all the tasks needed to complete a meeting
- ○ **B.** Needed as part of the project charter
- ○ **C.** Set and does not change throughout the project
- ○ **D.** Used to break down a project into manageable pieces

120. Which two of the following knowledge areas are part of closing?

- ○ **A.** Project communications management and project risk management
- ○ **B.** Project integration management and project scope management
- ○ **C.** Project scope management and project procurement management
- ○ **D.** Project integration management and project procurement management

121. Which of the following situations describes a violation of the PMI Code of Ethics and Professional Conduct?

- ○ **A.** Accepting a gift that is within the customary guidelines of the country or province you are currently working in
- ○ **B.** Using confidential information to advance your position or influence a critical decision
- ○ **C.** Complying with laws and regulations of the state or province in which project management services are provided
- ○ **D.** Disclosing information to a customer about a situation that might have an appearance of impropriety

122. At what point in a project does administrative closure take place?

- ○ **A.** When the project is cancelled
- ○ **B.** At the completion of each phase
- ○ **C.** Only when the project is complete or cancelled
- ○ **D.** As management sees fit

123. The project baseline

   ○ **A.** Encompass all the initial estimates for tasks and resource utilization

   ○ **B.** Is important only in the project initiation phase

   ○ **C.** Is the result of the original plans plus the approved changes

   ○ **D.** Is not needed to successfully manage a project

For Questions 124–126, use the following network diagram:

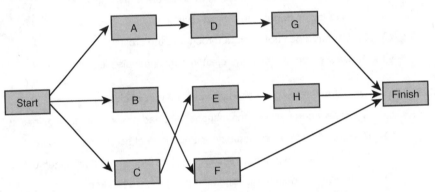

A = 5 weeks
B = 10 weeks
C = 2 weeks
D = 1 week
E = 1 week
F = 3 weeks
G = 11 weeks
H = 1 week

124. What would be the early start for activity H?

   ○ **A.** 11

   ○ **B.** 10

   ○ **C.** 4

   ○ **D.** 6

125. What is the critical path?

   ○ **A.** Start–A–D–G–Finish

   ○ **B.** Start–B–F–Finish

   ○ **C.** Start–C–E–H–Finish

126. Which project schedule represents the tasks outlined in the network diagram?

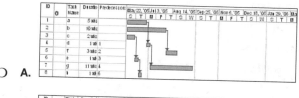

○ **A.**

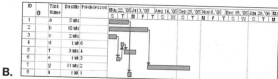

○ **B.**

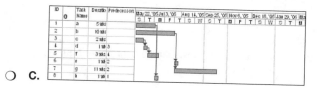

○ **C.**

127. Which of the following is NOT a good input to project cost estimation?

○ **A.** Work breakdown structures

○ **B.** Time estimates

○ **C.** Earn value analysis

○ **D.** Schedules

128. The major difference between project and functional management is that the project manager generally does not have control over which function?

○ **A.** Cost allocation

○ **B.** Staffing

○ **C.** Rewarding

○ **D.** Monitoring

129. Which of the following cost budgeting tools uses current and historical project information to calculate project cost estimates?

○ **A.** Cost cancellation techniques

○ **B.** Reserves analysis

○ **C.** Parametric estimating

○ **D.** Funding limit reconciliation

130. Which of the following is NOT an element of procurement management?

- ○ **A.** Inspection
- ○ **B.** Purchasing
- ○ **C.** Estimating
- ○ **D.** Expediting

131. Which tool is useful in determining what causes the majority of quality problems in a process?

- ○ **A.** Cause-and-effect diagram
- ○ **B.** Flowchart
- ○ **C.** Control chart
- ○ **D.** Pareto diagram

132. In the PMI realm, who is ultimately responsible for project quality?

- ○ **A.** Project team
- ○ **B.** Project manager
- ○ **C.** Quality assurance manager
- ○ **D.** Validation engineer

133. The process in which detailed resource assignments and responsibilities are formalized is called

- ○ **A.** Develop project management plan
- ○ **B.** Plan quality management
- ○ **C.** Develop project charter
- ○ **D.** Plan human resource management

134. How many communication channels will be required in a project in which 30 individuals are participating?

- ○ **A.** 150
- ○ **B.** 270
- ○ **C.** 444
- ○ **D.** 435

135. Which of the following terms describes the process of gathering, generating, and disseminating project information upon project completion?

- ○ **A.** Close project
- ○ **B.** Close project or phase

    ○ **C.** Administrative closure

    ○ **D.** Operational transfer

136. You are completing the closeout of a project to design a storage facility. The procurement contract is a cost-plus-incentive-fee contract. The target cost is $400,000, with an 8% target profit. However, the project comes in at $360,000. The incentive split is 75/25. How much is the total contract cost?

    ○ **A.** $410,000

    ○ **B.** $432,000

    ○ **C.** $442,000

    ○ **D.** $382,000

137. Who has the ultimate responsibility for making sure that a message in the project team is understood?

    ○ **A.** The project sponsor

    ○ **B.** The sender

    ○ **C.** The project coordinator

    ○ **D.** All of the above

138. Sound project objectives should be

    ○ **A.** General rather than specific

    ○ **B.** Established without considering resource bounds

    ○ **C.** Realistic and attainable

    ○ **D.** Measurable, intangible, and verifiable

139. The intent of the project risk management knowledge area is to

    ○ **A.** Underwrite all the risks affecting the company

    ○ **B.** Announce project risks

    ○ **C.** Address and implement how risk will be identified and mitigated

    ○ **D.** Increase the probability of positive outcomes in the project

140. Quality control is normally performed by

    ○ **A.** QA personnel

    ○ **B.** The project team

    ○ **C.** Operations personnel

    ○ **D.** Project management

141. As of today, $1,000 worth of planned work on Task A was supposed to have been done (PV). However, currently the EV is $850. What is the schedule variance (SV)?

- ○ **A.** −100
- ○ **B.** 100
- ○ **C.** −150
- ○ **D.** 150

142. Which one of these is NOT a typical way to deal with negative threats?

- ○ **A.** Avoid
- ○ **B.** Transfer
- ○ **C.** Mitigate
- ○ **D.** Share

143. Which of the following is a recognized contract type in the PMI context?

- ○ **A.** Fixed-price or lump-sum contract
- ○ **B.** Cost-reimbursable contract
- ○ **C.** Time-and-materials contract
- ○ **D.** All of the above

144. Which one of these is NOT used when preparing a statement of work?

- ○ **A.** Project scope statement
- ○ **B.** Work breakdown structure
- ○ **C.** Risk management plan
- ○ **D.** WBS dictionary

145. When a project manager receives a project change request, she should

- ○ **A.** Send it to the change control board for approval
- ○ **B.** Discuss it with the project team and leave it for phase 2
- ○ **C.** Evaluate its risk and potential impact before taking any action
- ○ **D.** None of the above

146. Which of the following is NOT part of the definition of quality?

- ○ **A.** Conformance to requirements
- ○ **B.** Fitness for use
- ○ **C.** Continuous improvement of products and services
- ○ **D.** Appeal to the customer

147. Resource leveling often affects a project by making the schedule

- ○ **A.** Shorter
- ○ **B.** Longer
- ○ **C.** More responsive to customer needs
- ○ **D.** Both A and C

148. Graphical displays of accumulated cost and labor hours, plotted as a function of time, are called

- ○ **A.** Variance reports
- ○ **B.** S curves
- ○ **C.** Trend analysis
- ○ **D.** Earned value reporting

149. The process of selecting and documenting the best approach to meet project objectives is part of

- ○ **A.** Scope baseline
- ○ **B.** Scope authorization
- ○ **C.** WBS
- ○ **D.** Scope planning

150. One method to determine how well a project is executing at a specific point in time is by using

- ○ **A.** Cost variance analysis
- ○ **B.** Historical data
- ○ **C.** Expert judgment
- ○ **D.** The cost performance index (CPI)

151. Quality assurance application in a project involves

- ○ **A.** Defining organizational quality practices
- ○ **B.** Ensuring Six Sigma compliance
- ○ **C.** Applying Pareto diagrams to project sample points
- ○ **D.** Applying organizational quality metrics to a project

152. Quality management is

     ○ **A.** Another name for recurrent inspections

     ○ **B.** Inversely related to productivity

     ○ **C.** Primarily the responsibility of management

     ○ **D.** Primarily the responsibility of the workers

153. Cost of quality is

     ○ **A.** Associated with nonconformance to specifications

     ○ **B.** Primarily caused by poor workmanship of workers

     ○ **C.** Used to determine whether a quality management program is suitable for a given project

     ○ **D.** Negligible for most large projects

154. The purpose of configuration management is to

     ○ **A.** Ensure that drawings are updated

     ○ **B.** Control change throughout a project

     ○ **C.** Control change during production

     ○ **D.** Generate engineering change proposals

155. Quality and _____ are directly related.

     ○ **A.** Productivity

     ○ **B.** Cost overruns

     ○ **C.** Scope control

     ○ **D.** Pareto diagram

156. You and your project team determine that external resources are needed. Which method would be best to secure these resources?

     ○ **A.** Acquisition

     ○ **B.** Pre-assignment

     ○ **C.** Negotiation

     ○ **D.** Contract management

157. As a project manager, you need to know how to manage conflict. Which one of the following is NOT a way to successfully manage conflict?

     ○ **A.** Problem solving

     ○ **B.** Compromising

     ○ **C.** Formal

     ○ **D.** Withdrawal

158. What type of inspection validates that quality requirements are met?

- ○ **A.** Inspection by attributes
- ○ **B.** Cyclical inspection
- ○ **C.** Quality conformance inspection
- ○ **D.** Original inspection

159. How much time should a project manager spend in communication activities?

- ○ **A.** 10%–25%
- ○ **B.** 36%–50%
- ○ **C.** 51%–69%
- ○ **D.** 70%–90%

160. Which of the following is NOT a basic element for successful communication?

- ○ **A.** Sender
- ○ **B.** Message
- ○ **C.** Analog line
- ○ **D.** Receiver

161. What is the name of the process that uses as primary inputs the procurement documents and the source selection criteria?

- ○ **A.** Plan procurement management
- ○ **B.** Conduct procurements
- ○ **C.** Control procurements
- ○ **D.** Close procurements

162. An approved corrective action is

- ○ **A.** A response to a management request
- ○ **B.** A quality management plan
- ○ **C.** A course correction to bring the project in line with the project plan
- ○ **D.** None of the above

163. Statistical cost estimating techniques that use historical data are called

- ○ **A.** Definitive
- ○ **B.** Analogy
- ○ **C.** Three-point
- ○ **D.** Parametric

164. What must management do to achieve long-term quality improvements?

   ○ **A.** Motivate the employees by using various techniques

   ○ **B.** Create a quality control department and give it authority over production

   ○ **C.** Implement a formal quality control program with worker and management involvement

   ○ **D.** Establish financial incentive packages for workers

165. A task-oriented list of activities organized into a tree is a

   ○ **A.** Detailed plan

   ○ **B.** Linear responsibility chart

   ○ **C.** Work breakdown structure

   ○ **D.** Cost account coding system

166. Fishbone diagrams, like the one in this figure, are used for

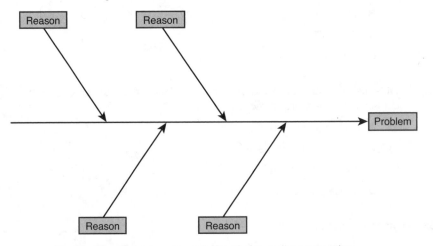

   ○ **A.** The cost management plan during project execution

   ○ **B.** Brainstorming

   ○ **C.** Finding the cause and effect in the project quality assurance process

   ○ **D.** All of the above

167. Pareto diagrams, fishbone diagrams, histograms, and Six Sigma are techniques used for implementing _____ in a project.

   ○ **A.** Quality processes

   ○ **B.** Quality metrics

   ○ **C.** Quality control

   ○ **D.** All of the above

For Questions 168–174, use the following problem:

You are the new project manager tasked with taking over for a project manager who left six weeks ago. Some of the numbers that you find in your initial research are as follows:

Estimated project cost: $675,000

Project timeline: 24 weeks

This is week 16, and accumulated costs are $300,000. In addition, only 25% of the work has been completed.

168. What is the budget at completion?

   ○ **A.** $300,000

   ○ **B.** $168,750

   ○ **C.** $675,000

   ○ **D.** There is not enough information to determine an answer.

169. What is the planned value?

   ○ **A.** $300,000

   ○ **B.** $168,750

   ○ **C.** $389,423

   ○ **D.** $452,250

170. What is the earned value?

   ○ **A.** $300,000

   ○ **B.** $168,750

   ○ **C.** $389,453

   ○ **D.** $483,103

171. What is the cost variance?

   ○ **A.** –$250,000

   ○ **B.** –$483,103

   ○ **C.** –$289,750

   ○ **D.** –$131,250

172. What is the schedule variance?

   ○ **A.** –$157,351

   ○ **B.** –$289,750

   ○ **C.** –$283,500

   ○ **D.** There is not enough information to determine an answer.

173. What is the estimated-at-completion cost?

- ○ **A.** $1,200,000
- ○ **B.** $675,000
- ○ **C.** $3,000,000
- ○ **D.** $1,050,000

174. Because the CPI is .5625, what do we know about this project?

- ○ **A.** It can be finished on time if we crash the schedule.
- ○ **B.** We will need an extra six weeks to complete it.
- ○ **C.** The project is experiencing a cost overrun for work completed.
- ○ **D.** None of the above.

175. Uncertainty refers to a situation where

- ○ **A.** The outcomes are known and the likelihood of their occurrences is high.
- ○ **B.** The outcomes and the likelihood of their occurrences are known.
- ○ **C.** Neither the outcomes nor their likelihood of their occurrences are known.
- ○ **D.** Current states can change at any time.

176. Which of the following phrases best describes Deming's definition of *quality*?

- ○ **A.** Conformance to requirements
- ○ **B.** Fitness for use
- ○ **C.** Continuous improvement of products and services
- ○ **D.** Customer focus

177. Maslow's hierarchy of needs talks about humans' need to satisfy various personal needs. What is the correct sequence for those needs, starting with the most basic need?

- ○ **A.** Safety, love, esteem and self-actualization, physiological
- ○ **B.** Love, physiological, safety, esteem and self-actualization
- ○ **C.** Esteem, physiological, safety, love, and self-actualization
- ○ **D.** Physiological, safety, love, esteem and self-actualization

178. Which of the following types of specifications identifies specific measurable capabilities or parameters for which a product can be tested during the acceptance procedure?

- ○ **A.** Performance
- ○ **B.** Functional
- ○ **C.** Technical
- ○ **D.** Baseline

179. Which leadership style would be most common in a car wash?

- ○ **A.** McGregor's Theory Y
- ○ **B.** McGregor's Theory X
- ○ **C.** Maslow's hierarchy of needs
- ○ **D.** Ouchi's Theory Z

180. Which phrase is most similar to business risk?

- ○ **A.** Profit and loss
- ○ **B.** Personnel turnover
- ○ **C.** Workers' compensation
- ○ **D.** Liability insurance

181. Which of the following contract types is the same as a cost-plus contract?

- ○ **A.** Firm fixed price
- ○ **B.** Cost reimbursable
- ○ **C.** Fixed price plus incentive fee
- ○ **D.** Progress payments

182. You have chosen to crash a project to avoid penalty payments for late deliveries. To crash the project, either overtime or additional resources should be assigned to

- ○ **A.** All activities
- ○ **B.** Activities with the longest time durations
- ○ **C.** Critical path activities, beginning with the longest time duration
- ○ **D.** Activities with the greatest risk

183. Which of the following statements best describes Pareto's law?

- ○ **A.** All problems that have measurable costs associated with them should be corrected to minimize quality control losses.
- ○ **B.** The majority of defects are caused by a small percentage of problems, and improvement efforts should be focused on those few problems.
- ○ **C.** All quality control problems should be corrected to achieve zero defects.
- ○ **D.** On average, correcting only 80% of quality control problems provides justifiable cost-effective benefits.

184. A project manager imposes judgment on a project team. Which of the following is the project manager doing?

- ○ **A.** Smoothing
- ○ **B.** Formalizing
- ○ **C.** Compromising
- ○ **D.** Forcing

185. S curves, histograms, and earn value analysis are examples of

- ○ **A.** Project justification
- ○ **B.** Capital acquisition requests
- ○ **C.** Performance reporting tools
- ○ **D.** None of the above

186. Which of the following are two procedures used to perform all the closure activities in a project or a project phase?

- ○ **A.** Management and stakeholder
- ○ **B.** Project team and stakeholder
- ○ **C.** Administrative and procurement closure
- ○ **D.** Management and procurement closure

187. You work for an organization that has no rules with regard to vendor kickbacks or special gifts. A vendor offers you a trip to Paris in exchange for your helping him get the contract with your organization. What would be the most prudent thing to do?

- ○ **A.** Accept the offer and help the vendor get the contract
- ○ **B.** Ask the vendor for an additional trip for your boss
- ○ **C.** Decline the offer and advise the vendor on the standard bidding process
- ○ **D.** Seek legal counsel before accepting the trip

188. As project manager, you offered a promotion to a team member that included a small increase in salary but substantially more responsibility. Which of the following needs would this promotion fulfill for the team member?

- ○ **A.** Monetary
- ○ **B.** Physiological
- ○ **C.** Esteem
- ○ **D.** Self-actualization

189. What is the purpose of a management reserve?

- ○ **A.** To implement additional unbudgeted scope
- ○ **B.** To compensate for inaccurate estimates
- ○ **C.** To cover major unforeseen catastrophes
- ○ **D.** To cover unforeseen problems in the project

190. You are offered a job as project manager for a fixed-cost project. At the same time, you are approached by another client to work on her project on a time-and-materials basis at a higher hourly rate. What should you do?

- ○ **A.** Tell the new client that you need some time to consider all your options before giving her an answer
- ○ **B.** Leave your current customer and start on the other project as soon as possible
- ○ **C.** Discuss the matter with your client and ask for more money
- ○ **D.** Try to squeeze in both projects without notifying anyone

191. Which of the following terms describes a formal invitation to submit a price for specified goods or services?

- ○ **A.** Request for proposal
- ○ **B.** Request for quotation
- ○ **C.** Tender invitation
- ○ **D.** Bid invitation

192. Which of the following is NOT an input to the plan quality management process?

- ○ **A.** Requirements documentation
- ○ **B.** Stakeholder register
- ○ **C.** Quality metrics
- ○ **D.** Risk register

193. As a senior leader in the project management field, you receive a voicemail message from one of your competitor's junior project managers, asking for help in the project management discipline. What is the most appropriate course of action?

- ○ **A.** Tell the other guy to stop complaining and get a couple project management books
- ○ **B.** Decide that it is not worth the risk and ignore the call
- ○ **C.** Start working with him after hours
- ○ **D.** Talk to your supervisor and apprise her of the situation before initiating contact

194. Which of the following is a graphical display of cumulative costs and labor hours plotted against time?

- ○ **A.** Trend line
- ○ **B.** Trend analysis
- ○ **C.** S curve
- ○ **D.** Percent completion report

195. An activity not on the critical path is completed in half the scheduled time. What is the impact?

- ○ **A.** The critical path is shortened.
- ○ **B.** The slack in the path containing this activity increases.
- ○ **C.** The total cost for this activity decreases.
- ○ **D.** Resources from this activity can be assigned to other activities.

196. You are assigned to lead a corporate project with a lot of diversity and several countries participating. What is your best course of action when it comes to giving assignments and setting up the schedule?

- ○ **A.** Try to standardize all activities based on the corporate calendar
- ○ **B.** Tell management that you need to implement a PMO at corporate in order to have everyone local
- ○ **C.** Learn about communication styles and local holidays and plan for process execution across time zones
- ○ **D.** Use external consultants who are willing to work locally

197. You are in charge of a project that is going to miss the milestones that were set at the enterprise level by two weeks. What do you do?

- ○ **A.** Advise management of the revised project plan and timeline
- ○ **B.** Wait and see if management notices when you do not give an update on the item
- ○ **C.** Crash the schedule to make the deadline
- ○ **D.** Do nothing

198. A good project manager tends to _____ above all else when it comes to active communications.

- ○ **A.** Write reports
- ○ **B.** Cold-call people
- ○ **C.** Listen
- ○ **D.** Help

199. Which of the following systems is designed to ensure the timely availability and oversight of non-personnel resources?

- ○ **A.** Inventory control
- ○ **B.** Materials management
- ○ **C.** Procurement
- ○ **D.** All of the above

200. In a fishbone diagram, where is the effect depicted?

- ○ **A.** At the right-hand end of the spine
- ○ **B.** At the end of a diagonal line
- ○ **C.** On a branch of a diagonal line
- ○ **D.** At the left-hand end of the spine

Answers to the PMP Practice Exam

Answers at a Glance

1. C	26. C	51. D
2. C	27. D	52. B
3. C	28. C	53. D
4. B	29. B	54. C
5. C	30. C	55. C
6. A	31. D	56. A
7. C	32. D	57. D
8. B	33. C	58. C
9. B	34. D	59. A
10. A	35. B	60. D
11. C	36. C	61. D
12. C	37. D	62. B
13. A	38. C	63. C
14. C	39. B	64. A
15. B	40. C	65. A
16. D	41. C	66. A
17. D	42. B	67. A
18. D	43. C	68. C
19. D	44. A	69. C
20. B	45. B	70. D
21. C	46. C	71. A
22. C	47. B	72. C
23. C	48. C	73. C
24. C	49. D	74. A
25. C	50. D	75. D

76. C	108. D	140. C	172. C
77. C	109. C	141. C	173. A
78. D	110. D	142. D	174. C
79. C	111. C	143. D	175. C
80. A	112. D	144. C	176. C
81. A	113. C	145. C	177. D
82. C	114. D	146. B	178. A
83. B	115. C	147. B	179. B
84. D	116. B	148. B	180. A
85. B	117. D	149. D	181. B
86. A	118. A	150. D	182. C
87. A	119. D	151. D	183. B
88. A	120. D	152. C	184. D
89. C	121. B	153. A	185. C
90. C	122. B	154. B	186. C
91. A	123. C	155. A	187. C
92. D	124. C	156. A	188. C
93. C	125. A	157. C	189. D
94. D	126. A	158. C	190. A
95. D	127. C	159. D	191. B
96. D	128. B	160. C	192. C
97. B	129. C	161. B	193. D
98. C	130. C	162. C	194. C
99. C	131. D	163. D	195. B
100. D	132. B	164. C	196. C
101. A	133. D	165. C	197. A
102. C	134. D	166. C	198. C
103. A	135. C	167. C	199. B
104. D	136. C	168. C	200. A
105. B	137. B	169. D	
106. C	138. C	170. B	
107. D	139. D	171. D	

Answers with Explanations

Question 1

Answer **C** is correct. For the PMP exam, the PMBOK is the final authority. You will be asked many questions that require you to apply the knowledge you've gained from the PMBOK. That is where your experience comes in. Answers A and B are incorrect because they do not place the PMBOK as the primary authority. Answer D is incorrect because it totally ignores the fact that your experience will allow you to apply the PMBOK content.

Question 2

Answer **C** is correct. You should not participate in the study group. Answer A is incorrect because it clearly violates the PMI Code of Ethics and Professional Conduct. Answers B and D are not good choices because of a lack of clear evidence that the questions are live PMP exam questions.

Question 3

Answer **C** is correct. You decide to include the business analyst because he possesses superior knowledge of the application area. Answers A and B are incorrect because his application area specific knowledge is the focus, not general management or interpersonal skills. Answer D is incorrect because it is not a specified area of expertise in the PMBOK. This question is an example of too much information. You will find many questions on the PMP exam that contain more information than you need. Use only what is necessary to answer the question. Don't get confused by extraneous information.

Question 4

Answer **B** is correct. A fishbone diagram, also called an Ishikawa diagram or a cause-and-effect diagram, is used to determine the cause or causes of a production problem. Answer A is incorrect because control charts are used to determine whether a process is stable. Answers C and D are incorrect because these tools depict the frequency of a variable or the relationship between two variables, not the cause of a production problem.

Question 5

Answer **C** is correct. The process of smoothing out resources over multiple periods is called *resource leveling*. The other answers refer to terms not associated with smoothing out resources.

Question 6

Answer **A** is correct. Risk and uncertainty are the highest at the beginning of a project. These two factors make the probability of failure the highest at the beginning. The more you know about a project, the better chance you will have of completing it successfully. Answer B is incorrect because a lot is known about a project by the time you publish any plan. Risk and uncertainty are lower than at the beginning. Answers C and D are incorrect for similar reasons. As you move closer to the end of a project, you gain a higher level of confidence in the project's outcome. This is largely due to the fact that as more work is accomplished, you can view and evaluate more and more of the project's output.

Question 7

Answer **C** is correct. The create WBS process is the process that follows collect requirements and define scope. Answers A, B, and D are incorrect because they do not follow the PMBOK process flow.

Question 8

Answer **B** is correct. Before continuing with any activity, you must have the authority to do so. Have the stakeholders sign the project charter and authorize the project. Answers A, C, and D constitute working on a project before it is authorized.

Question 9

Answer **B** is correct. Perform integrated change control, control schedule, and control quality are all processes in the monitoring and controlling process group. One of the primary concerns for processes in this process group is to identify areas in which changes to the plan are required. Manage communications is a process in the executing process group, which does not primarily focus on identifying areas in which changes are required.

Question 10

Answer **A** is correct. A lump-sum contract is the same as a fixed-price contract. Answer B is incorrect because it refers to an invalid type of contract. Answer C is incorrect because a purchase order does not hold the same weight as a formal contract. Because Answer A is the only correct answer, Answer D is also incorrect.

Question 11

Answer **C** is correct. "Quality assurance is the process of auditing the quality requirements and results from quality control measurements to ensure appropriate quality standards and operational definitions are used." Answer A is incorrect because "quality control is the process of monitoring and recording results of executing quality activities." Answer B is incorrect because quality planning is the process of planning for the activities that ensure the appropriate level of quality. Answer D is incorrect because quality improvement describes how to respond to the results of the quality assurance process.

Question 12

Answer **C** is correct. Any problem that is presented to management should be accompanied with a recommended solution. Answer A is incorrect because the project manager likely does not have hiring and firing authority. Answer B is incorrect because it does not address a solution for the problem. Answer D is incorrect because the demand to fire an employee transcends the scope of the project and is beyond the authority and boundary of the project manager.

Question 13

Answer **A** is correct. Communication between any people occurs based on the relationship between them. Formal and distant relationships yield formal and distant communications, and closer relationships tend to result in freer communication. Answers B, C, and D are incorrect because the project manager's standing or the size of the project do not have nearly as much impact on communication as the relationships in the project team.

Question 14

Answer **C** is correct. Calculate the expected value of an outcome by summing the result of the product of the value of each outcome and its probability. Answers A and B are incorrect because they define incorrect formulas. Answer D is incorrect because linear regression does not produce the expected value of an outcome.

Question 15

Answer **B** is correct. Expected monetary value is calculated as the sum of individual risk values ($P * I$). The weather risk (positive) impact is 0.25 * $80,000 = $20,000. The fuel price increase risk (negative) is 0.10 * –$45,000 = –$4,500. EMV = $20,000 + –$4,500 = $15,500. Answers A, C, and D are incorrect because they incorrectly calculate EMV.

Question 16

Answer **D** is correct. Although a lessons learned session should be held at project conclusion, these sessions should also be held throughout the project, especially at key milestones and when something goes wrong.

Question 17

Answer **D** is correct. The project manager is assigned to achieve the project objectives and is ultimately responsible for controlling quality.

Question 18

Answer **D** is correct. A notice to proceed is not part of the acquisition process. All other listed activities are components of the acquisition process.

Question 19

Answer **D** is correct. Because a project manager has primary responsibility over his or her project, it is important to involve the project managers of all involved projects as well as inform the functional managers. All interested parties should be able to work out a solution. Answers A, B, and C are incorrect because they fail to involve the project managers from the competing projects.

Question 20

Answer **B** is correct. You should address the problem by talking with the vendor about the rumor. Answer A is incorrect and would delay the project and likely cause future problems. Answer C is incorrect because it would probably violate the contract between the buyer and seller. Answer D is also incorrect because your agreement is between the vendor and the performing organization, not the labor union.

Question 21

Answer **C** is correct. A project team meeting is likely to embarrass the team member and breed resentment. All other answers refer to methods that direct communication with only the team member and would not incur the same embarrassment as a team meeting.

Question 22

Answer **C** is correct. A successful enterprise program starts with the tone at the top and the enterprise governance of your organization.

Question 23

Answer **C** is correct. A post-implementation review is a product or service performance review after the implementation has taken place.

Question 24

Answer **C** is correct. Lag is the delay between the start/finish of one activity and the start/finish of another activity. Answers A, B, and D are incorrect because slack and float refer to the amount of time an activity can be delayed without delaying the early start date of the succeeding activity.

Question 25

Answer **C** is correct. Subordinate-centered leadership empowers the project team to make most decisions. Answer A is incorrect because the laissez-faire leadership style empowers no one. It is a "hands-off" approach. Answers B and D are incorrect because they do not empower the project team to make decisions.

Question 26

Answer **C** is correct. Marketing is not an activity of procurement management. All the other options refer to valid activities in procurement management.

Question 27

Answer **D** is correct. Find out why the third vendor delivered an estimate that was unusual. A clear statement of work is needed for the vendors to provide accurate estimates. Answers A, B, and C are all inappropriate actions because they discuss another vendor's estimate. This information should be kept confidential between the buyer and seller.

Question 28

Answer **C** is correct. Requesting and obtaining feedback is the only way to really find out if a team member understands a message. All other answers refer to methods to increase the likelihood that a team member will receive a message but do not ensure that the message is understood.

Question 29

Answer **B** is correct. The critical path is the sequence of activities in which any delay will postpone the project completion date. All other answers are incorrect detractors.

Question 30

Answer **C** is correct. A project that ends in integration mode has had its resources assigned to other areas. A project that ends in extinction is a project that has ended before meeting its stated objectives, and a project that ends in inclusion mode is a project that has been accepted and has transitioned to be part of the organization.

Question 31

Answer **D** is correct. Among other components, the project charter includes measurable project objectives, a summary milestone schedule, and project approval requirements. Although each answer is individually correct, the best answer is "all of the above."

Question 32

Answer **D** is correct. A project that ends in extinction mode is a project that has ended before meeting its stated objectives. The other project modes are integration and inclusion mode. A project that ends in integration mode is a project for which resources have been assigned to other areas, and a project that ends in inclusion mode is a project that has been accepted and has transitioned to be part of the organization.

Question 33

Answer **C** is correct. It is important that project documentation maintain the original documents and all changes that have occurred over time. Answer A is incorrect because it disregards the original baseline. Answer B is incorrect because the change is only an annotation. That answer might sound correct, but it is important that changes be integrated, not just annotated. Answer D is incorrect because it, too, disregards the original baseline.

Question 34

Answer **D** is correct. Increasing the cost by 25% would be inappropriate. A risk assessment describing how the project might fail if the budget is not accurate is most appropriate. Answers A, B, and C are all incorrect because these choices are unethical. Always provide honest estimates of the project work.

Question 35

Answer **B** is correct. EV is the value of work performed and, in the case of work performed at a periodic rate, is calculated by multiplying the periodic rate by the duration of work (hourly rate times number of hours). Answers A and C are incorrect because they refer to incorrect formulas. Answer D is incorrect because the information necessary to calculate EV is available for a properly planned activity that has been completed.

Question 36

Answer **C** is correct. A project that ends in inclusion mode is a project that has transitioned to be part of the organization and its support infrastructure. The other project modes are extinction and integration mode. A project that ends in integration mode has had its resources assigned to other areas, and a project that ends in extinction mode is a project that has ended before meeting its stated objectives.

Question 37

Answer **D** is correct. A project must have a specific time frame, objectives, and resources. Answers A and B are incorrect because they do not reference a specific time frame and are ambiguous with respect to goals. Answer C is incorrect because it does not specify which goals the project will fulfill.

Question 38

Answer **C** is correct. The schedule compression technique of crashing is used to decrease the overall project duration. If the activity that is crashed causes the overall project duration to be decreased to less than the critical path duration, a new critical path emerges. Answer A is incorrect because the crashed activity might not appear on the critical path and might therefore have no effect on the overall project duration. Answer B is incorrect because slack changes depend on how other activities are dependent on the crashed activity. Answer D is incorrect because in includes the incorrect Answers A and B.

Question 39

Answer **B** is correct. According to the PMBOK, "Quality assurance is the process of auditing the quality requirements and results from quality control measurements to ensure appropriate quality standards and operational definitions are used." Answer A is incorrect because it refers to quality management. Answer C is incorrect because quality control is the process in which control charts are used to monitor the results of quality activities. Answer D is incorrect because it includes the incorrect Answer A.

Question 40

Answer **C** is correct. Because the executing phase of the project is where the actual work is accomplished, this phase is expected to incur the most expense. Answers A, B, and D are incorrect because they each refer to phases that require less work and, in turn, fewer expenses.

Question 41

Answer **C** is correct. Administrative closure pertains to all the tasks involved in closing all the activities pertaining to a specific project. Other outputs of the close project process are contract closure procedure, final product, service, or result and organizational process assets (updates).

Question 42

Answer **B** is correct. Product validation pertains to all activities that ensure that the products and services delivered by the project meet the needs of the customer and stakeholders.

Question 43

Answer **C** is correct. Remember that for the PMP test, you must select the most appropriate answer. In this case, you can argue that all of the answers could be correct at one time or another; however, the intent of the lessons learned is to record all the course corrections that might have affected the project baseline and the reasoning behind the preventive or corrective actions.

Question 44

Answer **A** is correct. Schedule variance (SV) is defined as the difference between EV and PV. Answer B is incorrect because the cost variance (CV) is the difference between EV and actual cost (AC). Answer C is incorrect because the estimate at completion (EAC) is the expected total cost of a scheduled activity. Answer D is incorrect because the actual cost (AC) is the actual cost incurred to accomplish work.

Question 45

Answer **B** is correct. Confusion and perception of a lack of direction is a common source of frustration and conflict in any team environment. Answers A, C, and D are incorrect because they do not represent common causes of conflict in any environment.

Question 46

Answer **C** is correct. First, find out what the local practices and customs call for in regard to hiring family members before others. Answers A and D are incorrect because they do not consider the qualifications of the project team leader and the project team. In addition, they do not take into account local customs. Answer B is also incorrect. Although it does consider the qualifications of the project team, it does not consider the local customs.

Question 47

Answer **B** is correct. Conflict during early stages can help identify issues that truly need to be addressed to help the project proceed more smoothly. Notice that the question asks "When CAN conflict be beneficial?" That is not to say that all conflict is beneficial. Answer A is incorrect because conflict should never be injected as a simple diversion. Answers C and D are incorrect because conflict in these situations tends to decrease productivity.

Question 48

Answer **C** is correct. The close procurements process refers to all procurements initiated during the lifetime of the project. Due to their legal nature, contracts have to be evaluated and follow formal legal dissolution or fulfillment.

Question 49

Answer **D** is correct. Work performance data is one of the outputs described by PMI for the direct and manage project work process.

Question 50

Answer **D** is the best response. You have a responsibility to refrain from accepting inappropriate forms of compensation for personal gain. Answers A and C are incorrect for this reason. Answer B is a poor choice because the appearance of impropriety is present.

Question 51

Answer **D** is the best response. A statement of work (SOW) identifies the business need for the project, the project or product requirements, and the strategic plan for the organization. Answers A, B, and C are individually correct, but Answer D is the better response.

Question 52

Answer **B** is the best response. The project manager, along with the project management team, directs the performance of the planned project activities and manages the technical and organizational interfaces necessitated by the project and occurring continuously throughout the project life cycle.

Question 53

Answer **D** is the best response. Earned value technique (EVT) measures the performance of a project as it moves through the entire project life cycle, from initiating through closing.

Question 54

Answer **C** is correct. The work breakdown structure (WBS) is a deliverable-oriented hierarchical decomposition of the work to be executed by a project team to accomplish project objectives and create the required deliverables.

Question 55

Answer **C** is correct. Receiving is the process of accepting, or assimilating, information. Answers A and D are incorrect because they each refer to processing received information. Answer B is incorrect because the term *communication* refers to the entire process of sending, receiving, and responding.

Question 56

Answer **A** is correct. Solving the problem reduces the likelihood that you will encounter the same issue on a recurring basis. Answers B, C, and D are incorrect because they do not actually solve the problem and likely result in having to revisit the problem in the future.

Question 57

Answer **D** is correct. Additional quality testing requires additional time and resources for the project. This is an example of integrated change control. Answer A is incorrect because scope creep is made up of small, undocumented changes to the project execution. Answer B is incorrect because change control falls within integrated change control. Answer C is incorrect because quality assurance is an organization-wide program.

Question 58

Answer **C** is correct. Decomposition is a planning technique that subdivides project deliverables into smaller, more manageable components until the project work and project deliverables are defined at the work package level.

Question 59

Answer **A** is correct. Creating a formal, documented change request is the best course of action for a change resulting from a law or regulation. Answer B is incorrect because the law or regulation likely overrides any existing project implementation. Answer C is incorrect because the project manager should first document the change through a change request. Answer D is incorrect because project work shouldn't stop just because of a change request.

Question 60

Answer **D** is correct. Applying sound project management techniques increases the likelihood that the project will be a success and all goals will be met but does not guarantee any outcome.

Question 61

Answer **D** is correct. The approved project scope statement is one component of the project scope baseline. Other components are the associated work breakdown structure (WBS) and the WBS dictionary. Answer A is incorrect because it is an unapproved preliminary, not detailed, project scope. Answer B is incorrect because even though it purports to be "approved," it is a preliminary, not detailed, project scope. Answer C is incorrect because it is not an "approved" detailed project scope statement.

Question 62

Answer **B** is correct. A project is a temporary endeavor undertaken to create a unique product, service, or result. A project by definition cannot be permanent nor ongoing. A project has a specific timeline and duration.

Question 63

Answer **C** is correct. A PMIS can assist a project manager the most during project execution. Answer A is incorrect because stakeholder analysis should have been completed during planning. Answer B is incorrect because change control boards can assist the project manager but not as much as the control and assistance offered through a PMIS. Answer D is incorrect because scope verification is proof of the project work, not an assistance to the project manager.

Question 64

Answer **A** is correct. Integrated change control requires detail for implementing the change. Without evidence of the need for a change, there is no reason to implement it. Answer B is incorrect because the project team's approval is not necessary for changes. Answer C is incorrect because a subject matter expert is not always needed to determine the need for change. Answer D is also incorrect because some changes might be discarded for reasons other than risk.

Question 65

Answer **A** is correct. Configuration management is documentation of the project product, including its attributes and changes to the product. Answer B is incorrect because integrated change control describes how to incorporate all of the project changes across the knowledge areas. Answer C is incorrect because scope control describes how to manage changes to the project scope. Answer D is also incorrect because the change management plan does not describe the project product, its features, or changes to the product.

Question 66

Answer **A** is correct. The risk of project failure is highest at the start of a project. The certainty of project completion increases as the project continues through its life cycle.

Question 67

Answer **A** is correct. Project changes from scope creep or error correction have a more significant impact on project cost as a project continues through its life cycle.

Question 68

Answer **C** is correct. Project cost and project staffing levels are low at the start of a project, peak during the middle phases of the project life cycle, and then drop rapidly toward the conclusion of the project.

Question 69

Answer **C** is the best response. A strong matrix structure within an organization supports a full-time project manager with considerable project authority, including budgetary and resource allocation ability, as well as a full-time project management administrative staff. Answer A is incorrect because a functional structure within an organization provides a part-time project manager with little to no authority and part-time administrative support. Answer B is incorrect because a weak matrix structure within an organization supports a part-time project manager with limited authority and only part-time administrative staffing. Answer D is incorrect because a projectized structure within an organization provides a full-time project manager with almost absolute authority and a full-time project management administrative staff.

Question 70

Answer **D** is correct. Rolling wave planning is a form of progressive elaboration in which the work to be performed in the near term is planned in detail while work scheduled for further out is defined at only a high level in the work breakdown structure (WBS). Rolling wave planning is a tool for activity definition. Answer A is incorrect because activity sequencing entails documentation of logical relationships among scheduled activities and is actually the task following activity definition. Answers B and C are incorrect because the precedence diagramming method (PDM), also called activity-on-node (AON), is a tool for activity sequencing.

Question 71

Answer **A** is correct. Finish-to-start is the most common type of precedence relationship used in the precedence diagramming method (PDM). The initiation of the successor activity is dependent on the completion of the predecessor activity in finish-to-start dependencies.

Question 72

Answer **C** is correct. The organizational process assets should guide the project manager and the decisions he or she makes when dealing with vendors operating in foreign countries. Answers A and B are incorrect because these documents are essential but usually do not reference allowed business practices. Answer D is incorrect. While the PMI Code of Ethics and Professional Conduct contains useful guidelines, organizational process assets are most specific to the project work and requirements.

Question 73

Answer **C** is correct. Chronological dependencies are not a type of dependency used in sequencing activities.

Question 74

Answer **A** is correct. Bottom-up estimating is a technique for estimating a component of work through the activity's decomposition. A bottom-up estimate is based on the requirements for each lower work package and then combined to estimate the entire component of work. Answer B is incorrect because there is no technique called decomposed estimating. Answer C is incorrect because should-cost estimating is an activity duration estimating technique. Answer D is incorrect because three-point estimating uses most likely, best-case, and worst-case estimates to generate a weighted estimate.

Question 75

Answer **D** is correct. It is the sponsor's call as to whether a potential conflict of interest will interfere with your ability to make fair decisions. If the sponsor is informed and has no issues with the assignments, you should not take any further action. Answer A is incorrect because hiding real or perceived conflicts of interest is unethical. Answers B and C are incorrect because the decision to take action belongs to the project sponsor.

Question 76

Answer **C** is the best response. Cost control involves determining and evaluating both the cause of a variance and the magnitude of the variance. Answers A and B are both individually correct, but Answer C is the best answer. Answer D is incorrect.

Question 77

Answer **C** is correct. No project should allow automatic change approvals. Also, Answer C is not a part of configuration management. Answers A, B, and D all describe the attributes of configuration management.

Question 78

Answer **D** is correct. The best choice is to appeal to the project sponsor to use his or her authority to address the conflicting opinions. Answer A is incorrect because it ignores the directive of an internal authority figure. Answers B and C are incorrect because they each allow the scope of the project to be changed without a change approval process.

Question 79

Answer **C** is correct. General management skills, status review meetings, and work authorization systems are the best tools described here that serve as part of the project plan execution. Answer A is incorrect because EVM and the WBS are not part of the tools used in the project plan execution. Answer B is incorrect because it includes EVM. Answer D is incorrect because it also includes EVM.

Question 80

Answer **A** is the correct response. Planned value (PV), in the earned value technique (EVT), is the budgeted cost for work scheduled to be completed on an activity up to a specific time. Answer B is incorrect because the budgeted cost for the work actually completed on the scheduled activity during a specific time period refers to earned value (EV). Answer C is incorrect because the total cost for work on the scheduled activity during a specific time period defines actual cost (AC). Answer D is incorrect.

Question 81

Answer **A** is correct. A cost performance index (CPI) value less than 1.0 indicates that a project has an overrun of the cost estimates. Answer B is incorrect because a cost underrun of the cost estimates is indicated by a CPI greater than 1.0. Answers C and D are incorrect.

Question 82

Answer **C** is correct. A statement of end users' needs is a basis of a project's functional requirements. The other answers are incorrect because they each reference documents that do not directly require definition of end users' needs.

Question 83

Answer **B** is correct. Schedule variance (SV) is calculated by subtracting the planned value (PV) from the earned value (EV). SV = EV – PV. In the example given, the PV is $200,000 and the EV is $100,000. Therefore, $100,000 – $200,000 = –$100,000. Answer A is incorrect, as is Answer C. Answer D is the cost variance (CV), not the SV, so it is incorrect.

Question 84

Answer **D** is correct. EVM, earned value management, is used throughout the project processes. It is a planning and control tool used to measure performance. Answers A, B, and C are correct in that EVM is used during these processes, but it is not as good an answer as D.

Question 85

Answer **B** is correct. If enough team members voluntarily offer to work overtime, you will be able to meet the schedule, although paying a higher overtime rate can affect the project budget. Answer A is incorrect because your responsibility is to ensure that the project stays on schedule, on budget, and produces a quality result. Answers C and D are incorrect because both actions exceed the authority of the project manager.

Question 86

Answer **A** is correct. TQM, total quality management, is a business philosophy to find methods to continuously improve. Answer B, ASQ (American Society of Quality), is not a business philosophy. Answers C and D are attributes of TQM but are not correct answers for this question.

Question 87

Answer **A** is correct. The cost performance index (CPI) is calculated by dividing the actual cost (AC) into the earned value (EV). CPI = EV ÷ AC. In the example given, the AC is $150,000 and the EV is $100,000. $100,000 ÷ $150,000 = .06667. A CPI value less than 1.0 indicates a cost overrun of the project budget. Answer B is incorrect because, if the project were under budget, the CPI value would be greater than 1.0. Answer C is incorrect because the CPI would be 0. Answer D is incorrect.

Question 88

Answer **A** is correct. The schedule performance index (SPI) is calculated by dividing the planned cost (PC) into the earned value (EV): SPI = EV ÷ PC. In the example given, the PC is $200,000 and the EV is $100,000. Therefore, $100,000 ÷ $200,000 = 0.05. An SPI value in conjunction with the schedule status allows you to predict the completion date for a project. Given the math done to arrive at Answer A, Answers B, C, and D are incorrect.

Question 89

Answer **C** is the best response. Monitoring project activities and results to evaluate whether the findings comply with applicable quality standards as well as identifying mitigation strategies are quality control activities. Answers A, B, and D are incorrect.

Question 90

Answer **C** is correct. When project work results are faulty and must be done over, it is attributed to the cost of nonconformance to quality. Answers A, B, and D are all incorrect because these terms do not describe faulty work or the cost of nonconformance.

Question 91

Answer **A** is correct. Confronting is the best problem-solving technique because it meets a problem directly. Answer B is incorrect because compromising requires both sides on an argument to give up something. Answer C is incorrect because forcing requires the project manager to force a decision based on external inputs, such as seniority or experience. Answer D is also incorrect because avoidance ignores the problem and does not solve it.

Question 92

Answer **D** is the best response. Answer A is correct because Ishikawa diagrams are also known as cause-and-effect diagrams and Answer C is correct because Ishikawa diagrams are also known as fishbone diagrams. Because both A and C are correct answers, Answer D, which includes both A and C, is the best response. Answer B is incorrect. Scatter diagrams show the pattern of relationship between two variables, while Ishikawa diagrams show how various factors (causes) may link to potential problems (effects).

Question 93

Answer **C** is correct. A Pareto diagram is a specific type of histogram, ordered by frequency of occurrence and showing how many defects were generated to show nonconformity. Answers A, B, and D are incorrect.

Question 94

Answer **D** is the best response. Project communication planning includes all these tasks: determining and limiting who communicates with whom and who receives what information, combining the type and format of information needed with an analysis of the value of the information for communication, and understanding how communication affects a project as a whole.

Question 95

Answer **D** is correct. The components in the question describe a seller's performance evaluation. Answers A, B, and C refer to analyses that do not specifically focus on a seller's performance.

Question 96

Answer **D** is correct. Procurement closing ensures that all contracts are properly terminated. Answer A is incorrect because there might still be money in the budget that was not used. Answer B is incorrect because some budget categories might have exceeded their limits. Answer C is incorrect because a client might be associated with multiple projects.

Question 97

Answer **B** is correct. Coercive power is power a project manager wields over the project team. Coercive power is the formal authority a project manager has over the project team. Answer A is incorrect because only referent power may come through lunch meetings. Answer C is incorrect because experience is expert power. Answer D is incorrect because interpersonal relationships are examples of referent power.

Question 98

Answer **C** is correct. When both parties give up something, it is a compromise. A compromise is an example of a lose–lose solution. Answer A is incorrect because win–win is accomplished through confrontation. Answer B is incorrect because win–lose allows only one party to get what they want from the scenario. Answer D is incorrect because a leave–lose solution is when one party walks away from the problem.

Question 99

Answer **C** is correct. Forcing happens when a project manager makes a decision based on factors not relevant to the problem. Just because a team member has more seniority does not mean this individual is correct. Answers A, B, and D are incorrect choices. Problem solving is not described in the scenario. Answer B, compromising, happens when both parties agree to give up something. Answer D, withdrawal, happens when a party leaves the argument.

Question 100

Answer **D** is correct. While Answers A, B, and C are all important decisions, it is crucial to know when a project should be cancelled to avoid further losses.

Question 101

Answer **A** is correct. Historical records give future project managers information to assess trends of past successes and difficulties. While Answers B, C, and D are each partially correct, the value in having access to historical records from multiple projects lies in the ability to generate trending reports.

Question 102

Answer **C** is correct. Small organizations have smaller staffs, and the project manager is sometimes the same person as the functional manager. Because all organizations are different, it is not accurate to say that project managers are "never" or "generally" the same person. Likewise, it is not a requirement that the project initiator be superior to the project and functional managers.

Question 103

Answer **A** is correct. Qualitative risk analysis occurs prior to quantitative risk analysis and is a method for prioritizing identified risks for quantitative risk analysis. Answers B, C, and D are incorrect.

Question 104

Answer **D** is correct. The project charter formally authorizes the project, assigns the project manager, and gives a high-level definition of the project and its deliverables; none of the other answers apply to the project charter definition.

Question 105

Answer **B** is correct as projects are seeded from the recognition of a regulatory or business needs. However, when it comes to measuring the actual organizational benefit, your client or company needs to make arrangements to secure the capital and reserve assignments. For this type of allocation, the aforementioned models are just a few of the tools at your disposal to find a measure of the enterprise benefit and the cost justification. Answer A is partially correct, but it does not express complete reasoning and consideration when selecting, justifying, and launching a project.

Question 106

Answer **C** is correct. Project control ensures that a project is executing according to the plan. Answers A and D are incorrect because planning of any type occurs in the planning process group. Answer B is incorrect because status reports are only one part of monitoring and controlling, not the primary purpose.

Question 107

Answer **D** is correct. With the information provided, it is not possible to determine the cause of the increased cost. Answers A, B, and C are incorrect because the question does not provide enough information to determine the specific cause of the increased cost.

Question 108

Answer **D** is correct. The project scope is a live document. Why? A project is a temporary endeavor, with a specific product, but external factors such as your business strategy can have a material impact on determining where the project might or might not go in the future. You might have thought of selecting Answer C, but the project charter is the document that formally launches the project and defines at a high level what are the project deliverables, who is the project sponsor, and who is the project manager.

Question 109

Answer **C** is correct. Collaborating is the ideal method when negotiating. The goal of negotiations is to work together for the good of the project. Answer A is incorrect because yielding is not working for the good of the project. Answer B, forcing, exerts power over one party without properly negotiating. Answer D, compromising, calls for both parties to give up something without necessarily working together for the good of the project.

Question 110

Answer **D** is correct. In the answers list, change requests is the only output for the control communications process. Answer A is incorrect because trend analysis is the study of project performance results to determine whether a project is improving or failing. It is a tool used as part of the control risks process, but it is not an output of the control communications process. Answers B and C are also tools used in processes, but they are not outputs of the control communications process.

Question 111

Answer **C** is correct. Rarely do you get to have a project for the sake of spending money. And, because a project is a temporary endeavor, the authority of the project manager is highly dependent on the support of senior management. Answer D is not correct because the job of the project sponsor is to represent management interest in the project and not to lead the execution of the project.

Question 112

Answer **D** is correct. Concessions are always determined during closure.

Question 113

Answer **C** is correct. Validate scope and control communications both occur in the monitoring and controlling process group, so Answers A, B, and D are incorrect.

Question 114

Answer **D** is correct. The project management plan is the entire framework and processes that are used to control the entire project effort. Answer A refers more to the mistaken interpretation that the project plan is the Gantt chart that people might prepare using products such Visio, Excel, or Project.

Question 115

Answer **C** is correct. Source selection happens during the executing process group. Answers A, B, and D are all incorrect because these process groups do not include source selection.

Question 116

Answer **B** is correct. Source selection criteria is an output to plan procurement management and an input to conduct procurements. Answers A, C, and D are inputs to control procurements.

Question 117

Answer **D** is correct. The primary function of the project manager is to integrate the project team and all activities that pertain to the project throughout the project life cycle. Answers A, B, and C are incorrect because they reference only part of the project manager's function, not the overall focus of the job.

Question 118

Answer **A** is correct. Fast tracking is attempting to shorten the schedule by performing activities in parallel, when appropriate. Answers B, C, and D are incorrect because they do not provide valid definitions for fast tracking.

Question 119

Answer **D** is correct. To have an effective work breakdown structure, you must take time to understand the project objectives and the risk involved. When this is accomplished, the next task is to compartmentalize the project into manageable pieces—but not to the extreme. Good examples are to stop at a point where a task is down to five days in duration or resource utilization can be measured. If you chose Answer A, you might have been thinking of a meeting agenda instead of the WBS. If you opted for Answer B, keep in mind that the project charter does not include or make reference to the WBS; remember that the intent of the project charter is to launch the project, announce the project manager, and present a general overview of the project deliverables.

Question 120

Answer **D** is correct. The closing project or phase is in the project integration management knowledge area, and closing procurements is in the project procurement management knowledge area.

Question 121

Answer **B** is correct. The PMI Code of Ethics and Professional Conduct disallows any use of confidential information other than its intended use in the context of the project. All other answers are allowable actions within the PMI Code of Ethics and Professional Conduct.

Question 122

Answer **B** is correct. Administrative closure should take place at the completion of each phase. Answer A is incorrect because administrative closure occurs more than just when a project is cancelled. Answer C is also incorrect because administrative closure does not take place only at project completion and cancellation; it can happen at the end of each project phase. Answer D is not a valid choice.

Question 123

Answer **C** is correct. The harsh reality of project management is that no matter how much time you invest in analysis during the execution of the project, critical elements may be missing, external forces can influence your project, and organizational changes can force a course correction. A project baseline helps you to account for all the course corrections you implement during the execution of a project. You might have been tempted to select Answer A, but the project baseline does not stay fixed; it changes as changes are implemented.

Question 124

Answer **C** is correct. Activity H should start in the first day of week 4 because it can't start executing until C (2) and E (1) are complete.

Question 125

Answer **A** is correct. In general, the critical path is composed of the activities that form the longest-duration path on a project. Answer A = 17-week duration, Answer B = 13-week duration, and Answer C = 4-week duration. Therefore, Answer A represents the longest-duration path on the project.

Question 126

Answer **A** is correct. The network diagram gives only three paths of execution: Start–A–D–G–Finish; Start–B–F–Finish; and Start–C–E–H–Finish. Answer A is the only one that shows the predecessors in the correct order.

Question 127

Answer **C** is correct. Earned value analysis is used during the execution of a project to determine resource consumption versus planned. On the other hand, the WBS, time estimates, and schedules are excellent sources for estimating the rate of consumption, timelines, and overall project resource needs.

Question 128

Answer **B** is correct. The project manager can request staff for a project but generally does not have direct authority to assign staff to the project. All the other answers list actions within the project manager's authority.

Question 129

Answer **C** is correct. Cost aggregation builds cost estimates by adding the tasks outlined in the work breakdown structures, and parametric estimates use historical data and project-specific characteristics. Cost cancellation techniques, reserve analysis, and funding limit reconciliation are not considered budgeting tools.

Question 130

Answer **C** is correct. Estimating is not an element of procurement management. All the other answers are part of procurement management.

Question 131

Answer **D** is correct. A Pareto diagram helps identify the cause of quality problems in a particular process. Answer A is incorrect because a cause-and-effect, or fishbone, diagram relates causes to effects of problems. Answers B and C are other graphic depictions of process flow and results.

Question 132

Answer **B** is correct. In the realm of project management, the project manager has the ultimate responsibility. You might have thought of the quality assurance manager, but quality goes beyond the project and is housed in the organization. The project team and the validation engineer are elements that support both the company quality policies and the processes required during the execution of the project.

Question 133

Answer **D** is correct. The plan human resource management process is where the core project team and the project manager plan for the request of resources from the functional manager and coordinate how to best approach the project demands versus the normal work duties of the resource.

Question 134

Answer **D** is correct. The number of communication channels can be determined using the formula $n(n-1)/2$, where n is the number of people participating in a project. The formula in this case will be $30 * (30 - 1) / 2$; that is, $30 * (29) / 2 = 870 / 2 = 435$, which is Answer D.

Question 135

Answer **C** is correct. Administrative closure is the process of generating, gathering, and disseminating project information. Answers A and B are incorrect because close project or phase involves more than just generating, gathering, and disseminating project information. Answer D, operational transfer, is the process of moving project deliverables into operations.

Question 136

Answer **C** is correct. The total contract cost is $442,000. Here's how the answer is calculated: Target cost is $400,000. The 8% profit is $32,000. The finished cost is $360,000, a difference of $40,000 between the target and the actual. The contract calls for a 75/25 split if the contract comes in under budget. The formula reads finished costs ($400,000) + profit margin ($32,000) + (.25 * under budget amount) ($10,000). Answers A, B, and D are all incorrect because these choices do not reflect the amount of the contract.

Question 137

Answer **B** is correct. For a message to be clearly understood, two things need to happen: The sender has to make sure that the receiver acknowledges the receipt and reading of the message, and the receiver needs to ensure that the sender has received the acknowledgement. None of the other options pertains to the message communication process.

Question 138

Answer **C** is correct. Sound project objectives should be realistic and attainable. Answer A is incorrect because sound project objectives cannot be general. Answer B is incorrect because resource bounds must be considered when stating project objectives. Answer D is incorrect because project objectives must be tangible.

Question 139

Answer **D** is correct. Risk can be catalogued in qualitative and quantitative terms. The project risk management knowledge area serves as a roadmap to reduce the effect of risk on the project. None of the other answers clearly articulate the scope and importance of the PMI risk management processes.

Question 140

Answer **C** is correct. Quality control is the process of monitoring and recording results of executing the quality activities and is normally performed by operations personnel. Answer A is incorrect because QA personnel normally carry out quality assurance activities (auditing quality control results), not quality control. Answers B and D are incorrect because they fail to specify quality personnel at all.

Question 141

Answer **C** is correct. The schedule variance (SV) is calculated using the following formula: SV = EV − PV. In the question, EV is 850, and PV is 1000, so SV = 850 − 1000, or −150. Answers A, B, and D are incorrect because they do not correspond to the correct formula.

Question 142

Answer **D** is correct. Share is a typical way to deal with positive risk. The other answers are examples of how a project manager might deal with a risk that might have a negative impact on the outcome of the project.

Question 143

Answer **D** is correct. All of these are examples of contract types that vary depending on the risk that the buyer and the seller are willing to assume.

Question 144

Answer **C** is correct. The risk management plan identifies how risk is managed throughout a project. Answers A, B, and D are examples of project plan elements that are used to define the work to be done and the deliverables expected out of the project.

Question 145

Answer **C** is correct. The project manager is ultimately responsible for the success of the project. Therefore, she should execute due diligence with regard to analyzing a change request before taking any action. Answers A and B might be actions you will take in the process; however, the number-one priority is to evaluate what impact a change will have on the outcome of the project.

Question 146

Answer **B** is correct. Fitness for use is not part of the definition of quality. Answers A, C, and D are all part of the definition of quality.

Question 147

Answer **B** is correct. Resource leveling often impacts the schedule by increasing the duration of one or more activities. This causes the schedule to be longer after leveling. Answer A is incorrect because resource leveling does not shorten the schedule. Answer C is incorrect because resource leveling either has no effect on responsiveness or reduces responsiveness to customer needs. Answer D is incorrect because Answers A and C are both incorrect.

Question 148

Answer **B** is correct. S curves are graphical displays of accumulated cost and labor hours, plotted as a function of time. Answers A, C, and D are incorrect because they each refer to a report that does not present a graphical display, as stated in the question.

Question 149

Answer **D** is correct. Scope planning is the process of deciding on the best approach to meeting project objectives. Answers A and C are incorrect because the scope baseline and the WBS are outputs of the create WBS process, not a process itself. Answer B is incorrect because the scope authorization is an approval of the scope baseline, not a process.

Question 150

Answer **D** is correct. The cost performance index (CPI) is the most encompassing answer as it divides the earned value by the actual cost of the project. A CPI value greater than 1 signifies that a project is running under budget.

Question 151

Answer **D** is correct. *Quality assurance* refers to the process of applying and measuring performance against enterprise quality policies. Six Sigma and Pareto diagrams are used to represent the execution trending of a process, and organizational quality practices refers to how quality is managed and considered in the enterprise.

Question 152

Answer **C** is correct. It is the responsibility of management to ensure quality. Answer D is incorrect because the responsibility for quality does not belong to the workers. Answers A and B are incorrect detractors.

Question 153

Answer **A** is correct. Cost of quality is the total cost of efforts related to quality. In other words, it is the cost of avoiding nonconformance to specifications. Answers B, C, and D are all incorrect statements with respect to the cost of quality.

Question 154

Answer **B** is correct. Configuration management provides the structure to control all changes throughout a project. Answers A, C, and D are incorrect because configuration management addresses many more areas than just the specific areas or phases mentioned in the answer.

Question 155

Answer **A** is correct. Quality is directly related to productivity. An increase in one results in an increase in the other. Answers B, C, and D present incorrect aspects of projects that are not directly related to quality.

Question 156

Answer **A** is correct. In the PMI realm, *acquisition* refers to the action of securing external resources. Pre-assignment, negotiation, and contract management are activities that a project manager might engage in during the process of securing the resources, but they are subprocesses when securing external resources.

Question 157

Answer **C** is correct. Answers A, B, and D are known ways to resolve conflict. From most long-lasting effects to least, they can be ranked problem solving, compromising, and forcing. Withdrawal and smoothing are part of this group, but they do not address the problem.

Question 158

Answer **C** is correct. A quality conformance inspection ensures that an inspected product meets or exceeds defined quality requirements. Answers A, B, and D are inspection terms that do not directly relate to quality.

Question 159

Answer **D** is correct. The project manager is the focal point for information for senior management, stakeholders, and the project team. As such, the project manager spends much of her or his time making sure that communication occurs and is effective at all levels affected by the product of the project.

Question 160

Answer **C** is correct. If you stand back and think of what it takes for successful communication, you think of an idea or a concept that needs to be communicated. You must build the entire message (words, syntax, and morphology); then talk to, write, or call the recipient to deliver the message; and wait for confirmation that your message was understood. On the other hand, the individual being communicated with has to do the same process but in reverse. He needs to receive the message, check if it is in a language or in a frame of reference familiar to him, and then proceed to decipher its meaning. Analog line is a technical term associated with old telephone lines over which modems modulated and demodulated messages.

Question 161

Answer **B** is correct. After you have defined your procurement plan, the equipment or service to be purchased, and how you are going to evaluate any responses, you are ready to conduct procurements.

Question 162

Answer **C** is correct. From time to time, external events, such as business strategy change or regulatory compliance, have a direct effect on the day-to-day execution of a project. Approved corrective actions are recognized changes throughout the entire organization of the project plan and are ultimately approved and authorized by the project sponsor and the project manager.

Question 163

Answer **D** is correct. Parametric estimating uses statistical relationships between historical data and other variables to calculate estimates. Answers A, B, and C refer to other types of estimating methods.

Question 164

Answer **C** is correct. Only a quality control program that includes worker and management input will produce long-term quality improvements. All other answers will generate, at best, temporary quality improvements.

Question 165

Answer **C** is correct. A work breakdown structure (WBS) is a task-oriented tree diagram of activities. Answer A is incorrect because a detailed plan is not necessarily task oriented and organized into a tree. Answers B and D are incorrect because neither option is a task-oriented list.

Question 166

Answer **C** is correct. The fishbone (also called the cause-and-effect) diagram, as shown in the following figure, was first developed by Kaoru Ishikawa in 1969. It is used to identify the root cause of a process going out of control. Brainstorming, Answer B, is an activity with the express purpose of collecting ideas, and Answer A refers to how costs might be managed through the life of a project.

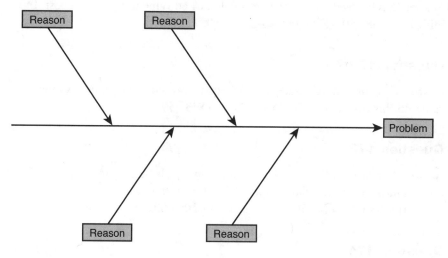

Question 167

Answer **C** is correct. The quality plan requires tools that enable the successful implementation of control programs that provide quality assurance, quality processes, and metrics that are used in support of the quality control activities.

Question 168

Answer **C** is correct. Budget at completion (BAC) equates to the original cost estimate of the project.

Question 169

Answer **D** is correct. Planned value (PV), or budget cost of work scheduled (BCWS), equates to the percentage of work that should have been completed according to the plan. In this case, you divide the 16 weeks by the 24 in the original plan; this equals 67%. You then multiply $675,000 (the budget at completion) by 67% and get $452,250.

Question 170

Answer **B** is correct. Earned value (EV), or budgeted cost of work performed (BCWP), equals the actual percentage of work performed times the budget at completion (BAC). In this case, EV = 0.25 * $675,000 = $168,750.

Question 171

Answer **D** is correct. Cost variance equals earned value minus actual cost. In this case, $168,750 – $300,000 = –$131,250.

Question 172

Answer **C** is correct. Schedule variance equals earned value minus planned value. In this case, $168,750 – $452,250 = –$283,500.

Question 173

Answer **A** is correct. Estimated at completion equals budget at completion divided into cost performance index (EV/AC). In this case, $675,000 ÷ (168750 ÷ 300000) = $675000 ÷ 0.5625 = $1,200,000.

Question 174

Answer **C** is correct. A CPI less than 1.0 suggests a cost overrun for work completed.

Question 175

Answer **C** is correct. Uncertainty means that neither the outcomes nor the likelihood of occurrence is known. Answers A and B are incorrect because in these answers, one of the variables is known. Answer D is an incorrect definition for uncertainty.

Question 176

Answer **C** is correct. Deming's definition of *quality* centers around continuous improvement. All other answers omit Deming's core focus and are incorrect.

Question 177

Answer **D** is correct. As project manager, you need to be aware of what makes employees and team members happy. One way to do this is to apply Dr. Abraham Maslow's hierarchy of needs. This theory postulates that the performance of an individual depends on how well his personal needs are satisfied. These range from basic needs (physiological), such as a roof over his head and food on his table, to self-actualization needs, such as finding self-fulfillment. You must recognize these as cyclical in the sense that self-actualization is only the destination; most individuals tend to treasure the journey as well.

Question 178

Answer **A** is correct. Performance specifications dictate parameters against which actual products can be measured for quality. Answers B, C, and D all refer to specifications that describe products in general, not necessarily with respect to quality.

Question 179

Answer **B** is correct. McGregor's Theory X postulates that people must be constantly watched and that they are incapable, avoid responsibility, and avoid work.

Question 180

Answer **A** is correct. Business risk is most similar to profit and loss. Answers B and C are incorrect because they each are common occurrences in a business environment. Answer D is incorrect because liability insurance is a response to risk (which is an example of risk transfer).

Question 181

Answer **B** is correct. A cost-reimbursable contract is the same as a cost-plus contract. Answers A and C are incorrect because they refer to other types of contracts, both based on fixed prices. Answer D is incorrect because it doesn't refer to a contract type at all.

Question 182

Answer **C** is correct. Adding additional resources or overtime to the critical path activities with the longest time duration has the greatest effect on the overall project by decreasing the overall project duration. Answers A, B, and D are all incorrect because adding resources to activities that are not on the critical path does not directly affect the overall project duration.

Question 183

Answer **B** is correct. Pareto's law states that because most defects are caused by a small percentage of problems, focusing remediation efforts on those problems has the biggest effect on quality. Answers A and C are incorrect because they arbitrarily waste money on problems that do not cause many defects. Answer D is an incorrect statement.

Question 184

Answer **D** is correct. The forcing conflict resolution technique forces a project manager's opinion(s) on the project team. This can solve the short-term need to make a decision but tends to create discord.

Question 185

Answer **C** is correct. Within the context of project communication management, these reports can assist in presenting a project's performance and resource utilization.

Question 186

Answer **C** is correct. As the name suggests, procurement closure addresses all the processes pertaining to procurement closures, and administrative deals with the processes internal to the organization.

Question 187

Answer **C** is correct. In accordance with the PMI Code of Ethics and Professional Conduct, you should always avoid any act that might be construed as a conflict of interest or unethical.

Question 188

Answer **C** is correct. Increased responsibility feeds the need for esteem. Answers A, B, and D are incorrect because they refer to needs that increased responsibility would not address.

Question 189

Answer **D** is correct. Management reserves are budgets reserved for unplanned changes. Answer A is incorrect because unbudgeted scope is scope creep and should be handled via change requests. Answer B is incorrect because inaccurate estimates should be handled via change requests as well. Answer C is incorrect because major catastrophes are addressed in the risk management plan.

Question 190

Answer **A** is correct. The PMI Code of Ethics and Professional Conduct clearly states that it is your responsibility to provide, maintain, and satisfy the scope and objectives of professional services unless otherwise directed by the customer.

Question 191

Answer **B** is correct. A request for quotation is a formal invitation to submit a price for specified goods or services. Although similar, Answer A is incorrect because a request for proposal is generally more generic and allows for more latitude with respect to the goods and services in the proposal. Remember, a request for quotation is for specific goods and services. Answers C and D are incorrect detractors.

Question 192

Answer **C** is correct. Quality metrics are an output of the plan quality management process. All other answers are inputs to the plan quality management process.

Question 193

Answer **D** is correct. As a PMP, you are expected to help in the advancement of the project management discipline and should do so whenever it does not detract from your primary responsibilities. Answers A and B are clearly inappropriate in that neither approach helps advance the discipline. Answer C is not the best answer because it ignores any potential conflict of interest issues.

Question 194

Answer **C** is correct. The S curve is a graphical display of cumulative costs and labor hours plotted against time. Answer A is incorrect because a trend line is a line superimposed on a graph depicting a trend in the common data points. Answer B is incorrect because trend analysis models future behavior based on historical data. Answer D is incorrect because it is a report on the status of completed work.

Question 195

Answer **B** is correct. If an activity is not on the critical path, completing it early increases the slack for that activity. Answer A is incorrect because finishing early with an activity that is not on the critical path does not affect the critical path. Answer C is incorrect because finishing an activity early does not always equate to lower cost. Answer D is incorrect because finishing an activity early does not always result in resource reassignment.

Question 196

Answer **C** is correct. You are the project manager and need to move away from making decisions solely based on the corporate environment. Probably the main reason for this international virtual team is to leverage the expertise of internal resources available to your client or employer within the corporate environment.

Question 197

Answer **A** is correct. You are ultimately responsible to your project sponsor and the rest of the executives affected by this delay. You need to have a meeting with management to apprise them of the new delivery date and offer crashing the schedule as an option.

Question 198

Answer **C** is correct. Only good listeners are capable of keeping long-term active communication with all the members of the project team up and down the chain.

Question 199

Answer **B** is correct. Materials management provides the facilities to ensure that all non-personnel resources are available when and where they are required. Answer A is incorrect because inventory control manages inventory after it has been acquired. Answer C is incorrect because procurement is the process of purchasing or producing resources but does not address the oversight of the resources after they are available.

Question 200

Answer **A** is correct. The effect is depicted at the right-hand end of a spine on a fishbone diagram. Answers B, C, and D are incorrect because they all refer to invalid locations for the effect on a fishbone diagram.

Index

A

W-X-Y-Z